AMERICAN HYSTERIA

AMERICAN HYSTERIA
*The Untold Story of Mass Political Extremism
in the United States*

ANDREW BURT

Guilford, Connecticut

An imprint of Rowman & Littlefield

Distributed by NATIONAL BOOK NETWORK

British Library Cataloguing in Publication Information Available

Library of Congress Cataloging-in-Publication Data Available

ISBN 978-1-4930-0334-1 (hardcover)
ISBN 978-1-4930-1765-2 (e-book)

♾™ The paper used in this publication meets the minimum requirements of American National
Standard for Information Sciences—Permanence of Paper for Printed Library Materials, ANSI/
NISO Z39.48-1992.

In memory of Millard Cass,
and for my parents

Contents

Chapter 1   Defining Hysteria: *What It Is . . . and What It Isn't.* 1

Chapter 2   America's First Time: *Jedidiah Morse*
and the Anti-Illuminati Movement. 21

Chapter 3   The Anti-Masons: *The Disappearance of William*
Morgan and the Rise of Third Party Politics 49

Chapter 4   The Red Scare: *A. Mitchell Palmer Takes*
On the Enemy within Our Gates 73

Chapter 5   The Dawning of McCarthyism: *From Communists*
to Blacklists, One Senator Channels the Fears
of a Nation. 99

Chapter 6   The United States after 9/11: *The American Right*
and the Threat of Sharia Law. 149

Chapter 7   The Way Forward: *A Practical Guide to Confronting*
Political Hysteria 183

Acknowledgments 197

Notes. 199

Index 227

About the Author 232

CHAPTER 1

Defining Hysteria

What It Is . . . and What It Isn't

Something momentous occurred on the morning of December 15, 2008—an event that was overlooked by the national press at the time and has gone largely unnoticed still. On that morning, a former Marine infantryman by the name of Kevin J. Murray filed a federal lawsuit in Michigan against the Treasury Department and the Federal Reserve, arguing that the government bailout of the insurance giant AIG violated the First Amendment of the Constitution. AIG was providing special types of financial products to Muslims that complied with the legal code of the Islamic religion, known as Sharia law. Now that AIG was funded by the government, Murray alleged, the government had violated the constitutionally mandated separation of church and state.

At the time, I was working as a reporter for *US News & World Report*, and the magnitude of the event wasn't immediately apparent—to me or to anyone else. Murray's claim was soon dismissed, and just as quickly forgotten. But as I read more about the case in the weeks after he filed suit, I began to see that something much deeper was at work.

Murray hadn't initiated the lawsuit on his own—he was aided by a network of conservatives on the far right, and chief among them was the Thomas More Law Center, a public interest law firm that filed the lawsuit on his behalf. Murray's lawyers clearly thought the suit was about much more than AIG alone. "Make no mistake," declared Richard Thompson, the president and chief counsel for the center, "there is an internal cultural jihad underway against our great nation, and I fear that many of our political leaders are unwittingly complicit in it." Others began to compare the lawsuit to a global fight against Islamic terrorism that was now being staged on two fronts. One was a violent struggle, which had been conducted overtly with hijacked planes and deadly roadside explosives, but the other battle was cultural—and was being waged in secret. This cultural war, they warned, had only now just gotten under way.

In the months after Murray first filed his suit, claims about the hidden threat of Sharia law began to slowly gather steam, moving from the fringes of American political discourse closer to the center stage. In March of 2009, for example, Fox News host Glenn Beck accused Harold Koh, the dean of Yale Law School and the Obama Administration's nominee for the position of legal advisor to the Department of State, of supporting the rule of Sharia law over the US Constitution. But instead of dismissing these claims as outright absurd, others soon rallied to Beck's cause. Prominent members of the GOP like Karl Rove and John Bolton, the former ambassador to the UN, began echoing versions of Beck's accusations.

By the next year, Republicans in the Oklahoma legislature had introduced a measure to make the use of Sharia law illegal in the state. "This is a war for the survival of America," Representative Rex Duncan, the politician behind the ballot measure, would say on national television. "It's a cultural war, it's a social war, it's a war for the survival of our country." In the following weeks and months, the movement would expand even further, winning over hundreds of state legislators, tens of thousands of grassroots supporters, and even a handful of members of Congress (as we will see in chapter 6). At the time of this writing, voters in nearly one in five states in the union have elected to ban Sharia law—an astonishing feat for any political movement, little less one premised upon demonizing the world's second-largest religion.

Was this nascent political movement a new type of phenomenon in American politics? Or did it channel something essential, something common to more than our era alone? How did these seemingly wild claims—vilifying a religion with more than 1.6 billion adherents—fit into historical context? With these questions in mind, I began to research the forgotten movements of our nation's political history—beginning with the dawn of the Revolution, and spanning to the present day—only to learn that there was much more to these accusations than meets the eye.

Consider, for example, the following claim, from an 1835 volume written by Samuel F. B. Morse, the inventor of the single-wire telegraph, describing a Catholic conspiracy to overthrow the US government:

> *Foreign spies have clothed themselves in a religious dress, and so awestruck are our journalists at its sacred texture, or so unable or unwilling to discern the difference between the man and his mask, that they start away in fear.*

Or this claim, part of the 1892 platform of the Populist Party, focused on the widespread belief that American monetary policy was being set by an international syndicate of bankers:

> *A vast conspiracy against mankind has been organized on two continents, and it is rapidly taking possession of the world. If not met and overthrown at once it forebodes terrible social convulsions, the destruction of civilization, or the establishment of an absolute despotism.*

Or this declaration from the 2010 bestselling book, *The Grand Jihad*, written by former federal prosecutor Andrew C. McCarthy, arguing that President Obama is in league with Islamic extremists, waging an ideological war against the United States from within:

> *A civilization fights to preserve itself or it dies. Has ours become so hollow, such a pale imitation of its former self? Do we lack the capacity even to speak of the evils arrayed against us? Have we become so cowardly that our censure is reserved for our saviors, not our pillagers? The conspirators are banking on it.*

While any one of these statements could have been pronounced at the height of McCarthyism in the early 1950s, these quotations were uttered several decades apart. As Mark Twain is said to have put it, history may not repeat itself, but it sure does rhyme. And in each case, huge portions of the American public bought into these accusations—not indefinitely, to be sure, but for a time.

A closer look at American history reveals that there is a marked trend underlying these claims. Every few decades, a striking political phenomenon emerges, based upon the fear that a secret network has infiltrated American society and threatens destruction from the inside. Even more fascinating is the fact that this type of movement is not relegated to the fringes of the political arena—it routinely takes center stage. Wide swaths of the American public, its leaders, and its intellectuals buy into the conspiracy theory, ready to sacrifice whatever they must—basic constitutional rights, for example—to keep the internal enemy at bay. Stranger still is the fact that the history of this tendency remains largely unexplored, in both the academic literature and in the popular press.

What explains this phenomenon? This book seeks to illustrate, through five separate examples, stretching from the 1790s to today, that America's sense of self-identity routinely comes under pressure, with the result that certain groups confront a loss in status. Engaging in political hysteria is how these groups seek to get it back. The following pages will detail stories of blacklists and scapegoating, conspiracies and cover-ups—tales that follow a similar shape and contour throughout American history. By looking at a handful of these movements, a startlingly recognizable pattern will emerge, one that sheds light on the state of American politics and identity today.

<hr>

But first, a note about the expression "hysteria" itself. Hysteria is a psychological term, used throughout history to describe different types of psychological illnesses, usually in the broadest terms. The word has its origins in the Greek term for "uterus," symbolizing the animal spirit women carried that craved children and created life. In ancient times, women who came down with fits of panic or rage were often described as hysterical—as having become possessed by their uterine spirit. The word has been used repeatedly to describe all sorts of mental ailments ever since, ailments that the best scientific minds of the day were unable to understand. Witchcraft, panic attacks, depression, sexual anxiety—all of these have been described as hysteria at different periods of time.

So too has this vague term been used to describe mass psychological phenomena, though again with little precision. Social trends throughout the last few hundred years have been labeled as "mass hysteria" when groups of people make the same senseless, and usually impulsive, decisions. The supposed epidemic of suicides in young European men after the publication of Johann Wolfgang von Goethe's 1774 novel, *The Sorrows of Young Werther*, in which the young protagonist brings his own life to an end, was described as an epidemic of hysteria. In the late 1930s, a New York radio station aired an all-too-convincing story about an invading army from Mars. Thousands of distressed listeners took to the streets, vacating their homes and panicking as if the apocalypse was near. This episode, too, was referred to as hysteria.

This book, however, aims at something different. In the following pages, I will use the term "hysteria" to refer to a specific type of political phenomenon, with specific features and common characteristics—a phenomenon that I will spend much of this introductory chapter defining. Unlike in past instances, I will not use the term to describe the psychological states of those who lead these types of movements, nor will I use the term to describe the psychological states of their followers. Here hysteria is a strictly political term, meant to describe American political movements—though there is no reason it could not be applied to movements in other countries as well. This is a book about American history, after all, and I leave the international dimensions of this analysis to others.

So just where, exactly, does the story of political hysteria begin? Like so many tales about America, this one begins not on American soil, but in France.

⚊ ⚊

Our story starts with Gustave Le Bon. Le Bon was a French doctor by trade, but it was his philosophical writings that would earn him renown and, at the age of thirty-five, enough money to stop working. Free from the standard concerns of daily life, Le Bon used the interlude from his professional life wisely, traveling the world, indulging his intellect, and learning about the latest scientific theories. Of all the theories in vogue, what struck Le Bon the most was the idea of the "unconscious," a theory of growing popularity in the 1890s, the decade that would turn out to be one of the most important of Le Bon's intellectual career. The unconscious was thought to be a mental force hidden from our minds, one that could affect what we think and how we feel without our knowing it. It explained how, despite the growing role of reason and of science in modern society, human beings still behaved in irrational ways. It would be a seminal theory, shaping the works of Sigmund Freud and Carl Gustav Jung, two of the most important figures in modern psychology. But for Le Bon, the theory of the unconscious also explained something different, something far more important than the operating principles of one single human mind: He thought that it governed the way that societies functioned at large.

And how did Le Bon come to this conclusion? Horses.

One of Le Bon's greatest fascinations had been the training of horses, about which he studied and wrote extensively. Le Bon had learned from horses that reason was less a matter of intelligence and more a matter of the forces of psychology—simple repetition, for example, could drastically alter the way horses thought. But Le Bon also noticed something else: Horses behaved differently when they were in groups, that the mind of one horse seemed to unconsciously affect the minds of the others. One rebellious horse, for example, could change the disposition of the entire group, even if none of the horses had been rebellious previously. Le Bon called this effect "mental contagion," in which the disposition of one horse spread to the others through the unconscious, somewhat like a contagious disease.

Soon Le Bon began to apply this idea to humans, and to human society. He found fame in this approach with the publication of *The Crowd: A Study of the Popular Mind* in 1895. The book was a seminal work in collective psychology, and in the study of society at large—one that continues to shape the thinking of psychologists, political scientists, and sociologists to this day. Here, for example, is how Le Bon believed crowds worked: First, as the individual begins to identify with the crowd, he becomes anonymous. Then, as more and more members of the crowd gain anonymity, the crowd becomes its own sort of entity, with its own form of collective unconscious. Lastly, the individual surrenders his own identity to the crowd, losing consciousness of his own behavior and acting without the constraints of logic or responsibility.

Le Bon had one more key insight, one that explains how groups of otherwise rational humans could act in astoundingly irrational ways: The crowd operates according to its lowest common denominator. According to Le Bon, the least intelligent member of the crowd sets the standard for the actions of the entire group; it was as if a crowd is composed of a chain of human intellects, and "higher" thoughts would fail to transmit at intellectual weak points in the chain. What the crowd could understand were the thoughts that every one of its members could grasp. In this way, the crowd was a deeply ominous force in society. It wasn't just the triumph of the collective over the individual, but the triumph of our basest impulses over our highest ones. The crowd was an outlet for human beings' most animalistic desires.

The explanatory power of Le Bon's theory was astounding. Le Bon explained, in the language of the psychological theories of the day, how groups of otherwise rational individuals could come together and act like uncivilized animals. These concerns were very real in the 1890s. Academics had spent the last century attempting to understand how the French Revolution, a political movement explicitly dedicated to reason and democracy, had given way to widespread public chaos. One of the most potent symbols of the French Revolution, after all, had been the guillotine, not the ballot box. Other instances of barbarism dotted the nineteenth century too—riots, pogroms, lynchings, and the like.

What made Le Bon's theory even more relevant was that, by the time of the 1890s, the masses—as opposed to less populous elite classes—were gaining more and more responsibility in countries throughout the West. In the United States, for example, African Americans and immigrants had become an increasingly large political constituency. By 1920, just a few decades off, women would be able to vote. "The entry of the popular classes into political life," wrote Le Bon, "is one of the most striking characteristics of our epoch of transition." How crowds functioned would thus determine the future of society, and Le Bon's pessimistic account was cause for great concern. If Le Bon was right, the twentieth century would be marked by the rise of mob mentality and senseless violence would soon ensue. Less than two decades before World War I, and four from the outbreak of World War II, these predictions were not so far off.

But Le Bon's account operated at the most abstract levels. It explained how otherwise rational individuals could come together to behave irrationally—a sort of baseline explanation for episodes that resembled political hysteria, but a very crude one nonetheless. It did not explain, for example, how these individuals united to form political constituencies, nor did it explain the motivations behind these groups or their timing. Why, for example, were some people attracted to irrational crowds while others were not? And it is here that Richard Hofstadter comes in.

A professor of history at Columbia University, Hofstadter blended Le Bon's focus on mass psychology with a deep understanding of American history and culture. His account of political hysteria would ultimately revolutionize the way that academics and journalists think about episodes of political hysteria to this day.

Hofstadter had watched the rise and fall of McCarthyism in the early 1950s from his perch at Columbia, but it was during the elections of 1952 that the subject of political psychology caught Hofstadter's eye. The election pitted the intellectual Democrat Adlai Stevenson against the plainspoken Dwight Eisenhower. And though Eisenhower won by a landslide, as was predicted, what surprised Hofstadter was what he called the "anti-intellectualism" of the American public—that Stevenson was not simply disliked for his pointed intelligence, but widely *hated*. There was something cultural about Stevenson's loss, Hofstadter thought, something beyond politics alone. What Hofstadter saw in the 1952 elections was a complete rejection of the academic class, and this intrigued him as much as it stung.

And so Hofstadter began one of the most productive stretches of his career, attempting to analyze the irrationalities of American politics. Why, for example, would Americans reject some of the most intelligent members of society, simply because of their intelligence? As Hofstadter looked to McCarthyism, which would begin to implode around 1954, he saw a similar type of irrationality at work. Why had the anti-communists been more focused on the threat of domestic communism, when a much more dire threat *actually* existed in the foreign policy arena? How could these political movements be so clearly irrational, and so clearly self-defeating, and yet gain widespread success?

8

The answer, Hofstadter believed, rested partially on timing and partially on psychology. First, Hofstadter thought that episodes of political hysteria only occurred *during periods of economic booms*. During booms, he argued, different classes of American society are freed from more materialistic worries—from concerns about taxes and economic policy, for example—and are able to engage in *status politics*. In status politics, social classes compete against each other for dominant positions in society, seeking influence and positions of power. Status politics is less about the competition for wealth, and more about the competition for *prestige*, generally defined as the approval, respect, or admiration accorded to one group by other members of society—a crucial concept for Hofstadter, and one that will be key to understanding the movements outlined in the pages to come. Whereas in class politics groups compete for economic resources, in status politics groups compete for prestige. Throughout the course of status competition, some classes win big, some lose big, and others fall in between. Hofstadter asserted that it is the losing classes that engage in the scapegoating and irrationality that characterized periods like McCarthyism. Driving periods of mass hysteria were thus some type of group-based social concerns. The groups that were lower on the totem pole, that had lost social prestige, were the ones most likely to engage in this type of hysteria.

But Hofstadter also thought there was more than timing alone to these periods of mass irrationality. He thought there was an element of psychology as well, and here is where he introduced his famous term "the paranoid style in American politics," first in a lecture and later in a book by that same name. The "paranoid style" was a political disposition that he thought afflicted segments of American society, one that caused certain Americans to see politics as a clash between good and evil, and one in which compromise—the cornerstone of democracy—became all but impossible. The paranoid American "does not see social conflict as something to be mediated and compromised, in the manner of the working politician," wrote Hofstadter. "Since what is at stake is always a conflict between absolute good and absolute evil, the quality needed is not a willingness to compromise but the will to fight things out to a finish. Nothing but complete victory will do."

It was thus much more than simple status politics that was at work in periods of hysteria. For Hofstadter, hysteria came about when periods of economic success aligned with a specific group's loss in social status—with the "paranoid" Americans' decline on the societal totem pole. As with genetic diseases, specific groups of Americans were "at risk" for hysteria, in Hofstadter's view. When these predisposed groups suffered a loss in status during periods of economic growth, periods of political hysteria would soon ensue.

—~—

A blending of Le Bon and Hofstadter's views has become the dominant explanation for periods of political hysteria, and widely persists to this day. This "traditional account" of hysteria focuses on collective psychology, explaining periods of political hysteria as the product of mob mentality among the declining classes.

And yet for all the genius behind Le Bon and Hofstadter's views, there is one major problem with their combined approach: The traditional account gets hysteria wrong.

Indeed, this traditional account obscures the actual factors behind political hysteria, and as I will contend in the pages that follow, hides its true importance. This failure has significant implications for an understanding of the processes at work in political hysteria—and for understanding American history itself. The rest of this chapter will outline the basic tenets of my theory of political hysteria, before turning to the stories themselves.

We begin by highlighting the most problematic aspect of the traditional account. That problem? The traditional account treats hysteria as the result of mob mentality, rather than national politics, and in this respect it is deeply mistaken. For the truth is that theories of mob mentality are better fit for explaining riots after football games than for explaining national political movements. "Crowds don't have central nervous systems," according to Clark McPhail, an emeritus professor of sociology at the University of Illinois at Urbana-Champaign, hinting at why the traditional account can only go so far when applied to national politics. Crowds simply cannot be analyzed as if they had a collective mind. So too do episodes of hysteria differ from mob mentality. Each episode is made up of coalitions of individuals, each with diverging needs and differing worldviews. Each is prone to factionalism. And each is ultimately rooted in political concerns.

Yet the traditional account of hysteria still dominates, and this book aims to correct this mistaken reading. It aims to show how political hysteria provides a window into American society, functioning as a sort of bellwether into the larger forces at work. Indeed, hysteria holds the key not just to understanding periods of so-called political irrationality, but to American politics and its history as a whole. Hysteria, at its core, boils down to an argument about group identity—it is a way of defining *who we are* by defining *whom we are against*. From this vantage point, there are two key points to understanding how political hysteria works. The first is that hysteria arises at times of profound change in America's national identity. The second is that each movement is focused on an outside threat. For those less interested in the theoretical underpinnings of political hysteria than in the characters and dramas that make up the movement's history, you will be forgiven for turning straight to the stories of the episodes themselves, starting with chapter 2. In the meantime, we will begin with hysteria's connection to national identity.

America's national identity has not been forged easily, nor has it ever been static. National identity is the "glue" that holds the country together, a common vision behind which Americans unite. It is affirmed and reaffirmed in popular culture, political speeches, patriotic songs, and in books and magazine articles. National identity is a tricky thing, for in one sense it is a pure abstraction, a series of arguments about what it means to be an American. Yet in another sense, it is very real: Millions of individuals help shape America's national identity every day, in the way a gun owner proudly cleans the barrel of his shotgun, for example, or when an immigrant tries to hide her accent in the checkout line at the grocery store. National identity is ultimately what America has gone to war to defend. It is, in essence, a process—and a fluid one at that.

Changes in America's national identity are constantly taking place—some subtly, others more overt—for this is precisely how national identity works. When the country was founded, for example, blacks were not perceived to actually be "American"—in most states they were expressly barred from exercising any political rights, both freed and slave alike. In 1862, President Lincoln would tell a delegation of free blacks visiting the White House to go back to Africa. A century later, though not without much struggle and bloodshed, the civil rights movement would change the nation, spelling the end for legalized segregation, and leading to huge advancements in the legal, economic, and social rights of African Americans. Nearly fifty years after that, an African American would be elected to the most powerful political office in the country—and this is just the most extreme example of these shifts.

So what, exactly, does America's national identity look like? Essentially, it can be summed up in three main arguments, each of which has been used throughout our history to define what the "United States" represents—what, in effect, keeps the United States *united*. Think of these arguments as "ingredients" in the American "recipe," as three separate stories—sometimes overlapping, sometimes contradicting—that Americans have told themselves to explain who they are. Each argument is crucial to understanding movements of political hysteria and can be summed up in the following phrase: *Americanism is based on Community, Descent, and Equality*, or *ABCDE* for short.

Community acknowledges that America comprises a patchwork of local entities, and that smaller allegiances often come before national ones. Call it a product of federalism or republican ideals, *community* is at its core a pragmatic argument about America's national identity, for it has allowed the country the room to compromise over some of its grander principles. A nation made up of local allegiances, after all, permits its communities to make decisions that might contradict each other on a larger scale—decisions like, for example, whether to abolish slavery. Under this view, communities in the North could put aside their differences with their Southern neighbors, at least in the short term, on the theory that regional disagreements needed to be subjugated to other, more pressing national concerns. For the first hundred years of the country's existence, this was the dominant view of American identity—that America's national identity was more local than national, more a patchwork of differing identities than one cohesive whole. For this reason community is a weak argument, precisely because it allows local identities to trump national interest. Before the Civil War, for example, Americans routinely referred to the US as "these United States," using the plural to emphasize local allegiances over national ones. By the end of the war, Americans would begin to use the singular "the United States," indicating that after nearly a hundred years of the country's existence, they were now finally part of *one* America, and it was around this time that *community* began to wane. A strong national identity, forged by years of profound physical and ideological struggle, began to set in.

If community no longer provides a sufficiently broad umbrella for national identity, what about the argument for *descent*, that it is ultimately the identity of our forbearers that makes us who we are? Since this argument defines Americans according to certain criteria of race, religion, or ethnicity, it is usually associated with the racist elements of American society and periods when blacks, Native Americans, Catholics, Asians, and Jews, among others, were excluded from playing an equal role in American society. And this is surely true. Most of the arguments for descent have emphasized the white Anglo-Saxon's place in American history, and they have been used to exclude immigrant or nonwhite populations. But descent has also been used to emphasize Americans' European roots in less overtly racist ways. The modern version of descent, for example, focuses on Judeo-Christian values as central to America's national identity, and many American politicians, in both the Democratic and Republican parties, have gone on record defending one or another version of this argument.

Finally, we might argue—and it is this argument that modern Americans are most familiar with—that what we most share in common is the belief in certain ideals, like opportunity and liberty, embodied in the Declaration of Independence and the Bill of Rights, and that these ideals apply to all of us equally by virtue of our Americanness. It was in defense of this principle of egalitarianism, for example, that President Woodrow Wilson once told a group of new citizens that being an American meant harboring allegiance "to no one" in particular, but rather to "a great ideal, to a great body of principles, to a great hope." Today, we define our national identity in terms of *equality*, and our contemporary political debates are largely focused on just what this means—it is generally framed by liberals as equal opportunity for all Americans (and associated with social welfare programs), while conservatives generally focus on equal access to universal freedoms (associated with the "small government" approach). What I call *equality* here is also known as the American Creed, a term first popularized by the sociologist Gunnar Myrdal in the 1940s. Some contemporary thinkers, however, argue that nations need more than mere common values to forge an identity—they need things like race, ethnicity, and geography—and this has been the case for most of American history as well. It is only in the last half of the twentieth century that equality has come to play such a defining role in our national identity.

These three main building blocks of America's national identity—*community, descent*, and *equality*—have been used throughout the country's history to create a common vision about what it means to be an American, and to unite America's myriad groups behind one national ideal. Each element's role has waxed and waned as the country evolved, as national crises like the Civil War or the civil rights movement brought out contradictions in Americans' shared self-image. The proportion of each element in America's national identity has, in short, shifted over time.

But just how, exactly, does America's national identity change?

Put simply, if national identity boils down to a series of arguments about what holds the country together, then all it takes to change the nation's identity is new arguments and new believers—a shift, for example, from *community* and *descent* to an identity that emphasizes *equality*. Politicians change the way they talk about America, journalists and academics emphasize new values, and the American public supports these changes.

A defining feature of this view of the shaping of national identity is that different groups may subscribe to varied notions about what it means to be an American—and indeed, they often do. Because forging a national identity is a process, *there is room for competing arguments among groups*. One period's conception of American identity might then manifest varying levels of tension. And the competing arguments offered by various groups are frequently connected to their own social status, to their own vision of their place in American society. To use the most striking example, the slave owner's vision of America was intimately connected to his own level of social prestige, and America's move toward greater equality in the aftermath of the Civil War undercut his standing in society. But this is also the case with groups that have less overtly at stake. Historically, for example, Christian groups have placed great weight on the declaration that America is "a Christian nation" as a way of ensuring their group's prestige and maintaining its dominance—and many such groups continue to do so today. In this way, status politics and national identity are deeply entwined. America's national identity is the ultimate codification of group prestige, an ever-shifting battleground in which groups vie for influence and approval on the national stage.

This means that when American national identity comes under pressure, certain groups will find that their vision of America's identity is no longer compatible with the rest of society's—just like the slave owners during the Civil War. The sociologist Joseph Gusfield called groups like American slave owners "doomed classes." During periods of profound change, he wrote, "social systems and cultures die slowly, leaving their rear guards behind to fight delaying action. . . . The dishonoring of their values is a part of the process of cultural and social change." It is precisely these groups that form the constituencies for movements of political hysteria. Hysteria is the way America's "doomed classes" confront their loss of prestige.

If political hysteria arises at times of abrupt ruptures in America's sense of itself as a nation, then it makes sense why such movements appear when they do—not simply in periods of economic booms, but when changes in national identity spur some groups to try to reclaim their declining prestige.

But what do such movements look like in the flesh? What marks their rhetoric? And what do their followers actually believe? The answer relates to a shared sense of threat. At times of profound shifts in America's national identity, a loss of prestige poses a very real threat to certain groups, one that helps motivate a movement's supporters to take action.

The dilemma for such movements, however, is that the threat is usually philosophical. It is cultural. It is an idea. It is ultimately intangible. And this is a big problem for political movements. Political movements are, after all, constructed through mobilization—they are built by convincing their constituents of the specific need to act. But it is hard to rally supporters around an invisible threat, around an abstract ideal, no matter how damaging the threat might be. It wasn't Nazism that Americans fought during World War II, for example—it was the Nazis.

Political hysteria overcomes this difficulty by projecting *real threats* onto *symbolic threats*, by creating a physical stand-in to symbolize the harm its constituency is actually confronting. Symbolic threats come in the form of outside groups or secret organizations—and the more conspicuous, the more compelling. Ethnic and religious groups, for example, have both served as symbolic threats for movements of political hysteria. The most persuasive symbols tend to be groups with powerful leaders and an operating ideology that is new or different, one that's easy to paint as an alien danger. The very act of labeling a group's ideology as alien, after all, can highlight what's indigenous and familiar to everyone else around. But there is more to symbolic threats than their foreign nature, just as there is more to political hysteria than xenophobia alone. Successful symbolic threats must be fashioned into compelling explanations for the real threat that Americans are actually facing—that a secret group of communists, for example, is manipulating American foreign policy, as was widely believed during the height of McCarthyism, based on American missteps abroad that seemed to favor the Soviet Union and a communist-like program of domestic welfare at home. The more conceivable the explanation, and the more plausible the connection between the symbolic and real threats, the more successful the hysteria will be.

Yet again, however, it is worth emphasizing that this explanation is not meant to serve as a psychological diagnosis of the supporters of movements of hysteria, as if they were projecting childhood traumas from the distant past. This type of psychological analysis has plagued past attempts at understanding political hysteria, and is precisely what we are trying to avoid in these pages. The projection from real to symbolic threats is merely meant to illustrate the appeal such movements wield among their followers, and the explanatory powers that movements of hysteria hold. It is precisely because such threats are symbolic, that they stand for some-thing much greater, that seemingly illogical arguments are able to play such a forceful role on the national political stage. Similarly, this is not to say that a movement's members do not actually believe the conspiracy theories they peddle—as we will see in the following pages, many of the members of the movements explored in this book actually believed in the righteousness of their cause, as if nothing less than the fate of the world depended on it. While it is doubtful that McCarthy actually believed the charges he made, for example, the same cannot be said for many of his supporters.

———

At this point, we have overviewed the traditional account of political hys-teria and the main reasons it leads us astray. We highlighted the way that America's national identity is formed from a series of overlapping arguments. We have shown how America's identity changes, how these changes create "doomed classes," and how political hysteria arises from these doomed groups' status concerns. And we outlined the connection between the real threats underlying each movement and the symbolic threat that each movement is purportedly focused upon. We have, in essence, explained why hysteria arises and what it looks like when it does. But what makes political hysteria different from other types of main-stream political movements? And how can we tell if a seemingly irrational movement is political hysteria or something else? These are intriguing questions, and the answers lie in comparing political hysteria to the gen-eral phenomenon it is most often confused with: political extremism.

Political scientists talk about extremism in a variety of ways. Some define extremism as the advocacy of violence over political compromise. Others plot segments of society across the political spectrum, and define extremism as any political movement that occurs on the far ends of that spectrum. The crucial point in all such notions lies in the fact that labeling a group as "extremist" marginalizes that group's role in the wider political discourse. To call a group "extremist" is to say that it occurs on the fringes of society, far outside the mainstream. The violent political movements of the 1960s and 1970s, such as the Weather Underground or the Black Panthers, were clearly extremist movements, as are many of the anti-government "Patriot" movements of today. They were rooted in the fringes of American politics, with relatively few adherents. And in this sense, they were clearly extreme.

At first blush, political hysteria seems quite similar to general political extremism. Both types of movements, after all, share a fascination with conspiracies, and they often take the form of crusades. To an outsider, both types of movements always seem irrational. But political hysteria isn't your ordinary flavor of political extremism—it is a *specific brand* of extremism. And that is because political hysteria does not erupt on the fringes of the political spectrum, as do other extreme movements, but rather it occurs in the mainstream. Movements of hysteria garner a widespread following. Key members of society turn out in support, state and national legislatures become infused with the movement's rhetoric, and huge swaths of the public subscribe to the movement's worldview. At the peak of McCarthyism, for example, 50 percent of the American public supported the senator and his witch hunts. This was no marginal phenomenon. Other movements of hysteria have followed the same pattern, moving from the fringes of political discourse to the center, with varying levels of success.

Another key feature of political hysteria is the way it treats the groups that make up its symbolic threat. When movements of political hysteria reject a group, for example, they generally do not espouse violence against that group, as most extremist movements usually do. Rather, they will attempt to prevent its members from playing a meaningful role in the formation of American identity, to denigrate their place in society, and ultimately to lessen their prestige. And this, after all, makes sense. Because political hysteria is ultimately about restoring each movement's vision of America's national identity, the movement's major aims are confined to the realm of status concerns. Political hysteria is not generally about physical expulsion, but about recapturing one group's role in America's identity by denigrating the role of another. It is ultimately about regaining social prestige.

The life span of each movement is another unique feature of political hysteria. Unlike most forms of extremism, which dwell at the margins of society for extended periods of time, hysteria flares up and dies out rather quickly, at least in relation to the threat it arose to purportedly confront. Political hysteria, as a mainstream phenomenon, is ultimately a transient one. It is as if a violent storm had swept through, the dark clouds vanished, and the perpetrators of the episode suddenly disgraced—despite the fact that the major threats continue to exist, such as the Soviet Union in the case of McCarthyism. The Soviet menace, after all, continued to confront the United States, both inside and out, for roughly four decades after McCarthyism's downfall. "The American people always see through a counterfeit," Harry Truman once quipped, it just "takes a little time."

Political hysteria occurs time and time again throughout American history, and it is a deeply disturbing phenomenon at that, with grave consequences to our laws and our freedoms. Movements of political hysteria routinely isolate and harm the most vulnerable among us, most commonly recent immigrants and minorities, inflicting long-term economic pain that can last generations. For each of the five episodes of political hysteria that I explore in the following chapters, I will look at the particular threat the movement rose to confront, its claims for who was to blame, the tools used to accomplish its ends, and how successful it was in convincing more Americans of its arguments over a longer period of time. The ultimate aim of this book is to describe not simply what political hysteria is, but how and why it is so successful, so that its past instances may be more fully understood and its future dangers avoided. But there is much more to political hysteria than can be described in this introductory chapter alone. Indeed, the real key to understanding the strange and fascinating tale of political hysteria lies in the stories of the five movements that fill the subsequent pages—in the characters and personalities that mark each episode, and in the stories of crime and intrigue at the heart of each movement. Our first begins on May 9, 1798.

CHAPTER 2

America's First Time

Jedidiah Morse and the Anti-Illuminati Movement

May 9, 1798, was much more than an ordinary weekday in the life of the newborn republic, and much more than an ordinary spring day at one Charlestown, Massachusetts, church. Just six weeks earlier, President John Adams, then only one year into his presidency, had declared the day a time of national fast and prayer, urging Americans to come together and atone for their communal sins. "The United States of America are at present placed in a hazardous and afflictive situation by the unfriendly disposition, conduct, and demands of a foreign power," declared Adams, referring to France. The former American ally had just begun seizing US ships—hundreds of them—in response to the United States's support for Great Britain, now at war with France for its fifth straight year. Adams asked that the nation's citizens pray that the conflict with France, later referred to as the "Quasi-War," not be allowed to worsen.

And so priests and worried citizens across the country gathered together to spend their day in prayer and contemplation. But for one New England pastor by the name of Jedidiah Morse, national fast day was about much more than mere prayer. To the parishioners who crowded the pews of the First Congregational Church of Charlestown, Massachusetts, that day, the tall reverend with beady eyes and powdered, silken hair would offer not just an explanation for the chaos that threatened to engulf the newborn nation—he would also offer a cure.

Today was a "day of trouble, of reviling and blasphemy," proclaimed the thirty-six-year-old minister. "Our newspapers teem with slander and personal invective and abuse. Our rulers, grown grey, many of them, in the service of their country . . . are yet stigmatized continually." The future, said Morse, was bleak, but it was not without hope. At least, not yet.

A secret network of conspirators had been operating within the country for years, he declared. "It is part of a deep-laid and extensive plan, which has for many years been in operation in Europe." From this plan "we may trace that torrent of irreligion, and abuse of every thing good and praise-worthy, which, at the present time, threatens to overwhelm the world." Morse, in short, had stumbled upon a conspiracy so immense, involving so many foreigners, that it threatened the very existence of the nation. And now, for the first time, he was willing to utter its name on American shores. The conspiracy, he declared, stemmed from an international society known as the *Illuminati*.

Morse went on to blame the Illuminati for everything from the French Revolution in Europe, which had begun nearly ten years earlier in 1789, to the political divisions in the United States. Loyal Federalist and supporter of President Adams that he was, it stood to reason that the political opposition, spearheaded by Thomas Jefferson and intellectuals like Thomas Paine, were members of the Illuminati as well. And so did Morse's sermon veer from an international conspiracy theory to one with domestic political ends. If America's problems were apparent before his speech, the solution was now even clearer—if only the country could expose the members of the Illuminati and uproot them, the nation could cipher the real Americans from the fake ones in the process. The increasingly complicated world of the 1790s, according to Morse's worldview, could now be viewed in black and white.

Had Morse been an average pastor, his sermon might have gone unnoticed—or at least been quickly forgotten. But Morse wasn't just any pastor. Raised in neighboring Woodstock, Connecticut, and educated at Yale, Morse presided over one of the oldest Protestant churches in America; his stature commanded the respect and admiration of senators and presidents alike. And that made Morse's speech more than just a sermon, but rather the beginnings of a crusade. America's first episode of political hysteria was about to occur.

Morse was an intelligent man, to be sure, but he was by no means clever enough to invent such an odd, sweeping theory on his own. The tales of conspiracies then swirling through Morse's mind had originated in Edinburgh, Scotland, the previous year with the appearance of a book not so succinctly entitled *Proofs of a Conspiracy Against All the Religions and Governments of Europe, Carried On in the Secret Meetings of the Free Masons, Illuminati, and Reading Societies*, upon which nearly all of Morse's sermon was based. The book's author was John Robison, a professor of natural philosophy at the University of Edinburgh and a relatively renowned intellectual. Only seven years earlier, the College of New Jersey—which would later become Princeton University—had awarded Robison an honorary degree for his academic work. For the third edition of the *Encyclopedia Britannica*, Robison had been asked to draft articles on seamanship, the telescope, optics, waterworks, resistance to fluids, music, and more—no small honor for an academic in those days. Robison, suffice it to say, was no run-of-the-mill kook. Which is what made his *Proofs* all the more strange.

Robison, though ironically a Mason himself, had apparently witnessed "matters of serious concern and debate" in the Masonic lodges he had been exposed to. These lodges formed the local chapters of the Freemasons, a fraternal organization that had sprung up in England and Scotland a couple of hundred years before. The organization was originally formed as a trade union, grown from groups of masons, or bricklayers, meeting to discuss their craft. Soon, however, the society sprouted into something much greater. It developed rituals and codes and a belief system that emphasized reason along with the devotion to a single deity. Some consider the lodges of Freemasonry, which often counted men of great power among their members, a driving factor behind the age of Enlightenment.

Despite his exposure to the inner workings of their lodges, the Masons aroused deep suspicions in Robison, suspicions that he would soon apply to a group known as the Illuminati. "I have found that the covert of a Mason Lodge had been employed in every country for venting and propagating sentiments in religion and politics, that could not have circulated in public without exposing the author to great danger," he would write in his *Proofs*. Here, in Robison's own words, is the danger that he had found:

I have been able to trace these attempts, made, through a course of fifty years, under the specious pretext of enlightening the world by the torch of philosophy. . . . I have observed these doctrines gradually diffusing and mixing with all the different systems of Free Masonry; till, at last, AN ASSOCIATION HAS BEEN FORMED for the express purpose of ROOTING OUT ALL THE RELIGIOUS ESTAB-LISHMENTS, AND OVERTURNING ALL THE EXISTING GOVERNMENTS OF EUROPE. . . . The Association of which I have been speaking is the Order of ILLUMINATI, founded, in 1775, by Dr. Adam Weishaupt, professor of Canonlaw in the University of Ingolstadt, and abolished in 1786.

The Illuminati, Robison would go on to assert, were bent on nothing less than world domination. "Their first and immediate aim is to get the possession of riches, power, and influence," he added, "and to accomplish this, they want to abolish Christianity . . . to overturn all the civil governments of Europe." Once the order has achieved this feat, the Illuminati will "extend their operations to the other quarters of the globe, till they have reduced mankind to the state of one indistinguishable chaotic mass." Robison, in the course of his "research," had uncovered quite the conspiracy indeed.

To be fair, Robison's accusations were not *entirely* baseless. An organization called the Illuminati had been formed two decades prior, though in 1776, not in 1775. It had been formed by an Adam Weishaupt, and in truth, it did pose a threat to the established religious order in Europe, for that order had placed limits on what men of letters such as Weishaupt could and could not say. Weishaupt's ultimate goal was to create an environment where reason was not confined by the limits placed on free speech by the Catholic Church. The order of the Illuminati would become powerful, mysterious, and secretive—much more secretive, in fact, than the Masons themselves, who Weishaupt determined were too open to the public to wield significant influence.

But Robison was also correct that the order was abolished. After rising to a position of influence in Germany, the Illuminati were quickly disbanded through a series of edicts outlawing the group, beginning in 1784.

As more and more members came forward about the group's activities, and were absolved of any wrongdoing as a result, the order's operations were gradually exposed to the public. Internal documents were discovered; mild intrigues in the name of a secular philosophy were set forth upon the public stage. All of this was true. But by 1787, when the duke of Bavaria issued his last edict against the order, the Illuminati were effectively dead; the order was reduced to a lifeless series of mutual associations and forgotten bylaws.

Indeed, take away the mysterious codes of the Illuminati, and the threat Robison saw was not even that novel. The order simply advocated a brand of humanism—dedicated, in essence, to Enlightenment ideals—that formed the basis for the American Revolution and the US Constitution itself. Thomas Jefferson put it best: "If Weishaupt had written here [in the US], where no secrecy is necessary . . . he would not have thought of any secret machinery for [his] purpose." It was the Church that had driven Weishaupt's ideals underground—ideals that, by the time Robison's book came out ten years later, were discussed openly in both Europe and America.

But that didn't stop Robison's accusations, nor did it temper the effort he applied in digging for facts to back up his wild claims. In attempting to show the global reach of the Illuminati, for example, Robison looked to the order's internal documents that the German government had released. These documents had been released in much the same way that a library's books are "released" after a fire; the order had been burned to the ground, and in making their papers public, the Bavarian government aimed to establish this fact. Nevertheless, on the basis of such documents Robison was able to claim the existence of fourteen lodges in Austria, eight in England, five in Strasburg, four in Bonn, and "many" in Poland, Switzerland, and Holland. As for America, Robison asserted that "several" existed there—a relatively trivial contention, as far as Robison was concerned, but one that would have profound implications on the other side of the Atlantic.

Robison's book quickly caught on. The fact that it was chock-full of juicy conspiracy stories helped it gain wide readership, but ultimately it was the explanatory power of *Proofs* that truly accounted for its success.

The 1780s and '90s were years of dramatic change. In the span of one decade, the United States colonies won independence from Great Britain (in 1783), the French Revolution ushered in a reign of democratic chaos in France (beginning in 1789), and the first successful slave revolt in world history occurred in Haiti (beginning in 1791). It was the chaos in France in particular that many found so appalling—chaos that needed explaining. In abolishing the monarchy, French revolutionaries had, for instance, even gone so far as to chop off the king's head. Such pandemonium was not the product of Enlightenment ideals; this was pure madness.

Underpinning all of these changes was a new kind of ideology, one that was similar to Weishaupt's own ideals—ideals summed up in the French Revolution's cry of resistance, "Liberté, égalité, fraternité." Such principles had resulted in democracy in the United States, to be sure, but they had also resulted in terror elsewhere, and in the rise of a new kind of secular life in the West. For preachers like Jedidiah Morse, highly devout and also highly traditional, many of these ideological changes were more than they could bear. As secular ideas spread across the national stage, for example, Morse saw the membership in his own church in Charlestown dwindle. By the 1790s, for example, "Morse was losing heads of households and his church was increasingly composed of widows, single women, and wives who joined without their husbands," according to one Morse biographer. And this at a time when New England's population, and Charlestown's in particular, was growing exponentially. The "idle, the intemperate, the unprincipled, and the poor" were sweeping into his town, Morse once lamented.

So too was a new type of politics sweeping the nation, one plagued with bitter rivalry and tensions. Just one year after George Washington had vacated the presidency, American democracy was marked by a new-found turmoil—the political climate was unpredictable, crude, and boisterous. As Morse himself once explained, the Revolutionary War would begin by unifying Americans with a common enemy in the British, but after the conflict ended, this unity began to fade and a number of political and social "defects" emerged. A "jealousy of power had been universally spread among the people of the United States," and Americans had lost "their habits of obedience." Morse couldn't even stomach the term

"Americans," but rather used the term "Fedro-Americans"—this was long before a unified national identity had even begun to take shape. Morse was living, in short, in an age of profound transformation, disrupting any semblance of what life was like in the colonies during British rule. For the many left terrified by the chaos of the western world, the idea that a small but powerful group was responsible for these changes had great appeal. And it was to these worries that Robison's grand conspiracy theory, and now Morse's, related.

Morse first got ahold of Robison's book in April of 1798. By his own account, he procured a copy while traveling in Philadelphia after "hearing the work spoken of in terms of the highest respect by men of judgment," men who had pronounced the manuscript "the most interesting work that the present century had produced." Robison's *Proofs* clearly struck a nerve in Morse, and quickly too. He would wait only a few weeks after first reading it before spreading Robison's accusations from his pulpit later that May. It was to be the first major warning against the Illuminati on American soil. And in the course of the next year, there would be many more warnings to come.

The truth was, however, that Morse wasn't the only one looking for secret societies to scapegoat at that time. During the early part of the 1790s, the political discourse had been very subtly prepared for this type of conspiracy to take hold. In the early part of that decade, groups known as "Democratic-Republican Societies" inspired by the French Revolution sprouted up throughout the United States with the goal of propagating ultra-democratic ideals. Though these groups were secretive, they were decidedly political: One of the main divisions between the two political parties of the day lay in choosing between the British or the French as America's main ally. The Federalists, led by Alexander Hamilton and later John Adams, favored an alliance with the British, whereas the Democratic-Republicans (or "Republicans" for short), led by Thomas Jefferson, favored France. It wasn't long after their founding until the Societies became political fodder for all sides of the spectrum. Federalist newspapers used the example of the Societies to decry French interference and plotting, whereas Republicans saw this as an attempt to rile up the population in reaction to little more than harmless social clubs. And though George Washington himself had managed to stay above the political fray—having refused to associate himself with any political party at all—he did not manage to stay above this one.

In July of 1794, a US marshal arrived in western Pennsylvania to restore order after a series of long-held protests against a new tax on whiskey. The marshal's presence, however, only made things worse. Hundreds of men attacked the federal tax inspector's home, prompting Washington to call in thousands of troops. The episode became known as the "Whiskey Rebellion," and here is how Washington justified his reaction to the protests in his 1794 State of the Union address. "Certain self-created societies" had "assumed the tone of condemnation" against federal efforts to collect taxes, and as a result "combinations" emerged against the national government that were "too powerful to be suppressed by the ordinary course of judicial proceedings." Washington, in short, had been forced to send in the troops by groups that were conspiring against the government's control, and his words planted a potent seed in the public's imagination. Not only were secret societies operating within the United States, but they were powerful enough to foment a rebellion. George Washington had said it himself.

Despite the conviction that flowed from Morse's pulpit in May of 1798, his first sermon on the Illuminati fell flat. The fight was not his own: It was Robison whom Morse cited, and he had largely rehashed Robison's accusations in domestic terms. Morse had even openly deferred to Robison himself. Robison's book "is my authority," Morse had explained to his congregation, and "ought to be read by every American." The New England reverend was merely the vessel, not the owner, of the conspiratorial charges he made. Bigger stories, such as the so-called XYZ Affair, which polarized American sentiment against the French even further, were claiming the nation's attention. And deservedly so: In that episode, French officials had demanded outlandish bribes in exchange for continuing diplomatic relations—no small insult to a new nation. The anti-French fervor this insult stirred up, however, would set the stage for events to follow.

"The fast discourse was received with very unexpected approbation," Morse would later write in a letter to Oliver Wolcott Jr., treasury secretary under John Adams, and an important figure in the hysteria that was to come. "This same discourse delivered two months ago would have excited such a flame, as would in all probability have rendered my situation extremely unpleasant, if not unsafe."

But if most Americans overlooked Morse's sermon, fellow members of the New England clergy did not. In a series of sermons throughout the summer of 1798, others began to cite Morse's speech and his accusations about the Illuminati, at first slowly, but later gathering steam. In June, a professor of divinity at Harvard would be one of the first, warning the graduating class that "a more recent system" of philosophy championed by the Illuminati had its sights set on the destruction of the world.

The reverend and president of Yale, Timothy Dwight, was the next and the highest profile yet to take up Morse's new cause. Delivering his Fourth of July sermon to an audience on the New Haven Green, Dwight traced Robison's accusations from the Illuminati up to the major events of the day. In Germany, "multitudes" of citizens "have become either partial or entire converts to these wretched doctrines." In France, "Illuminatism has been eagerly and extensively adopted," and its leaders have all "been members of this society." Neither Switzerland nor Italy, England nor Scotland had been spared. Even in America, Dwight declared, the Illuminati were operating secretly.

That Dwight echoed Robison's accusations was no small gesture. The president of Yale was a towering public figure; many even referred to him as "Pope Dwight" in a sign of his authoritative stature. And Dwight wasn't the only one who used the national holiday to buttress Robison's claims. In Hartford, Connecticut, for example, Dwight's own brother, Theodore Dwight, a distinguished lawyer, repeated these exact accusations. Others would soon follow suit. The public was slowly being primed for a grand fear of the Illuminati to take hold.

Soon, the press began to notice the growing pace of the accusations, helping to turn Robison's conspiracy theory into a controversy that would drive

Morse into the national spotlight. In late July, for example, one prominent Massachusetts paper published a bold article demanding evidence for Robison's assertions—directed, however, at Morse. Never one to be attacked in public, Morse responded attempting to back up his claims. He used a number of tactics to defend his allegations that would be repeated, time and again, in future episodes of hysteria. And it is for this reason that we can examine Morse's first attempt to justify his accusations while keeping his broader techniques in mind.

First, Morse sought to defend Robison. The fact that evidence for the entire Illuminati conspiracy boiled down to Robison's one book was a huge vulnerability—as with most episodes of hysteria, the actual evidence Morse could bolster was sparse. Take away that evidence and all of Morse's arguments would fall apart. And so Morse sought to protect the few facts he could merit by assuring the public that Robison's character and his reputation were both of the highest caliber. Demonstrating Robison's respectability, at least for the time being, was not all that hard to do. Robison was a notable academic, and there was nothing in the public record to cast doubt upon his credibility. Morse merely had to recite a few facts from Robison's biography, and voilà. Robison was a bona fide expert. Credibility achieved.

Next Morse moved on to the book itself. He noted the success the book had met across the Atlantic—implying that a volume so full of falsities, as Morse's accusers claimed, would not be so well received by the clergymen and academics that had recommended the work to Morse. Now, however, the weak point in Morse's defense lay in equating popularity with credibility. As we all know in the Internet age, just because something is well read does not mean it is well written, or even adheres to the facts. And it was here that Morse used a timeless ploy. Citing just *one* favorable assessment of the book from *one* English reviewer, Morse argued that at the very least there was a reasonable debate about the merits of the book going on in Europe. This, in turn, must have meant that the book was not entirely unreasonable.

Thus Morse created the illusion of legitimacy where it was lacking. A bogus book, a few notable believers, and one book review is not enough to turn a series of false accusations into a credible theory. But no matter—the game, in essence, had been won. Morse's goal was not to convince the reader that he was right, but merely to plant a seed of doubt that he *could* be, that the accusations *could* rest on reasonable grounds, that his theory was worth looking into. From there, Morse merely needed to recite the names of the men who had echoed Morse's own sermon throughout that summer to prove his point, which is exactly what he did. Robison's theory about the Illuminati, the message was, might not be 100 percent correct, but it could not be unfounded.

From this perch of false credibility, Morse could next claim to deal with the hard facts that Robison had revealed—despite, of course, that there were none. From this point on, Morse made two key moves. First, he rehashed a few of Robison's claims, mixed in with his own theories about the Illuminati and world events—the chaos in France, the discord at home. As a result, it became harder to distinguish Morse's theory from his accusations, to separate fact from speculation, making both seem more formidable. Secondly, he added the following crucial disclaimer: Morse was attempting to unveil a worldwide conspiracy, plotted by sinister but brilliant minds. Being but one man, Morse could not claim to understand the entire plot. But he *could* claim to have unveiled one. It was thus up to the reader to unravel the intrigue further.

Morse's ploy worked. He had planted a seed of doubt significant enough for even those who were previously cynical to now reconsider their skepticism. Even the author of the first article challenging Morse's assertions now admitted that his faith in the existence of the Illuminati was growing. Based upon the reputations of those who asserted the Illuminati existed, wasn't there at least some evidence that this was true? If so, how could we know for sure that the brotherhood wasn't secretly plotting to overthrow religious and civil institutions worldwide? And why did they meet in secret? What did they have to hide? The reader was now left with questions—ludicrous though they were—that Morse's arguments had granted the illusion of legitimacy. Questions that would, over the next few months, be asked with increasing frequency.

⸻

But the truth was these were only questions. Aside from Robison's book, there was no new evidence to suggest that either Morse or Robison were on to something. And as a result, in the months between August and November, the debate over the Illuminati stalled. Federalist proponents of the theory rehashed Robison's arguments and quoted those who had joined the cause. Republican opponents responded by calling for more evidence, to which Morse's supporters would simply repeat their theory again, sometimes accusing Jefferson himself of being a member of the brotherhood. And so on. All the while, however, the controversy was gaining notoriety, as was Morse himself.

As long as no new facts emerged to back up the theory, however, the fledgling Anti-Illuminati movement could gain no new ground. The best Morse could hope for was that his following would grow, even while his theory remained in standstill, with no new evidence to back up his cause. The nascent movement was essentially treading water. But it would not tread water for long.

In the fall of 1798 a new book entitled the *Memoirs Illustrating the History of Jacobinism* was translated into English, written by a Frenchman named Abbé Augustin Barruel. The book echoed much of Robison's claims, though it focused more directly on the Illuminati's role in the French Revolution and less on the Freemasons. How Barruel stumbled upon the same theory as Robison is unclear, though what is clear is that these two writers appeared to be the only ones ever to discover the grand conspiracy they claimed to have unearthed, and that Barruel was aware of Robison's work while writing parts of his own. Whereas Robison had written simply one tome, Barruel had written several; his *Memoirs* were in fact a multi-volume composition. One tackled the brotherhood's philosophical plans, another its governmental conspiracies. The third volume, however, would be the most important, for it detailed the inner workings and links among secret societies all over the world, all working in unison and all bent on global domination. Barruel's was a grand Conspiracy with a capital "C."

America, of course, had not been shielded from this threat. "As the plague flies on the wings of the wind, so do their triumphant legions infect America," declared Barruel. "So numerous were the brethren in North America, that Philadelphia and Boston trembled, lest their rising constitution should be obliged to make way for that of the great club; and if for a time the brotherhood has been obliged to shrink back into their hiding places, they are still sufficiently numerous." The appearance of Barruel's *Memoirs* thus gave the impression that he had found more evidence for Robison's theory—specifically, more evidence of the Illuminati's presence in America. At long last, the supporters of Robison, and of Morse, now had what they thought were new facts to bolster their budding crusade.

The differences, however, between Robison's version of events and Barruel's were significant. "Facts" were not uniform across their two accounts, and a close reading of both texts would have cast doubt on the reliability of both. The few who did notice the discrepancies called the whole theory into account. Articles were written exposing the hollowness of the Illuminati conspiracy, and of the claims by men like Morse. The appearance of Barruel's text thus gave new ammunition to the detractors of the Anti-Illuminati movement as well.

All the while, however, Morse had been careful about his role in the growing hysteria, letting his May sermon on the Illuminati speak for itself. Since his latest articles in defense of Robison's work, published in August of 1798, he essentially remained mum on the existence of the Illuminati, at least in public, busy with his church duties and his three young sons at home and his own writings. In addition to being one of the nation's foremost pastors, Morse also happened to be one of its most well-known geographers, writing treatises on America's landscapes, population, and culture in his spare time—so prominent were Morse's books that his eldest son would, while studying at Yale, earn the moniker "Geography Morse." Morse, in short, had a habit of keeping busy. There would be no new major speeches, no new grand theories about the threats that America faced—instead, Morse would guard his time. But by November, seeing that his first sermon had at long last caught on, a thorough debate sparked over the Illuminati, and fresh evidence for the conspiracy from Barruel, Morse spotted a prime opportunity, one that he could not resist. It would not be long before he again entered the fray.

—◆—

November 29, 1798. Thanksgiving Day, a day that was to catapult the Anti-Illuminati movement to the next level on the national stage. The theme of Morse's sermon was bounty. Harvest that year had been good, and Thanksgiving was a day of gratitude—but how in the midst of such chaos, of such plotting and conspiracies, could Americans ignore the threats that lay at their nation's door? The answer was that they could not. And so talk of gratitude quickly turned to an examination of the conspiracy that threatened to engulf the nation. Morse would spend the rest of the sermon discussing the Illuminati from his pulpit, expounding on the grand threat to his congregation for the first time in nearly half a year.

"The blessings of good government have been most imminently and immediately endangered by foreign intrigue," declared Morse, who described that plotting as a force that "has been operating in various ways for more than twenty years past." The list of their "insidious efforts" was long: They kept alive national prejudices, fought to make the government less efficient, attempted to weaken the president, to destroy the checks and balances, circulated controversial publications to stir up divisions, opposed the rule of law. In front of a rapt congregation, Morse tied the Illuminati's devious plots to the fall of every empire—the Greeks, the Romans, and of course, the French monarchy.

Ultimately, however, it was not the speech itself that would launch Morse into the national spotlight, but the forty-five-page appendix published alongside it. For Morse knew that the key to a successful sermon lay not just in its delivery—in the days when sermons were published and circulated across the country, the key was in its written form. And it was here in the appendix, citing copious amounts of new evidence, that Morse would mount the most convincing defense of the Anti-Illuminati movement offered to date. Here, at long last, Morse would offer details in support of his cause. There was, for example, a batch of original documents from actual French diplomats, which Morse juxtaposed with his own wild assertions, blurring the line between fact and conjecture. In one letter, a French diplomat declared it "useless, and even dangerous, to attempt [to inform] the people through the public papers," which Morse took as evidence that French spies had been placing propaganda in American newspapers. "Is it rash to suppose," inquired Morse, "that many of those virulent and calumnious pieces against our government, its officers and measures, which have appeared in our opposition papers, have been from the pens of the agents and spies of France in this country?"

Even Morse's appendix had its own appendix, replete with more details linking the Illuminati to the French, and the French in turn to the domestic opposition. In discussing the origins of the Democratic Societies in America, for example, Morse would argue that "they started into existence by a kind of magic influence, in all parts of the United States, from Georgia to New-Hampshire." Was it no accident that the leaders of these clubs were "uniformly devoted to the interests of France"? Did they not intend to produce a "revolution in our country, and to put it under the guardianship of France?" Digging for even more details, Morse included quotes from a conversation related to him between "an American gentleman of great integrity and respectability, in whose veracity full confidence is to be placed" and a "French emigrant of note." The French, this gentleman insinuated, lusted after the destruction of all countries that refused to take sides in its war with England—and with a special vigor reserved for the United States.

The details of Morse's proofs were, in the end, less important than the effort he placed in creating them. Here was, for the first time, an elaborate trove of evidence that did not originate from either Robison or Barruel. Here, for the first time, a detailed series of facts showed that not only did the Illuminati exist, but that its brotherhood was working through the highest levers of power—in this case, the French government—to foment revolution in the United States. Here, at long last, was new proof that the Illuminati was responsible for all of America's ills.

Morse's sermon was a hit. In the days before public polling, and two years before the national elections of 1800, we have no exact way of measuring the precise impact the exposé had on national politics; we have no way of knowing, in other words, how big a hit it was. But we do know that thirteen hundred copies were printed, all of which were sold. A second edition was printed in a matter of months. Businessmen in Boston volunteered the funds to print a free copy for every clergyman in Massachusetts. The editor of the *New York Gazette*, the state's first newspaper, was so inspired by the sermon that he published the entire seventy-five-page text in six successive editions. The ensuing pandemonium, according to one historian, became "an eighteenth-century version of a media event."

Meanwhile, clergymen across New England echoed Morse's call with new vigor, while both sides of the debate again took to the press. In January, one Boston newspaper published an anonymous article attacking the conspiracy by asserting that fears in Europe over the Illuminati had died down. If the Illuminati were truly a threat, the article asked, wouldn't the public on the other side of the Atlantic still be alarmed? Two weeks later, the same paper aired a counterattack. "The naked declaration of an unknown paragraphist, probably enough an emigrant illuminatist, will not be sufficient with enlightened Americans to convict Professor Robison or Abbé Barruel of criminality or even of error." And on and on such exchanges went, printed in newspapers from Boston to New York to Philadelphia.

Perhaps the greatest, if not the most surprising, measure of the success of Morse's sermon was the impact it had on men of great power. One senator from Massachusetts, the Federalist Dwight Foster, wrote to Morse that his sermon would "be of great service in the present situation. . . . Some gentlemen here are desirous to have it more generally circulated. Members of Congress from the South wish for copies to send to their constituents." The leading Federalist in the House of Representatives, Robert Goodloe Harper of Maryland, wrote that Morse's exposé on the Illuminati was "highly worthy of attention at all times, and especially at the present," adding that he would have his own printers republish it. John Jay, the founding father, diplomat, and first chief justice of the US Supreme Court, wrote to Morse in support of his efforts, as did Oliver Wolcott Jr., the secretary of the treasury and Morse's longtime pen pal.

And as if this outpouring of support was not enough, George Washington himself wrote to Morse that he had read both the sermon and "the Appendix with pleasure, and wish the latter at least could meet a more general circulation than it probably will have." The appendix "contains important information" that Washington asserted was "little known out of a small circle," and "dissemination of it would be useful, if spread through the community." But Washington, as it turns out, wouldn't be

Morse's most powerful supporter. That distinction would be reserved for John Adams, the sitting US president himself.

———

By March of 1799, the controversy was front and center on the national stage. Morse's sermon had given the Illuminati a central role in American politics, and nothing served as a greater testament to this fact than John Adams's Fast Day Proclamation of 1799. A year after Adams had first spoken to the nation of the "unfriendly disposition, conduct, and demands of a foreign power," he now took his anti-French rhetoric to another level—specifically, to Morse's level. And though he did not mention the Illuminati directly by name, there is no doubt that Adams knew exactly how his words would be taken.

"The most precious interests of the people of the United States are still held in jeopardy by the hostile designs and insidious acts of a foreign nation," warned Adams, "as well as by the dissemination among them of those principles, subversive of the foundations of all religious, moral, and social obligations, that have produced incalculable mischief and misery in other countries."

This was no ordinary call for national prayer—it was a call to action. At a time when fears over the Illuminati dominated much of the nation's attention, the sitting president's talk of hostile designs and subversive principles clearly echoed Morse's claims. Treasonous agents were among us, the message was, disseminating their poisonous ideas. Just who these agents were, and the precise nature of their ideas, Adams left the nation to work out on its own.

Morse, undoubtedly, took this as a personal vindication. The alarm that he had raised one year earlier was now being sounded by President John Adams himself. Morse now gained a new enthusiasm for his cause, one that would lead him to deliver his most vigorous diatribe against the Illuminati yet.

———

It is at a movement's political high point that its greatest weaknesses emerge. The boldest assertions are made. "Facts" are delivered so vehemently, so convincingly, that its leaders lose credibility when reality points the other way. So April 25, 1799, marked this point in the life of the Anti-Illuminati movement, the day when Jedidiah Morse, encouraged by members of the Adams Administration and even the president himself, made his third and final attempt to convince the country that the Illuminati were out there, plotting in secret, attempting to destroy the world. Morse would cite new evidence and, in doing so, again place his very reputation on the line.

"I intend, my brethren, to lay before you what I humbly conceive to be our real and most alarming dangers," Morse declared to his congregation. "The subtle and secret assailants are increasing in number, and are multiplying, varying, and arranging their means of attack, it would be criminal in me to be silent. I am compelled to sound the alarm."

And sound the alarm he did.

Morse made a series of declarations about the dangers of the Illuminati, and patriot that he was, the threat the brotherhood's very ideology posed to the nation's government. At the beginning of his sermon, all that was new about Morse's claims was his tone—Morse conveyed to his congregation that the United States had, by the spring of 1799, somehow reached a breaking point. The Illuminati had been operating in the country for years, and yet it was only now that the situation had become dire. All would soon be lost if Americans did not act to root out this evil. Even President Adams, Morse proclaimed, had said so himself.

"Do you ask for proofs of all this?" he asked. "They are so abundant, and so flagrant, that I scarcely know which to select." And here is where Morse set a precedent that future leaders of American hysteria would follow, time and again, in attempting to win over their skeptics—here he would offer details so precise, so particular, that his assertions couldn't be anything other than true. Morse, in short, would offer up *a list*. "I have, my brethren, an official, authenticated list of the names, ages, places of nativity, professions, etc. of the officers and members of a Society of Illuminati . . . consisting of one hundred members, instituted in Virginia, by the Grand Orient of France." And as if a grand list was not enough, this was not the only evidence Morse possessed. The list had been sent to him along with a letter that included confirmation of another society in New

York "out of which have sprung fourteen others, scattered we know not where over the United States."

As with the previous sermon that had won Morse such high praise, this sermon contained an appendix nearly as long as the speech itself. And it was here where all the evidence Morse cited was displayed, consisting of yet more letters translated from French. This time, however, the letters included new proofs laid out in meticulous detail. Added to that was a list of the members' names of one Virginia lodge, most of them foreigners, which led Morse to deduce that at least seventeen hundred members of the Illuminati were operating in the United States. "That there are branches and considerably numerous too, of this infernal affectation in this country we have now full proof," concluded Morse. "That they hold and propagate similar doctrines and maxims of conduct is abundantly evident from what is passing continually before our eyes. They even boast that their plans are deeply and extensively laid, and cannot be defeated, that success is certain. If then, Americans, we do not speedily take for our motto, *Vigilance, Union and Activity*, and act accordingly, we must expect soon to fall." The nation, Morse declared that day, stood at a precipice, and the bottom was a long way down.

Thus Jedidiah Morse laid down the gauntlet against the Illuminati. And yet what exactly was he attempting? What did he want his listeners to *do*? Certainly, he could not have expected those who believed in the conspiracy to do nothing. They would understand the threat for what it was—a war between civilizations, between pagans and believers, between good and evil itself—and "act accordingly," in Morse's own words. Morse played up the threat of the Illuminati in strikingly grandiose terms. But he left unsaid what cause, exactly, he was advocating for. And it is here that the source of Morse's evidence sheds light onto his deeper intentions.

Morse had received the documents from none other than Oliver Wolcott Jr., Adams's treasury secretary, political operative, and a key member of the administration, with whom Morse had been corresponding for years. Conspiracies were nothing new to Wolcott, who first began to stoke Morse's fears of secret societies before Adams had even assumed the presidency. In 1795, for example, then serving as a member of Washington's cabinet, Wolcott wrote to Morse that many events had occurred "which separately considered appear unimportant," yet when viewed as a pattern, a "general combination to involve the US in trouble" exerts "much influence." The country's greatest minds, added Wolcott, "are anxious to investigate the real cause of those agitations which exclusively happen in our great towns. . . . What do these things portend?"

Now, however, Wolcott furnished Morse with much more than vague questions, but with actual evidence of the Illuminati's internal machinations. Just how Wolcott came to possess these documents is unclear—whether he had forged the papers himself or acquired them from someone else remains unknown. The documents, on their own, were more confusing than incriminating, a jumbled mess of names and private correspondence, most of it surely made up. But Wolcott's role highlights the political underpinnings of the Anti-Illuminati movement and the support it drew nonetheless; though some surely feared the Illuminati, and believed the tales of their sinister plotting to be true, the hysteria was, at its root, a deeply political phenomenon, an ideological muckraking campaign. Thomas Jefferson, after all, was being made to look more and more like a member of the Illuminati every day. How could that not help the Federalist Party? And it just so happened that Morse's evidence about the Illuminati located a key lodge of the secret society in Jefferson's home state—and the Republican stronghold—of Virginia. Even better for the Federalists and their cause.

Morse and his hysteria, in short, played to the larger partisan efforts designed to halt the opposition party, to beat back Jefferson and the Republicans by demonizing the political order they espoused. The Republicans were anti-authoritarian at a time when the country needed stability; they believed that the soul of the new country was its farmer-citizens, not its elite. They were anti-banking and anti-industrialist, and strikingly open to secular ideas. The Jeffersonians were, quite simply, deeply threatening to traditionalists like Morse. As one Morse biographer and historian would later explain: "The community (family, church, state) always meant a hierarchy of ranks and degrees to which everyone submitted; peace, harmony, and virtue depended on people's submission to this reality. Morse saw hierarchy and the family metaphor increasingly challenged; particularly in national politics, the Jeffersonian challenge seemed to be a rebellion." At stake in Morse's crusade against the Illuminati was thus nothing less than the very structure of American society itself.

If Morse's second sermon on the Illuminati was a hit, his third was a breakaway sensation. As Morse would write to Wolcott that June: "I have disturbed a hornet's nest." And it was a good thing that Morse, in his own words, was "fearless" of his enemies' "stings."

A striking four separate editions of his latest sermon were printed— one in Boston, one in Hartford, one in Charlestown, and one in New York—in a testament to the hunger with which the public devoured Morse's most detailed accusations yet. By now, Morse's opponents had come to realize the gravity of the harm that his wild accusations could inflict, especially to the Republican Party. Hoards of Republican writers now took to the presses to expose the purely political nature of Morse's claims. Why not send the evidence to President Adams, they demanded, if Morse was so concerned? Why editorialize on the subject without taking direct action? How could he have anything but pure Federalist goals in mind? Others, however, came to Morse's defense, calling him an "enemy to bigotry" and "a real clergyman." The debate was heated, and newspapers across the country were gobbled up on account of this new intensity.

As with Morse's previous sermons, New England clergymen, lawyers, and philanthropists all came to his aid, sounding the alarm again and echoing his call. The following Fourth of July saw a number of speeches warning the nation of the immediate doom posed by the Illuminati. The brotherhood had created a trap, and America was now directly in its snares. Large swaths of the public were now on full alert, ready to fight the Illuminati as soon as they had the chance.

But heightened states of alarm do not last without continuous justification; like an athlete in full sprint, such intensity can only be kept up for so long. And unfortunately for Morse, along with increased intensity came increased scrutiny. Instead of finding its next opportunity to fight the Illuminati, the public would soon discover major cracks in Morse's call to alarm.

⌒〜

A German professor of geography, one anonymous letter, and a man once described as the "bête noire" of Morse, these were the seeds for Morse's unlikely downfall.

The improbable chain of events began in the early part of that decade, when Morse struck up a long-term correspondence with a man by the name of Christoph Ebeling at the University of Hamburg in Germany, one of Europe's foremost geographers, with the aim of improving Morse's own amateur geographies. "I consider the correspondence," wrote Morse in the spring of 1794, "as one of the most useful and important to me." Ebeling and Morse would write about the clergyman's efforts, with Morse relating the details of everyday life in America, while Ebeling provided the academic context to Morse's geographies from afar.

But Morse, as it turns out, was not the only one who had forged a relationship with the German professor. Ebeling had also struck up correspondences with other notable Americans of the day, such as Thomas Jefferson and, as fate would have it, one Reverend William Bentley, the minister of a neighboring church in Salem, Massachusetts, and a lifelong enemy of Morse. Why exactly Bentley and Morse were such vicious enemies has never been traced to a specific cause. Nothing indicates a pernicious episode between the two—no sleeping with the other one's wife, no fistfights or punches to the jaw. Whatever the specific origin of their shared animosity, however, their hatred arose from philosophical differences at the very least—where Morse was a staunch supporter of President Adams and the Federalists, Bentley was a Jeffersonian; where Morse was conservative, Bentley was a liberal and a Mason to boot. Hatred between the two men would span decades. After Morse began a lecture series for members of Boston's clergy years before, for example, Bentley was so appalled by Morse's orthodoxy that he confided in his diary that Morse was destined to bring controversy to the clergy.

Bentley, as it turns out, was right.

42

But even Morse could not have predicted how this rivalry would undermine his crusade against the Illuminati. Indeed, even after the pieces had fallen into place, and his reputation was reduced to tatters, Morse would spend the following years searching for the cause of his disgrace. And he would remain confused about the source of his downfall years after he found the answer he was looking for.

—◦—

The events that brought national shame upon Morse began, ironically, with his own attempt to verify his beliefs about the Illuminati. Sometime in the months leading up to the fall of 1799, Morse wrote to Ebeling inquiring about Robison and his *Proofs*. Professor Ebeling, respected man of letters that he was, would surely have new evidence for Morse about Robison's trustworthiness, or perhaps a good reason why Europeans had largely stopped worrying about the Illuminati—a reason that Morse could present to the public to buttress his claims. And so Morse asked his trusted advisor, academic, and friend for more information on the whole Illuminati affair.

Instead of aiding Morse's theories, however, Ebeling deflated them. "As to illuminism," Ebeling responded in a letter dated September 2, 1799, "we heartily laugh at it." Ebeling then proceeded to describe Weishaupt, the founder of the Illuminati, as neither a revolutionary nor a mastermind bent on the destruction of world religion; Weishaupt had even invited his accusers to bring charges against him in a court of law, but to no end, for the accusations were all baseless. Ebeling added that, "I cannot believe and no body does, that the order still exists since several years."

It is clear why Morse would not bring Ebeling's views to the public, for they totally undermined his own crusade. Clearer still is why Morse would attempt to hide the letter himself, to make sure that its information was contained. But did Ebeling's letter cause Morse to realize that the Anti-Illuminati movement itself was based on a lie? Pious man that he was, did Morse consider publicly renouncing his crusade? Or did he now harbor new doubts as to whether Ebeling himself was a member of the Illuminati? Deep down, in the hollows in his inner conscious, did Morse double down on his conspiracy theory, or did he back away from his suspicions?

What, exactly, Morse made of Ebeling's letter we do not know. We do know, however, that three weeks after Morse received the letter, an article describing a very similar letter from Ebeling to Morse appeared in a Connecticut paper, penned by an anonymous author and calling for Morse to make the full contents of Ebeling's letter public. "We have been informed," declared the anonymous author, "and in a way that authorises us to speak with confidence of the truth of the information, that a Rev. Doctor [Morse], a celebrated calumniator of Masonry, an eagle-eyed detector of *Illuminatism*, lately received a letter from Professor Eb[e]ling." The article went on to describe how Ebeling recounted to Morse that Robison had "lived too fast for his income," and had become insane even by his own friends' accounts. Robison had even fled Scotland to escape his creditors, to a country no worse than France itself. Robison, in short, was not to be trusted, little less respected—and even Morse's most esteemed advisor told him so.

Morse was outraged. He responded immediately by firing off an article of his own, demanding to know the identity of the author and denying the existence of the letter. The correspondence he did have from Ebeling, he asserted, was private, even if it might appear somewhat similar. It would betray Ebeling's confidence to air private letters to the public, he claimed, no matter what the cause. The matter soon became new fodder for the controversy, printed and reprinted in newspapers throughout the country. Unlike previous controversies about the Illuminati, however, this one was centered on facts. Did Morse receive such a letter? Why not publish it? What did *he* have to hide?

On October 9, 1799, almost a year and a half after Morse's first speech on the Illuminati, the final straw was laid. A Federalist-leaning newspaper called the *Massachusetts Spy* published portions of the text of the alleged letter between Ebeling and Morse, which described Robison as a lunatic and his facts as baseless. If ever there was a man who should not be taken seriously, wrote Ebeling to Morse, Robison was he. The text of the letter was reprinted in other newspapers, and later in full, unabbreviated form. The further it was disseminated, the weaker the Anti-Illuminati movement became. Here, at long last, was hard proof about Morse's claims—hard proof, however, that just happened to cut against them. And it was proof that Morse did not outright deny. There had been a letter, Morse again equivocated, but he could not publish it. Ebeling's letter about Robison was not the same one that had been printed in public, he claimed. But just how it differed Morse would not say.

In one area, at least, Morse was right: The public letter was not the same as the one that Ebeling had written him, though its contents were quite similar. Both the real letter from Ebeling and the public letter exposed Robison as an incompetent and disgraced man. But they were not identical. Where had this public letter come from? Who forged it? And how did the forger know about the real one?

Though Morse's search for these answers was prolonged, his fall from the national spotlight was not. The letter's publication, and Morse's awkward public response, immediately cast doubt upon his own motivations. The fact that he kept secret Ebeling's letter after he first received it, and then refused to release the actual copy after the other version had been printed, belied the trust he had gained with the public over the last two years. By 1800, the hysteria that Morse had almost single-handedly stirred up had dissipated—proving, not for the first time in the history of American hysteria, that the fewer a movement's progenitors, the easier it is to kill. It would be over a year before Morse discovered the man behind his downfall.

Morse did all he could to find the source of the letter. Somewhere, members of the Illuminati must have set him up. The hornets' nest had been awakened, and he had finally been stung. It took Morse more than a year to piece together that his rival William Bentley had corresponded with Ebeling, and that the two had written about Robison. If such were the case, Bentley might have received a letter from Ebeling describing the German professor's thoughts on the Illuminati—a letter very similar to the one that Morse had received on his own. And so, having come across a theory that at long last explained his public humiliation, Morse wrote to Bentley on February 20, 1801, asking whether the published letter "was in fact written to you by Professor Ebeling and whether or not, you handed it to the printer for publication." The answer Morse got back from Bentley was as understated as it was cold. Here, in full, is Bentley's reply:

February 21, 1801
Rev. Doctor—

The letter from Professor Ebeling, as published in the Massachusetts Spy of Oct. 9, 1799, was addressed to me, and printed at my request.

William Bentley

And so Morse's fall from grace was assured, though he would continue to devote himself to various crusades for the remaining two decades of his life. At one point, Morse would argue that New England secede from the union; in his view, the country had reached a point where the bonds uniting Americans were weaker than the factors that divided them. Later still, he would create a special-interest magazine devoted to his orthodox cause, though none of his efforts would again capture the national spotlight. By the 1820s, Morse had fallen into deep debt and been expelled from his Charlestown congregation. All of his successes had been fleeting, his failure prolonged. Morse would die, in 1826, thinking that he had no apparent legacy to call his own. But in this, too, Morse's judgment would prove wrong.

Morse left behind the blueprints for a type of political movement that would be repeated and refined throughout American history—a pattern that would, in fact, begin again within a few months of his death with the Anti-Masonic movement, the subject of the following chapter. Morse had, after all, been at the helm of the very first episode of American hysteria: an enduring legacy indeed. But beyond that, Morse's hysteria was unique in three respects. First, the Anti-Illuminati hysteria boasted no physical group of people that could embody the enemy—for, in the end, the Illuminati themselves were a nonexistent threat, an ideal with no representatives, having ceased to exist the decade before. If following periods of hysteria would take anything from the Illuminati episode, it was that a society is much better at rejecting people than ideas. It was this factor—the lack of a specific group to target—that would help make the Illuminati hysteria one of the shortest-lived episodes in American history.

Second, though at its height it had won over men as important as George Washington himself, it never translated into political power for its adherents. No elections were won because of promises to root out the Illuminati, and no party platforms were laid down with these plans in mind. Morse's was perhaps the weakest episode of political hysteria in the phenomenon's long and sordid history. Had Morse's theory not been debunked so quickly, perhaps the election of 1800 would have been the perfect venue for these accomplishments. It was Thomas Jefferson's party, however, the supposed scions of the Illuminati, that would take the elections of 1800, and with it the presidency.

The Illuminati hysteria was also unique in one further respect, for it was almost entirely created by Morse. If the story of hysteria in American politics tells us anything, it is that rarely is a movement so dominated by one figure. Episodes are usually stoked by a host of factors, from national figures to small-town ones, as we will see in the coming pages. Morse, however, managed to create a political movement almost entirely on his own. Perhaps it is this aspect that explains its short life span; perhaps the more minds that help create the hysteria, the longer it takes to die out. But perhaps, also, there was something unique about Morse—and about the whole Morse family itself. For it was Morse's eldest son, Samuel Finley Breese, later famous for the invention of the single-wire telegraph and Morse code, who would help give rise to another reactionary movement in American politics, the anti-Catholic Know Nothing Party of the 1840s and '50s, and who would help maintain his father's legacy by launching yet another crusade to defend America from the enemy within.

CHAPTER 3

The Anti-Masons

The Disappearance of William Morgan and the Rise of Third Party Politics

To this day, nobody knows the true fate of Captain William Morgan. A failed businessman and citizen of generally low repute, Morgan was abducted from his home, in the town of Batavia in upstate New York, in the early morning of September 11, 1826. He soon found himself in a Canandaigua jail cell, about fifty miles away, imprisoned for a debt of two dollars and sixty-five cents. The whole ordeal was doubtless confusing to Morgan, a man best known for his drinking. And it likely became even more confusing when a man he didn't know paid his bail. But that man had no intention of setting him free. Morgan emerged from the jail only to be physically forced into a carriage, reportedly screaming out "murder" while he was being dragged away.

This is the last anyone ever saw of Captain Morgan, about whom little else is certain. Some said that he was not really a military captain, while others claimed that he had earned that title in the War of 1812. Others asserted that both theories were technically true: that he fought the British in 1812 as a pirate seeking plunder, and was granted a pardon for his misdeeds by the president after the war. What we do know, however, is that whatever happened to him, trapped inside that northbound carriage and fearing for his life, Morgan never came back.

But the story of Morgan's disappearance has more than one twist. By some accounts, Morgan was simply banished from New York forever. One story places him in the city of Smyrna in modern-day Turkey a couple of years later, working as a wholesale fruit dealer specializing in figs. Another has him escaping to Arizona, where he became a celebrated Indian chief by the name of San Procope, confessing his real identity only on his deathbed. Yet another has a ferocious pirate conspicuously known as Guiliem Ganmore ("William Morgan") confessing his real identity just before being hanged in Havana in 1838.

Whatever Morgan's fate, it wasn't just his disappearance that set off a national firestorm. American history, after all, is full of murders and cover-ups, small-time conspiracies and pivotal larger ones. What turned Morgan's disappearance into a national political phenomenon was the suggestion that an organized group was behind it. For the evidence suggested that Morgan's abduction was carried out by members of a secret organization and, over the next few years, the details of their crime would slowly unfold, and along with it a remarkable period of American political hysteria.

—◆—

The story of Morgan's disappearance begins in the summer of 1826, when a new era was dawning in the nation's history. Fifty years after the Declaration of Independence, the last of America's founding generation was dying off—a turning point highlighted by the deaths of both Thomas Jefferson and John Adams on the Fourth of July that year. "It cannot be denied," said the politician Daniel Webster at the time, "that with America, and in America, a new era commences in human affairs." What would become of America's "great experiment" in democracy without the presence of its forefathers? Would the new country outlast its first generation? Or would it disintegrate into smaller entities, such as the so-called Republic of Indian Stream, a short-lived state that would have to be quashed by the New Hampshire militia? These questions were very real in many Americans' minds.

But in upstate New York, then on the outer edges of America's frontier, two men were occupied with a very different question: how to secure personal fame and fortune. The first was David C. Miller, the publisher of Batavia's *Republican Advocate*. Miller's was an opposition paper, pitted against the policies of New York's governor, DeWitt Clinton. Though he'd run the journal for over a decade, Miller was still a struggling newspaper-man searching for higher circulation. The second was William Morgan himself, who had moved his family restlessly throughout the countryside, first as a brewer, now as a stoneworker, hauling his wife Lucinda and two young children from one failed venture to the next. Only two years earlier, Morgan had written of his desperation: "The darkness of my prospects robs my mind, and extreme misery my body." The two men made an odd pair, but what they lacked in common background they shared in common circumstance—and now in common goals. For over that summer the two hatched a plan to expose to New York and ultimately the world the inner workings of the secret society of Freemasons. How, exactly, the two first came into contact is not known, but neither was held in high esteem by their community. According to one source, Miller was known to be a man "of irreligious character, great laxity of moral principle, and of intemperate habits"—and much worse things were said about Morgan. Not surprisingly, both men harbored deep-seated animosity toward Free-masonry, which served as a symbol for the establishment class.

Freemasonry is thought to have originated in England and Scotland sometime in the 1500s as a trade organization made up of local masons, or stoneworkers, but it soon took on a philosophical air. The triumph of reason began to be a focal point of the organization, as did dedication to deism, or the Enlightenment belief that the existence of God is apparent through observation and study rather than miracles or revelation. Over the centuries, the fraternity of Masons would expand throughout the world, as would its ceremonies and rituals, all of which involved strange sym-bols and bizarre oaths—in addition to their much more benign emphasis on civic-mindedness, religious tolerance, and communal learning. Most strikingly, the group met in secret. Their insularity would help create a sense of community within the organization, granting the air of privilege to new members while shielding the group from the world outside.

Perhaps most importantly, Masonry attracted elites. Masons were overwhelmingly men of middle and upper class status—doctors, lawyers, and businessmen—who had the time and leisure to join what amounted to a social club for the well to do. Many of the founding fathers them-selves had been Masons, including George Washington and Benjamin

Franklin—indeed, thirteen of the thirty-nine signers of the Constitution claimed membership in the Masonic fraternity. In the years between America's founding and 1826, Masonry had only grown more powerful—especially in New York State. The governor of New York, DeWitt Clinton, for example, was not only a Mason, but had been the Grand Master of the Grand Lodge of New York and the highest-ranking Mason in the country. By one estimate, more than half of all publicly held offices in New York were occupied by Masons. The combination of power and secrecy made the organization seem daunting in most Americans' eyes, which is exactly why Morgan and Miller thought they were on to something big.

Miller first hinted at some type of forthcoming revelation in an article published in the *Advocate* in August of 1826. Miller had discovered the "strongest evidence of rottenness," he wrote, evidence that compelled him and an unnamed collaborator, widely known to be Morgan, "to an act of justice to ourselves and to the public." This bombshell was a book, to be compiled by Morgan and printed by Miller, detailing Masonic rituals and misdeeds at the highest levels of power. Oddly, Morgan wasn't a member of the Masons, but he had somehow convinced other Masons that he was, and had been granted access to a neighboring Masonic lodge. Morgan was thus able to witness the Masons' ceremonies, recording their doings in a manuscript that would place Miller and Morgan directly in harm's way in the weeks to come.

News of Miller and Morgan's impending publication soon began to spread—exactly as Miller had hoped. The bigger the buildup, after all, the larger the audience. But Masons in neighboring counties also began to worry about the disclosures and soon became obsessed with Morgan's book. Reported one Mason at that time: "[I] never saw men so excited in my life." Committees of Masons were quickly organized to investigate the revelations, and "everything went forward in a kind of frenzy."

Groups of worried Masons began harassing the pair with prosecutions for petty debt, with the tacit cooperation of the county sheriff, who briefly placed Morgan in jail. Strange men, thought to be Masons from other counties, now began to make suspicious appearances in the villages and towns of upstate New York, putting not just Miller and Morgan on edge, but entire towns too. Miller even attracted a new business partner, one who offered to furnish his print shop with all the resources it would need to issue the new book. But the investor himself would turn out to be a Mason, sent by a neighboring lodge to spy on their plans.

The first declaration of war was issued on September 8, when a group of Masons attempted to destroy Miller's offices. Capping a night of drinking at a local tavern, a group of several dozen men descended onto the print shop. There they found that Miller had convened a posse of his own, equipped with firearms themselves and ready to fight. The Masons retreated, and Miller was safe—for the time being. Two nights later, Miller's office suddenly erupted into flames, though the fire was detected early and no serious damage was done. Cotton balls dipped in turpentine were reportedly found throughout the print shop, identifying the fire as an act of arson. The Masons, it seemed, were clearly to blame.

On September 11, the conflict escalated. Half a dozen Masons showed up at Morgan's home with an arrest warrant from the nearby town of Canandaigua. The charges: petty larceny for stealing a shirt and tie, lent to Morgan by the owner of the town's tavern, which Morgan had failed to return.

Soon Morgan was being whisked away in a carriage, though reportedly without worry. He apparently thought that testifying that he had simply forgotten to return the items would get him off the hook. And in this he was right. Once he was in Canandaigua, the charges fell through and he was released—only to be immediately arrested again for an outstanding debt of two dollars and sixty-five cents. This time the charges stuck.

Morgan would spend the following night in jail. Over the course of the next day, someone would pay his bail, securing his release but forcing him into a carriage that sped northwards out of town. It was while being shuttled between the jail and the carriage that Morgan reportedly cried "murder," suggesting that wherever he went next, it was not by his own free will. After that, Morgan simply disappeared.

And that wasn't the end of the ordeal, for a group of Masons soon came back for Miller. On September 12, roughly seventy armed Masons rallied at a tavern, while a constable presented the publisher with a warrant for his arrest on questionable criminal charges and conveyed him to the nearby town of Le Roy. Luckily for Miller, his lawyer and an armed posse from Batavia followed along, carrying him back home as soon as the charges fell through.

As Miller and his crew returned to Batavia, the story of his arrest spread like wildfire throughout neighboring villages and towns. Indeed, it was loose ends like Miller—and the family that Morgan had left behind—that would cause the Masons the most trouble. The fate of Morgan's wife, Lucinda Morgan, for example, would help to stoke up sympathy and support for Morgan's plight, deepening the public's anger over the Masons' crimes. The mother of two small children now no longer had a husband to depend on. Whether she was temporarily alone or forever a widow, no one knew.

But the broader significance of the Morgan affair wasn't just about the disappearance of one man. The crime had exposed the existence of a powerful group, shrouded in secrecy, manipulating the law for their own purposes. Both Miller and Morgan had initially been dragged away legally, after all. The story of Morgan's kidnapping, as it was told and retold throughout the coming weeks, focused on this aspect of the story—on how the elite Masons had turned the public interest into a private one, and how the government itself may have been perverted in the process. How, after all, could armed strangers simply walk into town, arrest Miller and kidnap Morgan, all under the guise of the law? Were the authorities in on the affair? Whose interests were they really working for anyway? And how could anyone now consider themselves safe? These questions began to be asked with increasing frequency—and with an increasing sense of fear. Soon, the Morgan affair reached a turning point as private sentiment began to shape public action.

Two weeks after the abduction, a series of heavily attended public meetings was held, beginning on September 25 in Batavia, New York, Morgan and Miller's hometown. Though the meetings were initially called to solve the mystery of Morgan's fate—in essence, these were "whodunit" gatherings—they were equally about calming the public's fear. There was no guarantee, after all, that what happened to Morgan could not happen to others.

As a result of the Batavia meetings, a panel was established, the so-called Committee of Ten, which began sending agents into neighboring towns to investigate the abduction, gathering facts and taking down testimony. Soon other neighboring towns followed suit with copycat committees, all bent on shedding light on the now infamous crime. Just as all of these public meetings were people's meetings, so too were these people's committees. No government authorities were called in, none were relied upon, and none, many suspected, could be trusted.

The irony of this development was that while the committees were created to calm the public's sense of fear, they in fact helped to deepen it. Throughout the months of October and November, citizen representatives of the committees traveled throughout upstate New York spreading the story of Morgan's abduction everywhere they went, serving to confirm the wild stories local newspapers were already printing about the kidnapping. Those who initially didn't believe what they read now heard witnesses attest to the truth of the affair. On top of this, the details of Morgan's fate were becoming more and more sensational. One version of the kidnapping, for example, ended with Morgan being murdered in some sort of occult Masonic ceremony, with his throat being cut "from ear to ear" and his tongue removed with a knife. Perhaps most importantly, the committees' actions laid new seeds of doubt about the government's ability to handle its own responsibilities—a group of citizens, after all, had taken the matter of justice into their own hands.

Up until this point, the public effort to get to the bottom of the scandal was straightforward, if impassioned. A group of men had conspired unlawfully against Morgan and Miller, and if they were not brought to justice, nothing prevented the same crime from occurring again. Once the criminals had been locked away, everyone could simply move on—or so, at least, it seemed in the early days after Morgan's disappearance. But this outlook would soon change.

The outrage over Morgan's kidnapping would transition from public fear to political hysteria, within just a few months. Though clearly only a few Masons were guilty of any crime, it was the reaction of other Masons that helped to convince much of the public that they weren't dealing with a simple crime, but with a widespread conspiracy. Many Masons began publicly—and inexplicably—to defend Morgan's abduction, and many of them were public figures to boot. "If they are publishing the true secrets of Masonry," said one former member of the New York legislature, we "should not think the lives of half a dozen such men as Morgan and Miller of any consequence in suppressing the work." Another Masonic judge on the Genesee County court stated that, "whatever Morgan's fate might have been, he deserved it—he had forfeited his life." As these statements proliferated, many respected and powerful Masons seemed to be practically defending murder. It was now less and less of a stretch to think that powerful elements within the state's government were in on the kidnapping too.

While the Masonic organization began to look more culpable as a whole, the nascent movement gained an expanded sense of purpose as the Morgan affair began working its way through the courts. In October, a group of Masons were indicted on charges of rioting and assault for the attempt to imprison Miller. In November, indictments were found against four other Masons—Nicholas Chesebro, Loton Lawson, Edward Sawyer, and John Sheldon, most of whom worked as farmers or mechanics in neighboring towns—for the conspiracy to seize Morgan from his jail cell in Canandaigua, and then for abducting him in the carriage that took him to wherever he went next. A second indictment was issued for executing the conspiracy. Here then was the appearance of a finale, a climax to the excitement over Morgan's disappearance—or, at least, this is what many hoped.

By January 1827, the trial was set to begin in Canandaigua, New York, where teams of lawyers, bankrolled by local Masonic lodges, assembled to represent the defendants. The district attorney prosecuting the case had amassed a large-scale team of his own, and crowds of onlookers gathered into the courtroom eager to watch the proceedings. The governor himself had taken an interest in the affair, requesting his own attorney general to attend the event on his behalf.

On Tuesday January 2, 1827, the trial began routinely enough. The four defendants had pleaded not guilty to kidnapping Morgan, and David C. Miller, Morgan's partner and publisher, who had been subpoenaed by both the prosecution and the defense, was called as the first key witness in the trial. In anticipation of Miller taking the stand, a grand silence filled the courtroom. But Miller, it seemed, was nowhere to be found. The confusion that ensued was so great that the judge adjourned the court until the next day.

The reasons for Miller's absence are still unclear. According to his own account, Miller apparently simply forgot that he was meant to appear in court, and then was waylaid by some business in a neighboring town. He also claimed to lack the money to travel, despite the mere fifty-mile distance between his home in Batavia and the courthouse in Canandaigua. Many would later allege that he had been blackmailed or bribed into refusing to testify.

When the trial reconvened the next day, the court was in for another surprise, one that would shock the public much more than Miller's absence. Three of the defendants immediately changed their pleas to "guilty" for the conspiracy to abduct Morgan (and the fourth now acknowledged the kidnapping had taken place). They now admitted to removing Morgan from his jail cell in Canandaigua and forcing him into the carriage that spirited him away. None of them, however, claimed to know where Morgan was headed, or what had happened to him once the carriage departed.

The effect of the new plea was to reduce the scope of the trial considerably—it was no longer a matter of convicting the four men of kidnapping or murder, or shedding light onto the larger conspiracy as a whole. The trial was now simply about proving whether or not the Masons were in Canandaigua the night of September 12, and whether or not they were seen removing Morgan from his cell. The jury's verdict came quickly: Witnesses now corroborated exactly what the indictment charged.

And so the first conviction of the Morgan affair was made with surprisingly little fanfare. The four defendants were sentenced to lenient terms, ranging from two years to one month in prison, for nothing more than forcibly moving Morgan from one place to another.

If the public wanted justice, this surely was not it. But for those deeply concerned about the conspiracy against Morgan, the trial proved fulfilling in another sense, for it gave renewed purpose to their outrage. Indeed, it was at this trial that the real significance of the public's alarm first became clear, thanks in no small part to Judge Enos T. Throop. When it came time for the judge to read the sentencing statement to the four guilty men, Throop read much more than a simple description of their punishment. What he told the Masons, in front of a rapt courtroom, and reprinted in papers across the state, revealed that their trial was now about something greater than their criminal offense alone.

Throop began by describing the four Masons' crimes. Theirs was a "daring, wicked and presumptuous" act, he said, one that had "polluted this land." The men had robbed the state of a citizen, left the victim's wife and his children "helpless," and somehow shielded the rest of the culprits from being brought to justice. But this act on its own was not even the "heaviest part of your crime," as Throop explained:

> *Your conduct has created, in the people of this section of the country, a strong feeling of virtuous indignation. The court rejoices to witness it—to be made sure that a citizen's person cannot be invaded by lawless violence, without its being felt by every individual in the community. It is a blessed spirit, and we do hope that it will not subside—that it will be accompanied by a ceaseless vigilance, and untiring activity. . . . We see in this public sensation the spirit which brought us into existence as a nation, and a pledge that our rights and liberties are destined to endure.*

The public's outrage, in other words, was now no longer about one crime, or even the conspiracy to cover it up. And it wasn't simply about outrage, either. It was about the "spirit which brought us into existence as a nation," in Judge Throop's words, and about the fear that this spirit was threatened.

At its core, the Morgan affair centered on the scandal of his disappearance in broad daylight. What Judge Throop saw in the public indignation was a dedication to America's founding spirit. The citizens, it seemed, were willing to enforce the laws themselves, if that's what it took to protect American ideals—that all men were subject to the law, that democracy was based on equality among citizens, and that no group could pledge loyalty to itself above others. What began as the public's reaction to a local kidnapping was now, somehow, evolving into a common dedication to protect America's core values.

But the deeper significance of the outrage was that Freemasonry served as a compelling symbol for the real threat that many Americans were facing. The 1820s were, after all, a decade of great uncertainty, one in which industrialization posed profound challenges to American society. The rise of manufacturing threatened to reorganize the American labor force on a massive scale, as did immigrants and population booms in eastern cities. The Jeffersonian vision of an agrarian republic was less and less applicable to Americans' daily lives. At its core, the idea of what it meant to be an American was changing, and industrialization was the vehicle for these changes. "In fastening on Masonry as the foremost evil in the Republic," writes historian Paul Goodman, "Antimasons were responding to the emergence of industrial society which clashed with the remnants of a pre-industrial order." The old order was based on social homogeneity and stability; the new order was driven by the swings of the market and constant economic competition. America, many thought, was entering an era of chaos, and one in which equality was fundamentally threatened. This was what the outrage of the citizens in upstate New York was really all about.

Indeed, the higher a town's exposure to the effects of industrialization, the higher the levels of Anti-Masonic support. In Genesee County, for example, the county in upstate New York that formed the heart of the movement, the towns with the highest Anti-Masonic sentiment were those with the highest rates of economic development. The converse was also true: the towns with the lowest levels of economic development formed the movement's weakest base. So too was Anti-Masonry organized by the county's commercial elites. Over 80 percent of the Anti-Masonic committee members and candidates were professionals or businessmen, with attorneys holding leadership positions over 70 percent of the time between 1827 and 1833.

Anti-Masonry was thus not about lower classes confronting economic uncertainty, or engaging in class conflict. Anti-Masonry found support among those whose vision of America was threatened by changes in the American way of life, and consequently had much to lose. The Anti-Masonic movement, even at its earliest stages, was about the very need for an organization like the Masons, one whose ranks were growing in the 1820s, thanks to the materialistic spirit American society was adopting. And it was about how this new spirit conflicted with traditional American ideals.

Exclude or be excluded—this might have been the motto of the Freemasons, and it certainly fit the hyper-competitive times. But the Anti-Masons liked neither option, and they did not want to choose.

━◦━

With the trial now complete, the movement reached another turning point. Furious over the court's inability to bring all of Morgan's abductors to justice, and now cloaked with a deeper sense of purpose, alarmed members of the public began to advocate action in the political realm. In February, a joint meeting was held by the people of the towns of Batavia, Bethany, and Stafford, who resolved to "withhold their support at elections from all such men of the Masonic fraternity." The people in the town of Seneca committed that "they would not vote for Freemasons, for any offices whatever." And it wasn't only Masonic politicians who found themselves under attack. Newspapers run by Masons, which many felt had been conspicuously silent on the Morgan affair, were also the target of the public's ire. A public meeting of the towns of Pembroke and Alexander passed a joint resolution to "discourage the circulation of any paper" that did not cover the Morgan affair accurately. In meetings throughout the towns of upstate New York, scores of similar resolutions followed suit. By February of 1827, five months after Morgan had gone missing, the Anti-Masonic Party was born.

But it wasn't just the symbolism of the Morgan scandal, the political dynamics of the moment, or the sheer luck of its timing that helped propel the Anti-Masons onto the national stage. Political hysteria, like any movement, revolves around people and personalities, mental ingenuity and human flaws, and the Anti-Masons found their galvanizing force in the canny figure, equal parts politician and propagandist, named Thurlow Weed.

A tall printer with a wide forehead and firm chin, Weed was born into a farming family in rural New York, working alternatively as a tavern boy, a farmhand, and even a volunteer in the War of 1812. By 1828, at thirty years of age, what he lacked in formal education he made up for in political savvy. For between the fall of 1826, when William Morgan had first gone missing, and 1827, when the Anti-Masons first participated in state elections, Weed had spotted a political movement—one that he now thought had clear national potential.

Even in the early days of the outrage over Morgan's disappearance, Weed had been quick to affix himself to the movement's rising star. He was among the first to serve on Rochester's Anti-Masonic "Morgan Committee," for example, one of the most prominent bodies set up in the aftermath of the kidnapping. The following year he waded deeper into Anti-Masonic politics, helping to recruit Anti-Masonic candidates for local elections, and stirring up public support for the Anti-Masons' platform—which consisted, at this point, in simply removing Masons from elected office—and making a name for himself in the process. Indeed, for both the Anti-Masons and for Weed, the elections of 1827 were an astounding success. The party of the sitting US president, John Quincy Adams, elected twelve members to the New York legislature. The newly minted Anti-Masons elected a shocking fifteen. Weed's status as a prescient political operator was growing.

But Weed's largest contribution to the movement wasn't simply his political skills; it was his talent as a journalist. After the elections, he founded Rochester's *Anti-Masonic Enquirer*, soon the most prominent Anti-Masonic newspaper in the country, pumping Anti-Masonic literature into communities throughout the nation. The party adhered, at first, to a single-issue platform, based solely on the fact that Freemasonry undercut American values, and with the consequent goal of removing all Masons from positions of power—though it would evolve over the coming years to include measures such as support for Native American rights, the belief in limiting the power of the executive branch, and the necessity of a national bank.

The Morgan affair offered more than just an ideological platform for Weed. It also offered what every newspaperman thrives on: a scandal. The Morgan trials blended murder mystery with populist ideology and public outrage, the perfect mix for a man with both deep-seated political and journalistic ambitions. And there were so many trials to boot. From

October 1826 to the middle of 1831, for example, in various counties throughout the state, over twenty grand jury investigations were held, and at least eighteen separate trials involving up to thirty-nine different defendants, comprising all the combinations of routes and persons that the Anti-Masons imagined were involved in the kidnapping, each one an opportunity to stir up populist furor and public controversy. In a very real sense, the ebb and flow of the Morgan trials formed the heartbeat of the Anti-Masonic movement—a heart that Weed needed very much to keep alive.

By the following summer, just a few months before the national elections of 1828, Weed had more at stake in the Anti-Masonic movement than ever. President Adams himself had made Weed his campaign manager in western New York, openly aligning himself with the Anti-Masons by declaring that "I am not, never was, and never shall be a Freemason"— no small feat for both Weed and his new party.

Meanwhile, next up for trial was the Niagara County sheriff Eli Bruce, the most potent symbol of the Masonic conspiracy yet. The New York governor had just relented to the Anti-Masons' calls for a special legislative committee to look into the Morgan affair—a long and arduous political battle—and the symbolism of Eli Bruce's role in the abduction carried significant weight. Not only was Bruce thought to be linked to the kidnapping—Morgan likely traveled through Niagara County while being abducted—but Bruce was a Mason as well. At the very least, Bruce must have tacitly allowed the kidnappers transit, with full knowledge of the crime. At the worst, he may have actively participated in the kidnapping—though the details here vary, depending on whose version of events we follow.

In either case, all signs pointed to Bruce's guilt: Bruce had been called as a witness during previous trials and had pleaded the Fifth, drawing on his constitutional right not to incriminate himself. Even the New York governor had publicly stated his belief that Bruce was "a participant in the said abduction." Here, then, was a man charged with upholding the law and yet one with apparently dual loyalties. Bruce was a symbol of the very evils the Anti-Masons believed Freemasonry stood for: corruption, self-aggrandizement, hidden agendas. But the problem was that Bruce was being tried for conspiracy to kidnap Morgan, and to find him guilty, the prosecution needed to prove that he had in fact been kidnapped— something that no trial had previously been able to do. Earlier trials had merely proven that he had been removed from his jail cell and placed in a carriage. What Morgan did next, and whether it was done forcibly or by account of his own free will, was all still speculation.

With the Eli Bruce trial, however, the Anti-Masons hoped to shed more light into Morgan's disappearance, to prove in a court of law that he had in fact been kidnapped, and to place Bruce behind bars in the process. The investigatory committees had traced Morgan to an arms depot in Fort Niagara, just across the border from Canada, where Morgan was last imprisoned before his whereabouts became unknown. The committees had discovered that Elisha Adams, a soldier living at Fort Niagara, had allegedly taken care of Morgan throughout his confinement, feeding him meals and ensuring his captivity. Adams may have been the last non-Mason to have seen Morgan alive, making him the key witness who could prove that Morgan had been kidnapped, and perhaps even murdered— thereby incriminating everyone who had played a part in the conspiracy to abduct Morgan, including Eli Bruce.

There was only one problem: Elisha Adams had gone missing.

Since the investigations into Morgan's disappearance had commenced, Adams had simply vanished. No one had seen him or heard from him in the preceding two years. Without Adams, the Anti-Masons worried, there would be insufficient testimony to prove Bruce's connection to the crime, the charges would be dismissed, and the Masons would win again. The trial needed a producer, someone to assemble the missing pieces, to dramatize the proceedings and to stir up public support—someone to, in effect, turn the enforcement of justice into a public spectacle.

Thurlow Weed was the perfect man for the job.

Over the summer of 1828, Weed had received a tip that Adams was hiding out in a cabin in the foothills of Vermont. Within no time Weed had received permission from the Vermont governor to arrest Adams as a fugitive from justice if he found him in the state, and set out for the mountain town of Brookfield, Vermont, some 350 miles distant from Weed's home in Rochester.

Weed arrived at the cabin near midnight, accompanied by a local sheriff in case Adams put up a fight, an unlikely scenario given that Adams was both elderly and handicapped, but Weed didn't want to take any chances. At his approach to the cabin, the door was opened by Adams's brother-in-law. When Weed inquired about Adams, a voice from upstairs interrupted, "I'm here, and have been expecting you." Adams wobbled downstairs, and soon Weed and Morgan's reputed prison guard were standing face-to-face. Shortly thereafter, Adams agreed to testify at Bruce's trial and began packing his bags.

On the long journey back to New York, Adams would tell Weed what he knew about the Morgan affair, according to Weed's own account. For three days, Adams heard Morgan make loud noises in the magazine, crying repeatedly for help. While Adams kept watch over the prisoner, a group of Masons were planning to conduct Morgan across the river to Canada. One night four Masons took Morgan out of the magazine and onto a boat, while Adams was asked to stand guard on the shore in case any witnesses approached. When the boat returned, only the four Masons were on board. Adams asked no questions, and the Masons went their separate ways. Here at long last was the inside story of what happened to Morgan that September night, at least according to Weed.

The good news for Weed was that Adams's story alone would have been enough to prove that Morgan had been abducted, and thus to convict Bruce of conspiracy to kidnap Morgan. The bad news was that Adams said nothing like it once he took the witness stand. Once in the courtroom, he denied any knowledge of Morgan, or of his time in the Fort Niagara magazine, or of hearing anyone's calls for help. He denied knowing practically anything about the Morgan affair at all.

In the end, despite the lack of evidence from Adams, Bruce was convicted for his role in the abduction and given a minor sentence. Weed and the Anti-Masons were enraged. As far as they were concerned, Bruce had gotten off easy. To top it off, the justice system had failed to shed any light on Morgan's fate yet again. Was Morgan dead or alive, held hostage or simply missing? No one knew. Denunciations of the trial rang throughout the Anti-Masonic press.

But the truth was that from Weed's own perspective, the trial was a great achievement. It had increased the public's interest in the continuing saga while feeding its outrage too—a political win-win. If the public's reaction to the trial was any indication, the election of 1828, coming just a few weeks later, would be a grand success.

Success was an understatement. In fact, the 1828 elections marked a major turning point for the Anti-Masons, when the party shifted from a local political force into a national one. From that point on, the movement would only continue to gather steam. As Anti-Masonry spread from New York to states like Vermont, Ohio, Massachusetts, and Maryland, new candidates sprouted up like garden weeds. Said one historian of the Anti-Masonic movement, it was "to New York that the other States looked for guidance, for leaders, and to a large extent for political material and methods." More precisely, from that point on they now looked to Thurlow Weed—he was "the magician," said one New York politician, "whose wand directs and controls the operations of the Antimasonic party." Anti-Masonic candidates won seats in state legislatures across the country, but the party's gains were not simply at the local level. The Anti-Masons became the first third party in the United States to send its candidates to Congress, electing nearly half a dozen members to the House of Representatives.

Even more significant than the Anti-Masons' transition from New York politics to the national stage was the elevation in its standing. Not only had the party won seats in the US Congress, but President Adams had practically endorsed the party by allying himself with Weed. This implicit support would help give increased credence to the Anti-Masons' allegations, lending the illusion of credibility to some of their most outrageous claims. Stated Thurlow Weed: "Mr. Adams had made the path of duty smooth by becoming an Anti-Mason."

Perhaps more notably, the Anti-Masons had now gained the mantle of the opposition party. President Andrew Jackson, an avowed Mason himself, had ousted Adams and was now in power. That the Anti-Masons had in turn supported and been supported by Adams legitimized their animosity to Jackson. The Anti-Masons would have four years to organize against him, allying with other elements of the opposition. Now members of the public who disagreed with Jackson's policies had an alternate, and simpler, explanation for why the US president was steering the country in the wrong direction: He was the leader of a grand Masonic conspiracy, bent on diluting America's founding values and secretly pledging loyalty to foreign ideals. Indeed, the Anti-Masons now not only had a prominent political platform, in both state and national legislatures and in the media. They had a villain in the White House.

By 1830, the push for a national organization was under way, aided by opposition to Jackson and the growing sense that American society was fracturing. On September 11 of that year, precisely four years after Morgan had been abducted from his Batavia home, the Anti-Masons held their first national convention in Philadelphia, with delegates from New York, Massachusetts, Connecticut, Vermont, Rhode Island, Pennsylvania, New Jersey, Delaware, Ohio, Maryland, and Michigan in attendance. It was here that the party hatched its grandest plans for nationwide dominance—and, ultimately, where the seeds of the movement's downfall were first sown.

With growing national power came increased opportunity, and divisions were already stirring within the Anti-Masons' ranks. For many of the moderates in the party, some of whom viewed Andrew Jackson's policies as a danger equal to, if not greater than, the threat posed by Masonry, the need to build coalitions with opposition figures outside the Anti-Masonic Party soon became clear. If the party wanted to keep the Jacksonians out of power, Anti-Masons and Republicans would have to join forces, and that would mean compromise was in order.

The problem, however, was that many of the opposition figures refused to publicly denounce Masonry, while others were suspected of being Masons themselves. A large number of Anti-Masons, zealous in their beliefs, did not have the stomach for compromise—they simply refused to deal with any politicians who would not denounce all of Freemasonry as un-American and evil. Questions about the party's ability to handle routine political tasks now began to be asked with increasing frequency. Would the Anti-Masons be able to strike political bargains at all? Would allying themselves with Jackson's Republican opposition undermine their cause? Put simply, would compromise dilute the Anti-Masons' strengths or would it make the party stronger? During the 1830 national convention, as the Anti-Masons readied themselves for the next level of national prominence, these questions were very real. Yet the party was neither unified nor organized enough to answer them.

In the face of such disarray, the delegates agreed to postpone major decisions, such as whom to nominate for the 1832 presidential elections, until the following September, when the party would hold a national nominating convention, the first of its kind in American politics, and one that is emulated by political parties to this day. Instead of party leaders choosing whom the convention would nominate, delegates to the convention, each representing their local supporters, would elect the party's candidates—just as the American public would elect their representatives at large. This new type of convention was a way of bridging ideological differences within the party, of importing the democratic process into the party itself. At the same time, it underscored the party's increasingly weakened leadership. Before the Anti-Masons even reached the zenith of their power, the practicalities of maintaining a political organization had already proven troublesome.

Thurlow Weed himself became embroiled in the rising tensions, as warring factions within the party jostled over issues of compromise. The party needed a high-profile newspaper, one that could disseminate Anti-Masonic literature from New York to the rest of the country, and to keep the diverse elements of the party united behind a common cause. Yet again, Weed was the perfect man for the job. By 1830, Weed had moved to Albany, the state's capital, to found the *Albany Evening Journal*, soon one of the most widely circulated papers in the country.

The problem was that Weed's was a nearly impossible task. From his seat in Albany, the pragmatic Weed was increasingly accused of abandoning the Anti-Masons' ideals in favor of supporting other members of Jackson's opposition—of placing the party's future prospects above its own principles. The radical elements of Weed's own party now accused him of having "been guilty of a mean and base deception" and of duping "the honest Antimasonic yeomanry" into supporting politicians with Masonic sympathies, or even of withholding new accusations in the name of compromise. Because the radical Anti-Masons required outright denunciations of Masonry from any politician they were willing to trust, "politicians with Masonic sympathies" was an impossibly large group.

The divisions between Weed and the radical dissidents were magnified in the party membership at large. One newspaper covering a local 1831 Anti-Masonic convention highlighted the now increasingly popular view "that Antimasonry had other and higher objects in view than the prostration of the Masonic fraternity." Samuel Miles Hopkins, a longtime New York politician and one of the state's most prominent Anti-Masons, declared that Andrew Jackson was a greater threat to the country than Freemasonry, and that in the last election he himself had voted for Masons rather than let pro-Jackson candidates win. By 1831, a year before the presidential elections, the Anti-Masonic Party was rotting from within.

The new tensions within the party would not stop Thurlow Weed, however, whose ambitions were growing larger and larger still. Weed was a driving force behind the nominating convention of 1831, attempting to secure candidates that the increasingly disparate wings of the Anti-Masonic Party could agree upon. When it came to the presidential nomination, Weed's was an especially hard task. But Weed thought that he had found the perfect candidate in William Wirt, a Virginia politician and former attorney general, and one of the last vestiges of old-style American politics—a man who Weed believed could help the party, and the nation, overcome its internal tensions.

Wirt was a stern moralist and a devoutly religious man, and he had been tapped by Thomas Jefferson himself as a political heir. "You will become the Colossus of the republican government of your country," Jefferson had once assured him. Wirt was a good match, for his concern with America's moral status echoed many of the Anti-Masons' deepest concerns. Wirt, for example, once described himself as a profoundly disappointed man: "disappointed in my country and the glory that I thought awaited her . . . disappointed most sadly in the intelligence and virtue which I had attributed to our countrymen." It was the selfish pursuit of profit that Wirt thought was the animating evil of the times. The growing object of Americans of every stripe was simply "to grow rich: a passion which is visible, not only in the walks of private life, but which has crept into and poisoned every public body." What Wirt identified as the growing flaws in American society were the same evils that the Anti-Masons saw in Freemasonry itself: selfishness, moral decay, and a system in which the few benefited at the expense of the many.

The problem was that not only had Wirt himself once been a Mason, he had never explicitly renounced the order. Now, he was calling the entire conflict between Masonry and Anti-Masonry "a fitter subject for farce than tragedy," and bemoaning the "wild and bitter and unjust persecution against so harmless an institution as Free Masonry."

The most radical of the Anti-Masons were obviously outraged by Wirt, which likely came as little surprise to Weed. Here was a candidate who neither believed in the evils of Freemasonry nor had explicitly denounced the order. He had even himself been a Mason. Increasingly sidelined, the radicals watched as Wirt was selected to carry the party's banner in the fight against Andrew Jackson, allying with other elements of the opposition.

But by and large the rest of the party supported him, perhaps to a fault. Wirt would ultimately carry only the state of Vermont in the presidential elections, winning Anti-Masonic counties in states across the country but falling severely short of any meaningful support at the national level. Simply put, enthusiasm for the Anti-Masonic cause was dying out.

The greatest cause for this lack of enthusiasm wasn't simply Wirt, but the end of the Morgan trials themselves. By 1831, after nearly twenty trials with more than three dozen defendants, the New York statute of limitations kicked in, and new trials were now restricted by law. The Morgan affair had been instrumental in identifying the Masons as a looming evil, denounced in papers and pamphlets and town halls across the country. Now that the scandal had petered out, forever unsolved, the symbolic threat was deflated. After Wirt's failed candidacy, the Anti-Masonic Party "seemed as if by magic, in one moment annihilated," wrote one nineteenth-century historian. Men "who had repeatedly most solemnly declared, they would never vote for an adhering Mason for any office whatever, in one day, ceased to utter a word against Masonry."

Some of the radical elements of the party had already begun to anticipate the end in the lead-up to the election itself, admitting that Anti-Masonry was dying, if not already dead. John Crary, one of the party's founders and once its candidate for lieutenant governor of New York, wrote to a New York newspaper that "if Antimasonry was right in 1828, it must be wrong now, for it is different both in principle and practice from what it was then." The party had made room for members and ideas that even some of its founders could not tolerate. It would take only a year for Weed himself to admit the same. After the Anti-Masons met with failure yet again in the local elections of 1833, Weed conceded that the party's run was over. "The election of 1833 demonstrated unmistakably not only that opposition to Masonry as a party in a political aspect had lost its hold upon the public mind," he would write, "but that its leading object, namely, to awaken and perpetuate a public sentiment against secret societies, had signally failed." Thus the reign of Anti-Masonry, and this episode of political hysteria, came to a gradual end—though not without lasting effects. The fraternity that the party had set itself against was forever damaged. Over the course of the hysteria, Masons across the country resigned or denounced their membership, and hundreds of lodges were shuttered in the process. "Lodges by scores and hundreds went down before the torrent and were swept away," according to one Mason at the time. "In the State of New York alone upward of 400 lodges, or two thirds of the craft, became extinct."

For men like Weed, the Anti-Masonic hysteria had not been for naught. During Andrew Jackson's second term, the separate elements of the opposition began to organize, realizing the strength of their combined power, if only they could achieve unity. It was with these goals in mind that the Whig Party, the predecessor to the modern Republican Party and the party of Lincoln, was born—a party comprised of a wide variety of beliefs, and many contradictions. The party tended to support all things anti-Jackson, including measures in favor of a national bank, prison and educational reform, along with the temperance movement, though it ultimately lacked a single coherent ideology. The Whigs would slowly gain strength throughout the 1830s as former Anti-Masons and others gradually came into the new political fold. It was an ambitious task, unifying so many differing interests, and Weed himself would rededicate the *Albany Evening Journal* to the new cause.

But the rise of the Whigs did not mean the political hysteria was dead and gone. Like a virus introduced into the bloodstream, it simply went into retreat. Throughout the following decade, a few politicians would still make their names proclaiming the evils of Masonry. Some of them faded into obscurity, but others met with limited success. As late as 1836, Pennsylvania's Thaddeus Stevens led an Anti-Masonic committee in the state legislature that held public hearings on the threat of Masonry, interrogating Masonic witnesses and drawing some national attention (a tactic that would be employed in episodes of hysteria to come). Stevens would ultimately rise to become a congressman, and later one of the US House of Representatives' most outspoken abolitionists during the Civil War.

In Massachusetts, Ohio, and Vermont, local groups of Anti-Masons met to purge their states of Freemasonry's influence throughout the 1830s as well, and some still harbored national ambitions for their party. But cracks had emerged in the Anti-Masonic movement that were too big to plaster over, and no longer did the threat of Freemasonry captivate as large a political audience or maintain its wide appeal. The Anti-Masonic movement now operated on the fringes of American political discourse, where it truly belonged.

As for the former Anti-Masons themselves, numerous members of the party went on to greater achievements, first as Whigs and then as Republicans. Millard Fillmore, a New York Anti-Mason from the very start, would begin his only term as US president in 1850. William Seward, another New York Anti-Mason, became Abraham Lincoln's secretary of state, serving as a key member of Lincoln's wartime cabinet. Thurlow Weed would become a key national figure, engineering presidential elections for the Whigs and the Republicans throughout the following decades. Meanwhile, William Morgan's lonely widow, Lucinda Morgan, would herself rise to higher levels of fame. She moved west and reportedly remarried a man by the name of Joseph Smith, the founder of the Church of Jesus Christ of Latter Day Saints, or the Mormons—a group that, like the Freemasons, would find itself the unwelcome target of future political crusades.

CHAPTER 4

The Red Scare

A. Mitchell Palmer Takes On the Enemy within Our Gates

Walking down Georgetown's cobblestone streets one summer evening, Carlo Valdinoci had no idea he was about to die. If you asked him why he had traveled to the nation's capital that day, he probably would have told you it was to make a statement. At a mere twenty-three years old, Valdinoci was an ambitious man—he wanted to change the course of history. He might have spoken in grandiose terms, and perhaps even talked about how some day his actions would reshape the American system of government. Oddly enough, he would have been right.

What Valdinoci did on June 2, 1919, helped set in motion one of the most intense periods of political hysteria in American history—a period in which fears of an internal revolution became the nearly singular focus of American politics. This period would see the American public tolerate breaches of fundamental rights in the name of rooting out the Bolshevik enemy. What is commonly known as the "Red Scare," lasting from 1919 through 1920, was not your ordinary movement of political hysteria. It was political hysteria on steroids.

But like most Americans at the time, Valdinoci had no way of knowing what was on the horizon. He was an Italian-American immigrant, and a member of a small band of anarchists who believed that violence was the only way to change the existing political order, one in which the masses were dominated by capitalists through something akin to slave labor. He had been on the run since 1917 for urging resistance to the national draft—a crime at a time when the United States found itself fighting World War I. Today, we would call Valdinoci a domestic terrorist. Back then, they had other words: radical, Bolshevik, anarchist, hyphenate, un-American. The country had been worried about men like Valdinoci ever since President William McKinley had been assassinated by an anarchist's bullet eighteen years before. Men like Valdinoci had been demonized for decades, and they were hunted by federal and state authorities too.

But that day, Valdinoci was not in hiding—if anything, he stood out. Dressed in a multi-colored striped shirt and a polka dot bow tie, he wore his finest clothes, with the odd combination of brown leather sandals to match. He even sported a new fedora, which he had bought earlier that day in Philadelphia while waiting between train stops from New York. Beneath his pinstriped suit, Valdinoci also wore two guns—one Colt Automatic and a Smith & Wesson revolver. Inside the large leather satchel he carried were twenty pounds of dynamite.

We know what Valdinoci was wearing because at around 11:15 p.m. that night the explosives in his briefcase mistakenly went off, scattering bits and pieces of his body over two city blocks, and blowing up the first floor of Attorney General A. Mitchell Palmer's home in the process. No one was hurt in the blast except Valdinoci, whose torso was later discovered on the rooftop of a nearby building, blown dozens of feet into the air from the explosion, but Palmer's neighbors were frightened, as was Palmer himself. One of his neighbors, for example, a young Franklin Delano Roosevelt then serving as assistant secretary of the Navy, was the first to arrive on the scene. Roosevelt would later recall finding a deeply spooked Palmer and a badly damaged house, covered in debris and blood and gore.

But the explosion frightened more than just the members of Palmer's elite Georgetown neighborhood. In a very real sense, the bombing captured the nation's psyche. Amidst the fragments of Valdinoci's body were fifty copies of a pamphlet that declared this attack was just the beginning. "There will have to be bloodshed," the flyer read, "there will have to be murder; we will kill, because it is necessary." The fact that multiple other bombings occurred that night, in seven separate cities across the country, showed that these were more than mere words—they were serious threats.

Indeed, less than a year after World War I ended on the European continent, Valdinoci's actions helped convince the American public that a new war was coming. It was a war that would be waged on America's soil. And it would be waged by none other than A. Mitchell Palmer himself.

⸺

It all started in Seattle. On January 21, 1919, thirty-five thousand shipyard workers began to strike for higher wages and shorter hours. In itself the strike was nothing new—thousands had occurred during the war years, at times crippling industries and sending brief but painful shocks to the country's consumers. Americans had quite simply become used to these strikes. Small in scope and relatively brief in duration, the labor movement had been careful to use strikes as a targeted weapon, aimed at Big Capital without causing too much pain to the American consumer. And the labor movement had been pretty good at this dance—rocking the boat enough for their bosses to cave to their demands, without causing much broader damage.

But the Seattle strike was different. This time, the boat nearly capsized.

Shortly after the first strike began, the Seattle Central Labor Council, which represented all unions in the area, announced that it would begin a strike of its own—a *general strike*—in support of the shipyard workers. The idea was to combine the power of all of Seattle's workers to make sure their demands were met. If the workers had leverage in one industry, they'd have even more leverage if they banded together in *all* industries. After years of hard work and sacrifice in order to meet the country's mobilization efforts during World War I, the labor movement was ready for new concessions, for higher pay and for an increased standard of living. Beginning in Seattle, just months after the end of the war, the movement sought to improve its lot.

The problem was that the Seattle strike would be the first time an official, citywide general strike occurred in American history—the labor movement's plans were new, and entirely scary. Suddenly, the strike was not about the demands of a group of workers in one industry, as most labor strikes had been up until that point. It was about the demands of workers *as a whole*—about a separate class of Americans with interests that were unique to their status, leveraging their power to the potential detriment of society. Over one hundred local unions would be involved in the upcoming strike, affecting the cities of both Seattle and Tacoma, and the public in both Washington and across the country was deeply alarmed.

This strike was no targeted weapon. It was a chemical bomb.

In the days between the Labor Council's announcement and the date when the general strike would begin, Washingtonians bought out the stocks of drugstores, supermarkets, and even gun shops. With all of the city's major unions on strike, how would the city function? Who would take out the trash, ensure the hospitals and the firehouses were working? How would the city even feed itself if the strike dragged on? The nation's eyes were fixed on Seattle, wondering and worrying if what transpired there portended a more unstable future for the country.

Making matters worse was the Labor Council itself, which gave Washington's citizens anything but reassurance. Two days before the strike began, the Washington labor movement's own daily paper ran an editorial announcing that, "We are undertaking the most tremendous move ever made by labor in this country," and repeatedly emphasizing that "no one knows where" the general strike would lead. Far from calming fears, the Labor Council exacerbated them. Was the editorial some type of veiled warning? Was more at stake than the simple demands for increased wages and better working conditions? God forbid, was this the beginning of some type of communist revolution?

Such questions weren't entirely outside the realm of possibility. Just over a year before, communists in Russia had undertaken the Bolshevik Revolution, overthrowing their pro-western government and instituting a reign of chaos, violence, and anarchy. In the years afterward, that chaos would spread. Around the time of the Seattle strike, half a million workers rose up in Berlin in an attempt to establish a socialist government in Germany. In Hungary and Bavaria, communist regimes were actually put in place. Bolsheviks were feared to be sweeping Europe and the world. During the Seattle strike, Americans would begin to fear that agents of Russian communism were sweeping the United States too.

<hr>

It took little time for Americans to view the Seattle strike through the lens of revolution. The actual controversy between Seattle's workers and their bosses, the one surrounding hourly wages and working conditions, was all too quickly forgotten—this was now a conflict between foreign elements, bent on revolution, and American ones. Among the best examples of the framing of the strike came from one of Seattle's main newspapers, the *Seattle Star*. The day before the strike began, the paper described the strike as an "acid test" between American principles and communist ones:

> *A part of our community is, in fact, defying our government, and is, in fact, contemplating changing that government, and not by American Methods. This small part of our city talks plainly of "taking over things," of "resuming under our management."*
>
> *We call this thing that is upon us a general strike, but it is more than that. It is to be an acid test of American citizenship—an acid test of all those principles for which our soldiers have fought and died. It is to determine whether this is a country worth living in and a country worth dying for. The challenge is right up to you—men and women of Seattle.*
>
> *Under which flag do you stand?*

Editorials like the *Star*'s were not unique. The *Washington Post* would call the strike "the stepping stone to a bolshevized America," while others would assert the strike was flat-out Marxist. In the public imagination, the general strike was now a symbol of something much greater. Soon, everything that was threatening about the strike was labeled "Bolshevik" and equated with the Russian communists—including groups that clearly had nothing to do with the Bolsheviks at all. It was a catchall phrase, one that would be applied broadly and thoughtlessly throughout the coming days, and in the crusade to come.

By the time the strike actually took place, it was as if a mini World War I were occurring on Seattle's soil. On the morning of February 6, some sixty thousand workers went on strike, amounting to roughly 20 percent of the city's entire population. The city was totally paralyzed as a result. Fearing general mayhem, groups of veterans formed voluntary militias to help keep the peace. Committees were formed to ensure that food was distributed throughout the city. Seattle's mayor, Ole Hanson, called in over a thousand federal troops to guarantee the safety of the city, personally escorting them into Seattle in an American flag–draped car—mixing emergency measures with theatrical ones.

However overblown reactions were to the strike, to most Americans, what took place in Seattle seemed like apocalyptic stuff.

Americans' need for reassurance, combined with the Seattle mayor's proclivity for attention, proved a dangerous combination. On the second day of the strike, Hanson issued a proclamation to the people of Seattle guaranteeing their safety, decrying the anti-American tendencies of the enemy strikers, and boasting that the strike would be over and done with soon. "The time has come," proclaimed Hanson, "for the people in Seattle to show their Americanism." Thus began Hanson's fifteen minutes of fame, a period he would exploit for all its glory. And glorious it was indeed: Public opinion, in both Washington State and around the country, heralded the mayor's efforts as both patriotic and brave. Everyone was now predicting the strikers' impending defeat.

The Labor Council—along with the national labor unions—soon began to realize how deeply mistaken they had been. They had demanded too much, too quickly, and isolated the entire working class as a result. By February 11, a mere five days after the strike had begun, they called it off. The nation's first general strike had ended in failure for Seattle's workers.

"The rebellion is quelled," declared Hanson gleefully, "the test came and was met by Seattle unflinchingly." The rest of the nation celebrated Seattle's victory, elevating Hanson's status to a national hero and sending him on a countrywide speaking tour. The Seattle strike had pitted foreign elements against American ones, and Americanism had won the day.

❧

There is, of course, much more to the story of the Seattle strike than the way that it unfolded, just as there is much more to the anti-Bolshevik hysteria than the Seattle strike itself—a strike that would form its touchstone, its point of ascendance onto the national political stage. An entire country, after all, does not unify around an event with such fervor without greater forces at work. Indeed, the forces at play in the Seattle strike had been stirring for years, if not for decades.

By 1919, America was changing. Disruptive forces confronted Americans at nearly every turn. At the economic level, inflation was up, prices were skyrocketing, and jobs were a scarcity. Meanwhile, four million veterans were coming home from the war, and they returned to a different society than the one they had left. During the war, blacks had moved north, crowding inner cities, and racial tensions throughout the country had increased as a result. With so many men off fighting the war, women had assumed increased importance—so much so that soon they would receive the right to vote. Meanwhile, the era of Prohibition, which would outlaw alcohol across the land, was just around the corner. Changes to the American way of life were ubiquitous, and the status quo was in peril. It was this sense of uncertainty that formed the basis for the nation's reaction to the Seattle strike, and ultimately gave rise to the anti-Bolshevik hysteria itself.

Perhaps most importantly, nativist forces were also stirring within the American public, forces that had been steadily growing in the years before the war—and not without reason. The rise in anti-immigrant sentiments correlated to the drastic increase in immigration into the United States itself. In the first two decades of the twentieth century, the country welcomed an unprecedented fourteen million immigrants, many of them Catholics and Jews from Southern and Eastern Europe, to its shores. Many of these immigrants retained their native languages, lived in isolated, and at times squalid communities, bringing with them their old ways of life.

But immigrants didn't just import foreign customs and languages into the United States, they also brought with them strange new ideas. The American Socialist Party, for example, counted the immigrant population among its key constituents—indeed, socialism itself was a strange new ideology imported from abroad. And thanks to the rise in immigration, American socialists met with increasing political success. In 1912, for example, the socialist presidential candidate garnered 897,000 national votes. By 1914, the party had thirty members in legislatures across twelve states.

The American public met these changes with deep suspicion—and with deep concern. With so many foreigners clinging to their old identities, and importing new ideologies into the body politic, what would be America's future? Were these foreigners intruding on the American way of life? Or were they improving it? Indeed, what did it even mean to be an American anymore? The issue of "Americanism" soon became one of the main problems of the day.

At few points in the course of American history has national identity been in such a fragile state. Many publicly worried that immigrants would never assimilate, that the tide of immigration would forever dilute the sense of self that unified Americans from shore to shore. America wasn't a "melting pot," these voices argued, it was a "salad bowl," where immigrants might never adapt. Immigrants who described themselves as "Italian-American" or "German-American"—so-called hyphenates, in the slang of the day—were viewed as a testament to this fact, aiming to keep their dual identities indefinitely. Men like former president Theodore Roosevelt declared that, "No good American can have any feeling except scorn" for hyphenates. Just before America's entry into the war, the Democratic Party declared the problem of hyphenates "the supreme issue of the day." President Woodrow Wilson himself had run for reelection on a campaign of "anti-hyphenism" just a few years before. If the melting pot was boiling before the United States entered the war, by the time the war ended, it had been knocked over.

All of which made the atmosphere surrounding the Seattle strike electric. When Americans saw Seattle's workers implement a new and potentially more powerful method of striking, they saw an immigrant community with foreign sympathies demanding more and more out of American society. They saw a newly divided country, with Bolshevik workers on one side and "real" Americans on the other. Here was a defining moment in America's search for its new identity, a moment when the public could identify what was *not American*, and rally around that. At long last, Americans had found their symbolic threat.

~~~

If the Seattle strike was a hallmark moment in the birth of the anti-Bolshevik hysteria, it was also an odd moment too, for the movement suddenly emerged at a national level without a leader. Instead, myriad groups—from the national media to veterans organizations, to members of the business community, and beyond—all began to decry the impending threat of Bolshevism with a new sense of alarm, and each to their own advantage.

In many senses, each group saw in the Bolshevik movement a different threat. Sexual and gender norms were changing—the 1920s would be the decade of "flappers," short skirts, and birth control—and many anti-Bolsheviks would find a way to connect Bolshevism with new sexual mores, often accusing Bolsheviks of perverted sex acts and of defiling the institution of marriage. There was also the obvious anti-immigrant component: Anyone resistant to the tide of immigration, or anyone still harboring anti-German sentiments from the war, saw value in a movement dedicated to ridding the country of all these dangerous foreigners. So too did the prohibitionists join in, for they saw in foreign communities a dependence on alcohol they viewed as undercutting the traditional American values of self-restraint, propriety, and independence. And the business community readily joined in as well, viewing the fear of Bolsheviks as a way to halt the increasing demands of labor. Meanwhile, newspapers used the scare to increase circulation, while politicians and veterans groups viewed the Bolsheviks as a new way to drum up support. By uniting against the Bolshevik threat, it seemed, so many segments of American society could defend their own values.

To put it simply, there was no singular constituency—no immediate group to which the movement appealed over others. Rather, the constituency crossed groups and classes of every order. And this is one of the many factors that made this period of hysteria so unique. Unlike previous episodes, which appealed to a handful of specific segments within American society, the anti-Bolshevik hysteria was widespread. The hysteria arose at a time of deep national crisis. As a result, the movement's supporters would come from nearly every quarter at the movement's peak.

But just because the movement lacked leadership did not mean that no one attempted to lead. One such attempt came from Lee Overman, a Democratic senator from North Carolina. Overman had been the chair of a committee created to investigate the threat of the domestic German population during the war. Beginning in early 1919, however, Overman switched the subject of his investigations from the Germans to the Bolsheviks, all in an effort to stir up national alarm. Indeed, the resolution that made this switch official was passed on February 4, almost exactly a year after the Seattle strike began. Over the course of the following month, the committee would suss out the Bolshevik conspiracy, calling in outside "experts" to convincingly explain how Bolshevik spies were sabotaging American society from within.

On March 10, Overman ended his first investigation, soon releasing a report made up of twelve hundred pages of anti-Bolshevik propaganda, declaring that the Seattle strike was the first attempted revolution of many more to come. The report advocated new laws that would make it easier to deport Bolsheviks and their sympathizers, and to throw them in jail. The report lumped all radical groups as being part and parcel of the Bolshevik threat, reaffirming the view Americans already had of the Seattle strike. Declared Overman, "We must bring home to the people the truth that a compromise with Bolshevism is to barter away our inheritance."

And just as the Overman report was alarming, the national media's reaction was sensational. "EXTREMISTS HERE PLAN A REVOLT TO SEIZE POWER," read one headline in the *New York Times*. "ANARCHISTS, SOCIALISTS, IN CONSPIRACY TO OVERTHROW GOVERNMENT," read another in the *Los Angeles Times*. Reporting like this—and sometimes even more bombastic—abounded. All across the country, politicians began to react. In New York, the state legislature created its own committee to further investigate the Bolshevik threat. Legislatures in other states took similar, and at times drastic, actions too.

But the truth was that as the nation's sense of alarm over the Bolshevik threat grew, so too was the actual threat rising. Later that same month, the Soviet government in Moscow convened an international congress of socialists, communists, and radicals, publishing a manifesto on the need for a worldwide Bolshevik revolution. The result of this congress wasn't simply a manifesto, it was also an organization itself—known as the Comintern—backed by the Soviet government with the express aim of fomenting revolutions across the world. If ever there was evidence of an international cabal of Bolsheviks plotting the destruction of the American way of life, this was it.

⌐ ⌐

Over the course of the following months, the American public was presented with even more alarming evidence of the growing threat of domestic Bolsheviks, this time in the form of bombings. Just as the Overman committee was releasing its warning about Bolshevism, the *Chicago Tribune* uncovered a radical plot to plant bombs all over the city. "The situation is a delicate one," the Chicago police chief would say, exacerbating the public's fears without clarifying them. "Further than that I do not care to talk."

In the weeks afterward, more and more bomb plots and conspiracies would be discovered just in the nick of time, only to be publicly revealed with sweeping headlines, but with no actual harm inflicted. But on April 28 that pattern would change.

On that date, a small brown package, seven inches long and three inches wide, arrived at Ole Hanson's office in Seattle. What made the package so strange was that it was leaking some kind of fluid—fluid that appeared to be eating away at everything it touched. A similar package arrived at the home of former Georgia senator Thomas W. Hardwick in Atlanta, though in this case it wasn't leaking. When the Hardwicks' maid opened it, the package exploded, blowing off both her hands and badly damaging Mrs. Hardwick's face.

The mail bombing made big headlines. The threat of domestic Bolshevism was no longer just about the general strike—it now portended actual violence, of the kind that the police could not stop. Sure, the bombings were minor in scale—only two households had been targeted, and only one successfully. But for the first time, the revolutionaries were successfully using arms.

"Why don't they attack me like men," challenged Hanson, "instead of playing the part of cowardly assassins?" But it was cowardly assassins Americans were afraid of.

And soon things would get a lot scarier.

At 2:00 a.m. on the night of April 30, two days after the mail bombings, Charles Caplan was riding the New York subway home after a

83

late-night shift at the post office when something strange caught his eye. While reading that day's paper, he came across the description of the package sent to the Hardwicks' house, which matched the one delivered to Hanson. The odd thing was that the packages were familiar—Caplan had set aside sixteen identical packages three days earlier for insufficient postage.

Caplan rushed back to the post office, only to have his suspicions confirmed. When the bomb squad arrived to inspect the packages, they announced the boxes were the real deal—it took almost six hours to dismantle just one bomb. These were the work of experts, said the lead investigator, confirming that he had "never examined a bomb of more skillful construction or deadlier possibilities."

After Caplan's revelation, another eighteen packages were intercepted in post offices across the country. All told, thirty-six prominent individuals, from Supreme Court justices to senators and even Attorney General A. Mitchell Palmer himself, had all been marked for death. The perpetrators of the plot were never identified, but it was obvious that the assassinations were planned to take place around May 1, better known as International Workers' Day, or May Day, the annual celebration of the international labor movement. This connection was not lost on the American public, its politicians, or the press. Americans took these attacks seriously—they weren't simply headlines in the newspaper, they were direct affronts to the American way of life. One newspaper, the *Chicago Tribune*, even went so far as to warn all readers of any box that arrived through the mail—such was the gravity of this new and violent threat.

By the time that May Day actually came around, Americans were ready for a showdown with the labor movement—and that is exactly what they got. Demonstrations on behalf of the labor movement turned violent all across the country. Veterans groups and "Patriot" clubs confronted labor rallies, and each time violence ensued. Riots broke out in Boston, New York City, Chicago, and Detroit. One of the worst took place in Cleveland, with simultaneous riots breaking out across the city in response to socialist parades. By the end of the day, Army trucks were needed to disperse the rioters. The final count stood at one dead, over forty injured, and 106 arrests. Yet again, the public saw the Bolsheviks as responsible. They were fomenting unrest and violence, dividing the classes, and preying on immigrants' minds—just as the Comintern had promised. The war against the Bolsheviks was clearly underway, and it had only just begun.

— — —

Amidst these rising tensions stood Palmer, the resolute attorney general who, if anything, was publicly disinclined to take sides—despite the fact that he had been a target of the May Day bombings himself. If anything, it was Palmer's personality and beliefs that kept him from taking a role in the growing hysteria. Palmer had grown up in rural Pennsylvania a devout Quaker, and he remained dedicated to the principles of pacifism, tolerance, and compromise long into adulthood. When President Wilson had offered Palmer the position of secretary of war just a few years before, Palmer responded that "the United States requires not a man of peace for a war secretary, but one who can think war." Adding to Palmer's reluctance was the fact that he actually considered himself a friend of labor.

And all of this showed.

In his only public comments on the May Day riots, Palmer reminded the nation that all men had the right to urge changes in American laws and institutions—even socialist changes—as long as they did not advocate the use of violence. The American public not only heard Palmer's measured message, it reacted angrily. "The policy of tolerance which has marked the attitude of the Department of Justice," wrote the *New York Times*, "must be dropped for one of vigorous prosecution if the Bolshevist movement is to be held in check." Indeed, Palmer was widely maligned for his reluctance to take on the Bolshevik threat, for his stubborn adherence to his Quaker principles.

Principled and reluctant, this was the way Palmer seemed for the first half of 1919, for the first few months that he served as attorney general.

But then, on June 2, a strange thing happened. In the late hours of that Monday night, surveying Valdinoci's blood and body parts spread out over his front lawn, something in Palmer's mind clicked. He had had enough of the Bolsheviks, he decided, and so had the country. Whether it was because he truly believed in the threat, or because he thought it offered him the surest means to fame and fortune, we do not know. But what we do know is that in the hours immediately after the bombing, Palmer suddenly decided to take on the Bolsheviks, to ride their movement into the ground, using all the tools of the national government at his disposal—no matter what the collateral damage might be. Here was a moment with huge implications for the country, and for the movement of hysteria only then in its infancy. Valdinoci had awoken a demon, and Palmer's reign of terror was about to occur.

Palmer reacted quickly. One of his first moves was to convene an all-day meeting with his top deputies, and to devise a battle plan. That plan? The mass roundup and deportation of alien radicals, one that would take place on a scale never seen before in the United States. "Those who cannot or will not live the life of Americans," crowed Palmer, "should go back to the countries from which they came."

But first Palmer would bide his time. Mass deportations required much groundwork—a whole new bureaucracy would need to be created, the nation's policemen and local government officials would need to be educated about the threat, and the public would need to be brought in on the government's new plan. To this end, Palmer's Department of Justice began distributing anti-Bolshevik propaganda, warning of the communist revolution taking place on America's shores, all with the official seal of the attorney general. One such pamphlet, sent to all major media outlets, began with a letter signed by Palmer himself: "My one desire is to acquaint people like you with the real menace of evil-thinking which is the foundation of the Red movement." If the country's reaction was sensational before, it would soon be totally overblown.

Meanwhile, within the Department of Justice itself Palmer established a new division called the General Intelligence Division, appointing a twenty-four-year-old J. Edgar Hoover to lead the effort. Soon the GID was gathering masses of information on the Bolshevik movement, all in an effort to craft the government's impending deportations. The division would boast a catalogue of over two hundred thousand index cards detailing the activities of radicals within the country, profiling over sixty thousand individuals themselves.

And this was a brilliant plan indeed. Palmer's legal authorities stopped short of any real action against radical American citizens. Little things like the First Amendment, which guarantees the rights of Americans to free speech, got in his way. If Americans expressed radical ideals or Bolshevik sympathies, there simply wasn't much he could do to stop them. But immigrants—alien Reds!—those he could deport, thanks to wartime laws that allowed the deportation of foreign agitators.

And this, in a sense, was all the anti-Bolshevik movement needed. Americans were waiting for a show of force, an attack against the tide of immigrants and their radical ideals, something that could prove once and for all that Americanism wasn't that badly threatened, that the American way of life was here to stay.

There was only one problem: Americans couldn't wait long enough. Over the next few months, public opinion would push Palmer further and further toward action, exerting pressure from every quarter, even as he drew up his plans. Even while Palmer was readying to strike against the Reds, the public wanted immediate results. Americans would again begin to doubt Palmer's resolve.

By the fall of 1919 the United States was entering a period of profound unrest. It wasn't just that one event portended domestic chaos, it was that so many of them did. The inflation rate, which had skyrocketed during the war, now stood at 15 percent. Meanwhile, false alarms about Bolshevik plots and anarchist attacks were wearing on the American public. The tensions between capital and labor were mounting. And the demands of the labor movement would terrorize the nation yet again, this time in a series of spectacular strikes.

The first strike began on September 9 in Boston, when over one thousand policemen walked off their jobs. The police had wanted to unionize to pressure the city for better hours and pay, but the city government blocked all such efforts. These were public employees, after all. Whose interests would they represent as a union? And what would happen if they went on strike?

Union or not, their strike began, and this time the nation reacted even more fearfully than it had with the Seattle strike. Private citizens and veterans created their own militias. Harvard even offered its own students to the cause. Despite these efforts, examples of lawlessness—looting, rioting, and minor spates of violence—soon abounded. President Wilson called the strike "a crime against civilization," while the *Wall Street Journal* proclaimed "Lenin and Trotsky are on their way." The Massachusetts governor and future president Calvin Coolidge announced that, "there is no right to strike against the public safety by anybody, anywhere, any time"—an announcement that would soon bring him national fame.

As with the Seattle strike, this one did not last long. A whole new roster of policemen was soon recruited, and all of the strikers, amounting to some 70 percent of the entire police force, permanently lost their jobs—a harsh measure, but a popular one. The public now widely accepted the notion that the strikers were "Bolsheviks." If the Boston strike proved anything, it was that Bolshevism led to anarchy, and this the American people would not tolerate.

A range of even larger strikes would follow. On September 22, the nation's steelworkers went on strike, amounting to nearly four hundred thousand workers across the country. This not only wrought havoc on the nation's economy, but it raised the specter of real class warfare, organized across state lines and in numbers comparable to an actual army (the strikers numbered, in fact, roughly the same size as the US Army at that time). Six weeks after the strike began, another broke out, this time amongst the nation's coal workers—and just a few weeks before winter too. Declared President Wilson, the strike was "not only unjustifiable, it is unlawful."

The Bolshevik threat was multiplying right before Americans' eyes. If Americans were alarmed before the fall of 1919, the public was now shocked—the Bolsheviks were operating on a scale hitherto unimagined. The American Communist Party had even warned as much. "Strikes of protest [will] develop into general political strikes and then into revolutionary mass action," according to their own manifesto. American communists "shall participate in mass strikes," it read, "not only to achieve the immediate purposes of the strike, but to develop the revolutionary implications." As the Bolshevik threat appeared to be growing, so too did the need for action.

—◆—

Soon, Palmer would hit the Bolsheviks and he would hit them hard. But the circumstances under which Palmer's actions took place highlight another bizarre fact about this period of hysteria: While in one sense Palmer was the leader of a national movement, he was also its pawn. What marked Palmer's tenure in the spotlight was a curious back-and-forth between leadership and public pressure—Palmer would increase the public's fear of foreign elements within American shores, and then the public in turn would force Palmer to act more vigorously than he preferred. To call Palmer the leader of the anti-Bolshevik hysteria is thus to only tell half the story.

By October, with the major strikes causing deep alarm across the country, Americans were ready for action. And so, in fact, was Congress. On October 19, the Senate unanimously passed a resolution demanding Palmer to "advise and inform the Senate whether or not the Department of Justice has taken legal proceedings . . . for the arrest and punishment" of aliens who had "attempted to bring about the forcible overthrow of the Government of the United States," and if not, to explain the cause of his inaction. This resolution served to highlight Palmer's apparent ineffectiveness in the public mind, despite his own plans to the contrary. The world's greatest deliberative body was doing exactly what it was supposed to: channeling the people's will. The Bolshevik threat was rising, and Americans demanded a larger and faster and more deliberate response.

And so Palmer sprang into action. On November 7, the two-year anniversary of the Bolshevik Revolution in Russia, federal agents raided supposed Bolshevik offices in twelve cities across the country, rounding up hundreds of men and women. The official target of the raids was the Union of Russian Workers, a national organization with some four thousand members, all of whom were Russian immigrants and all of whom were "atheists, communists and anarchists," according to the organization's own documents. The only problem was that many members hadn't even read the organization's charter, nor were they radicals in any real sense. The Union was little more than a social club for Russian immigrants; no real criminal or subversive activity had ever come out of the group.

But facts like that couldn't stop the raid, which was conducted brutally and indiscriminately. Men walking by the New York offices who simply admitted to being Russian were apprehended, and a number of others inside the headquarters were badly beaten. Although Palmer had only obtained twenty-seven arrest warrants in New York, roughly two hundred men and women were detained. Once in custody, some spent several months in jail.

If the raids were carried out without regard for the law, the public barely noticed. In fact, this was exactly what the public had been waiting for. Finally, a sign not only of the Bolshevik threat, but of the American response. Palmer was heralded as a hero, more noble and more charismatic than Ole Hanson himself. One week after the raid, Palmer penned an official response to the Senate's earlier resolution, now boasting his many efforts against the Bolshevik threat. He detailed some 471 radical papers distributed in the United States, and asked for increased legal authorities to confront the impending revolution—not just against immigrants, but against American citizens as well. And that wasn't all. Lest Congress or the American people believe that Palmer was not a true warrior, he ended his letter with the following line: "I have caused a number of other lines of activities to be pursued by my department which from the confidential nature thereof I can not disclose at this time." In other words, a war was coming, and Palmer was fighting it in the shadows. If Congress wanted victory, it should trust him, back down, and shut up. All of which it did—at least, for a time.

And that was that. The November 7 raid marked Palmer's ascension to the national spotlight, his name and reputation as good as gold. The Bolshevik threat might not have been receding, but he could finally declare that it was under attack. Meanwhile, the public had gotten its first taste of blood. And in the weeks and months to come, it would prove hungry for more.

Friday, January 2, 1920. This would be the climax of Palmer's attacks against the Bolshevik movement, the day that would set Palmer's place in history as one of the most ruthless attorney generals the country has ever known. Federal agents in more than thirty cities culminated months of preparation by simultaneously raiding Bolshevik organizations across the country. And thanks to the meticulous tracking methods developed by the General Intelligence Division, they were well prepared. Agents carried with them pictures of each Bolshevik target, along with information about where he or she would be at every hour of the day. Within the first forty-eight hours of the Palmer raids, some five thousand persons were arrested across the country.

Although strict procedures were put in place for both the capture and the interrogation of suspected Bolsheviks, these procedures were grossly violated, as were many Americans' basic constitutional rights. In Lynn, Massachusetts, for example, thirty-nine bakers were arrested on suspicion of plotting a revolution. In truth, they were merely meeting to establish a cooperative bakery. Fifteen miles away in Boston, a woman named Minnie Federman, suspected of storing radical literature in her home, was mistakenly arrested in her bedroom at 6:00 a.m. on January 3. It was only later discovered that she was an American citizen with no ties to the radical movement at all. In Newark, New Jersey, one man was walking down Charlton Street when he was reportedly arrested because he "looked like a radical."

Such stories abounded in cities across the country, but many more violations of American laws were less amusing. In Pittsburgh, for example, one man was arrested without warrant and held in jail for over a month before his friends petitioned for his release, and all without explanation. In Detroit, nearly eight hundred persons were arrested and held for up to six days in a dark, windowless hallway, sharing only a single toilet. Nearly half were released when it was discovered that their arrest had been a mistake all along.

No apology or sign of regret came from the US government, not to mention Palmer himself. In fact, precisely the opposite. Palmer reminded the public of the impetus for the raids in the first place. "Like a prairie-fire, the blaze of revolution was sweeping over every American institution of law and order," he announced. "It was eating its way into the homes of the American workmen, its sharp tongues of revolutionary heat were licking the altars of the churches, leaping into the belfry of the school bell, crawling into the sacred corners of American homes, seeking to replace marriage vows with libertine laws, burning up the foundations of society."

The public was, on the whole, supportive of Palmer's efforts, even if they violated some basic rights. Crowed the *Washington Post*, "There is no time to waste on hairsplitting over infringement of liberty." The raids would continue on a sporadic basis throughout the month of January.

But the truth was that Palmer's raids did not take place without criticism. Indeed, like all movements of hysteria before it, it was at the height of its success that the seeds of its downfall were planted, this time in the realization of the harm the anti-Bolshevik hysteria was inflicting on American values. Liberal magazines and newspapers began to voice their concerns with increasing openness. The number of influential Americans who were now openly opposed to Palmer began to increase. On January 12, Francis Kane, the US attorney for the Eastern District of Pennsylvania, submitted his resignation to Wilson over Palmer's "anti-radical policies" and "his method of carrying them out." Granted, the opposition to Palmer was not widespread. But beginning with the January raids, it would continue to grow.

Palmer, of course, paid no mind. For now, he had his sights set on larger things like the White House. On March 1, he would announce his campaign for the presidency to much fanfare. The elections were, after all, eight months away, and Palmer aimed to ride the wave of anti-Bolshevik hysteria to the country's highest office. His only problem? It wouldn't last long enough to get him there.

~❦~

At first, everyone hated the assistant secretary of labor, Louis Post, the number two official in the Department of Labor. At seventy-one years old, Post's appearance was both dreary and antiquated, his face framed by an old-fashioned beard on one end and a wild sprout of gray hair on the other. Once an assistant US attorney in New York, he had been the editor and publisher of a liberal magazine and had espoused some unpopular views. Post had called for easy divorce and supported the single tax movement, for example, which advocated that the nation's citizens pay one tax to support the government and one tax alone. Post was also prone to fiery populism. To the public, he was an odd man, one whose tenure in national government should have expired long ago.

And when—through an unlikely turn of events—Post became acting secretary of labor in March 1920, the public was even more suspicious, and with good reason too. By law, the Labor Department was responsible for all alien deportations. The Justice Department would capture the Reds, and the Labor Department was supposed to send them away. But Post, the man now in charge of the nation's deportation program, stood quite clearly against it. He had asserted it was unconstitutional, an abridgment of immigrants' constitutional rights, and he began to systematically reverse all of Palmer's hard work. Within his first month as head of the Labor Department, Post decided sixteen hundred deportation cases, cancelling warrants in 1,141, or 71 percent of them, and releasing hundreds more suspected Bolsheviks.

Palmer's nemesis had arrived on the scene, and the attorney general was growing more furious by the day.

But Palmer wasn't the only one outraged by Post's actions. The American public was too. Newspapers roundly condemned Post. He was widely labeled a Bolshevik, and the department he ran a cesspool of Bolshevism. By April 15, Congress was ready to take action. Kansas's representative Homer Hoch offered a resolution directing the House to investigate Post, and to impeach him if the facts warranted. Post had thrown sand into Palmer's gears, and Congress was now intent on cleaning them.

By April 27, the first hearings into Post's conduct had begun. Ironically, however, it was these hearings that marked the beginning of Palmer's downfall. In publicly examining Post, Americans were forced to confront their assumptions about Palmer, about Bolshevism, and about the Red crusade itself—the investigation would soon reveal that not only was Post innocent of all wrongdoing, but he was in fact justified in his actions. Hoch's investigation revealed that Post had done nothing wrong. By May 1, the House committee investigating Post offered a weakened resolution, merely censuring Post for his leniency. The censure was more of a tribute to Palmer than the intended rebuke of Post. An investigation that began with the threat of impeachment ended with nothing more than a slap on the wrist.

The House's failure to discover any of Post's wrongdoings coincided with another national scare, one that also helped to hasten Palmer's fall from national grace. May 1, 1920, marked May Day yet again, and Palmer and his department predicted that the Bolsheviks would attempt to hit back with a vengeance. The General Intelligence Division prophesied massive riots, political assassinations, and bombings of the kind that had taken place in 1919. Palmer himself warned that Americans of all kinds were marked for death. Newspapers reprinted these claims verbatim.

And so the nation once again stood alert. Police forces across the country readied themselves for the coming attack. In New York, the entire police force was on duty from midnight April 30 to 8:00 a.m. on May 2. In Boston, trucks mounted with machine guns stood ready throughout the city. In Chicago, 360 radicals were placed under guard for the day "just in case."

The strange thing was that nothing happened, despite Palmer's wild prophecies. The day came and passed without one single incident. It now began to dawn on the public that Palmer and his warnings, and perhaps even the Bolshevik threat itself, were ginned up, perhaps even exaggerated entirely. Palmer had been crying wolf for months. On May 1, 1920, he finally began to look a fool.

Meanwhile, Post had been waiting for his turn on the national stage. And on May 7, when the House committee investigating Post allowed him to testify, that was exactly what he received. The hearings would be Post's first chance to defend himself before Congress and the American people, a chance he had been demanding. The committee likely relented to Post's demands assuming he would be an easy target. Post was, after all, an old and slight man. Perhaps he would incriminate himself somehow, or at the very least, justify their failed inquiry into his record in the first place. Perhaps he would give them new justifications for their investigation.

Congress, and the public at large, was in for a surprise.

If Post ever had off days, May 7 was not one of them. His brilliant mind was on full display, stunning the congressmen and the press who assembled for his testimony. At once, he mounted a sweeping defense of his record, of the Constitution, of American values and of US history, all the while attacking Palmer as a ruthless, unprincipled madman. When congressmen brought up obscure facts about deportation cases, attempting to goad Post into revealing his supposed Bolshevik sympathies, he brought up even more obscure details about the same cases, correcting their mistakes and assumptions. The seventy-one-year-old had mastered the facts with more nuance than anyone else in the room, including even the congressional staffers. Of all the raids that Palmer had conducted, Post pointed out that only a meager three pistols were ever discovered. As one newspaper headline described the scene: Post "71, full of fight—Flays Attorney General's work of persecuting men found innocent of wrong." Hailed the article, "Despite his 71 years he seemed 25."

Post's testimony, combined with the hollow warnings of May Day, proved a game changer. Here was, on the one hand, a clear indication that the fears of Bolshevism were overblown. And on the other was an old underdog, at first scorned by the public but fighting for his beliefs in the face of immense pressure. "Unterrified by the unreined emotionalism," described one national magazine, "stood one little man, cool but fiery, who set his belief in the Constitution of the country above all fears."

Soon the public began to realize that Post's fight was their fight, that the enemy of true "Americanism" wasn't the Bolsheviks. The real enemy had been Palmer's own crusade all along.

Almost as quickly as the anti-Bolshevik hysteria had captivated the American public, it began to wane. A few weeks after Post's testimony, an embattled Palmer tried to mount his own defense in front of Congress, but Palmer fired blanks. He hurled epithet after epithet at Post and his ilk, accusing his own detractors of Bolshevik sympathies and warning the public of the impending attacks and the wider revolution. Men like Post harbored "tender solicitude for social revolutionists and perverted sympathy for the criminal anarchists of the country," Palmer asserted. But it was too late.

Around that same time, a group of twelve of the country's most respected lawyers released a stinging denouncement of Palmer and his

Justice Department, among them Felix Frankfurter, a future Supreme Court justice, and Roscoe Pound, the dean of Harvard Law School. This was the most high-profile rebuke of Palmer to have appeared in public, detailing how his actions had personally threatened the American system of government. "Here is no question of a vague and threatened menace," the report read, "but a present assault upon the most sacred principles of our Constitutional liberty." Palmer, they argued, was a graver threat to the country than the Reds. This was an attack from which he would not recover.

But Palmer, newfound warrior that he was, tried to fight back still, even as the tide of public opinion ran against him. He and his department continually warned of new and nefarious threats. Meanwhile, his campaign for president was still underway. He marshaled every ounce of political capital he had gained throughout his career. And he doubled down on his own "Americanism." Describing his campaign platform to voters before the Georgia primary, Palmer announced, in all seriousness:

> I am myself an American and I love to preach my doctrine before undiluted one hundred percent Americans, because my platform is, in a word, undiluted Americanism.

In the end, however, all his efforts would end in failure. Palmer's name was now synonymous with his anti-Bolshevik crusade, with the violation of American civil liberties, with crying wolf. The crusade was now over. And so too was Palmer's career.

As a sign of how far the public had come after the spring of 1920, the country barely flinched when, on September 16, a bomb exploded outside J. P. Morgan's Wall Street office. Thirty-eight people were killed in the blast, and hundreds more were wounded. The heat from the explosion was so intense that those standing near open windows six stories above street level were badly burned. The bombing would be the deadliest act of terrorism in American history up until that time. And yet the public reacted with calm, if not with reason. Wrote the *Cleveland Plain Dealer*: "Capitalism is untouched. The federal government is not shaken in the slightest degree. The public is merely shocked, not terrorized, much less converted to the merits of anarchism." The hysteria had passed; the public had moved on.

As for Palmer himself, he would be the last victim of his own crusade. In November, Warren G. Harding would be elected president. A few months later, Palmer would vacate the last position in government he ever held. Meanwhile, Congress asked Palmer to account for his wrongdoings, and the American public itself began to blame Palmer for the hysteria that had taken place under his watch.

To all this, however, Palmer remained defiant, even proud. "I apologize for nothing that the Department of Justice has done in this matter," he would testify. "I glory in it." And this was, in effect, all that Palmer would ever say about his raids and his broader legacy. He had defended his country proudly against a Bolshevik attack. He had been right back then. It was only now that the public sentiments were wrong.

But Palmer's private actions spoke louder than his public words. In his last remaining days as attorney general, he removed almost all of his official correspondence from the government's files. By the time he died, in 1936, Palmer had destroyed nearly all of his personal papers. Perhaps Palmer did not trust the historians to tell his story, his faith in the public now broken over his meteoric loss in reputation. Perhaps he really believed in the righteousness of his own crusade.

But it is more likely that Palmer realized the folly of his actions, and the dangers of the movement that had taken place under his watch. For at the climax of an episode of political hysteria, the public's hunger for action is insatiable, restrained by neither the nation's most vaunted laws nor its values—nor, in this case, by the conscience of its leaders. If the country was soon ashamed of the anti-Bolshevik hysteria, Palmer's final actions suggest that, not long afterward, he was too.

CHAPTER 5

The Dawning of McCarthyism

From Communists to Blacklists,
One Senator Channels the Fears of a Nation

Her name was Elizabeth Bentley, and she was a Soviet spy. Born in New Milford, Connecticut, in 1908, Bentley fit the profile of the quintessential East Coast elite. A Vassar graduate with a major in English and a minor in Italian, she would go on to work as a teacher at a selective single-sex boarding school in Virginia, spending time in Europe over the summers to round out her language skills and to better educate her girls back home. She was a blue-blooded Episcopalian, prim and proper with blue eyes and light hair, just the kind of woman many young American girls were expected to be.

But on July 31, 1948, in testimony before the House Committee on Un-American Activities, also known as the HUAC, Bentley destroyed that image and revealed something sinister underneath. On that morning, she wore a simple dark dress, her back perfectly straight in her chair and her hands perfectly folded on the desk in front of her. Surrounding her was an army of microphones, newsreel cameras, and lights. When the members of the committee began asking her questions, she answered calmly and politely. She told of how she had met a man named Jacob Golos in October of 1938 in New York City, though she first came to know him as "Timmy"—the pseudonym he used while working as an agent of the USSR. Golos operated a New York–based travel agency known as World Tourists, which he had set up a decade before with communist funds, giving him the time and ability to operate a large-scale spy ring in the United States. Bentley, who had fallen in love with Golos, carefully described how she gradually came to assume responsibility for a number of his contacts in Washington, DC.

"What type of contacts?" inquired committee member John E. Rankin, a Democratic congressman from Mississippi.

Here Bentley responded with two words that would soon come to symbolize Americans' worst fears: "Government employees."

Bentley went on to name names, providing details of whom she met with and when, outlining which government officials were members of the Communist Party and which ones were agents of the Russian Secret Police. All were veteran civil servants, and all were secretly devoted to overthrowing the US government from within, she claimed. There was Nathan Gregory Silvermaster, for example, an economist in the Bureau of Economic Warfare and his wife Helen, who led a "ring" of Soviet spies working in the government out of their Rock Creek home. There was Solomon Adler, the US Treasury representative to China during World War II. And then there was Lauchlin Currie, an economic advisor to President Roosevelt from 1939 to 1945. All told, she named a total of seventeen government employees throughout the course of her testimony.

Bentley would describe in more lurid detail the espionage ring she managed, both on that day and in testimony in the days afterward, outlining her biweekly trips to Washington and the tradecraft she used to hide her meetings, her falling out with Golos and why she had turned on her country, only to air all her secrets to the nation she now loved again. But to the congressmen sitting in the hearing room of the HUAC, where Bentley's testimony took place that day, or to the American public at home, it wasn't just these details that they were after. In fact, it wasn't really Bentley they cared about at all. If a woman like Bentley could have played such a pivotal role in undermining the US government, then there was a very real possibility that there were more Americans like her. Hers was no simpleminded conspiracy theory—the threat she symbolized was real. The Soviet Union, recently emboldened from the Allied victory during World War II, harbored ambitions of spreading communism around the world. It had dropped the "Iron Curtain" over Eastern Europe, effectively conquering half the continent and imposing communism on millions of persons there. It had networks of spies and sympathizers to spread com-munism further. And here Bentley was—model American citizen on the outside, but red and traitorous down below.

How many more Bentleys were there? And why hadn't she been caught in the first place? Why did the nation need to wait for spies like her to come clean on their own accord? Such questions were not lost on the Justice Department, which sought to cover its failures by indicting twelve leaders of the American Communist Party. Despite these seem-ingly decisive actions, the American public would soon find itself con-sumed with such worries, stretching into the middle of the next decade. Neighbors would accuse neighbors of spying for the Soviets, in big cit-ies and small towns alike. Teachers were suspected of brainwashing their classrooms. Loyalty oaths became a fact of life—by 1956, a whopping 13.5 million Americans were estimated to have undergone a loyalty test or background investigation. Fear swept a nation of 150 million like a tsunami. And in the middle of it all, a little-known Wisconsin senator named Joseph McCarthy would manage to ride the wave.

The story of McCarthyism, one of the most sweeping episodes of politi-cal hysteria in American history, is much more than the story of Joseph McCarthy, whose few years in the national spotlight lent this period of hysteria his name. One of the biggest mysteries of this era, officially span-ning the late 1940s and into the mid-1950s, is how one man—virtually unknown before the scare, and disgraced once it had ended—managed to affix his personal brand to a political movement that involved nearly every segment of American society, and one that enjoyed the approval of the majority of Americans at its height. To this day, explanations of McCarthyism give the junior senator from Wisconsin more credit than he is due—it was *his* phenomenon, the story commonly goes, and *he* was to blame for the political climate of fear and repression at that time. Without McCarthy, such accounts suggest, we might not have even had McCarthyism at all.

But McCarthyism traces it roots to long before the junior sena-tor from Wisconsin even came on to the scene—back to a time when

McCarthy was a small-town lawyer, in fact, working in Shawano, Wisconsin, far from the national limelight. By 1938, for example, when Democratic representative from Texas Martin Dies declared that "subversive" communists had infiltrated the US government and staged a national campaign to clean its ranks, McCarthy was a failed politician, having lost his first attempt at elected office in a race for Shawano County district attorney. In June 1940, when Congress passed the Smith Act, outlawing any activity deemed "subversive" to the US government, and broadly violating modern conceptions of the First Amendment's right to free speech, McCarthy was nothing more than a circuit judge barely one year into his tenure, making a name for himself as a careless, publicity-seeking arbiter from his Appleton, Wisconsin, courthouse. And by the time President Harry Truman signed Executive Order 9835, on March 21, 1947, creating a loyalty program for federal employees and an official blacklist of "subversive" persons or organizations—laying the groundwork for much of the hysteria to come—McCarthy was merely a much disliked first-term senator who, by some accounts, focused more energy on gambling and women than he did on legislating.

The real story of McCarthyism, of the phenomenon that helped define domestic American politics for more than one decade, didn't need McCarthy as much as it made use of him—McCarthy would eventually channel a political movement whose birth preceded him, and whose powers were beyond his control. Ultimately, the episode of hysteria known as McCarthyism involved three US presidents, hundreds of congressmen, and thousands of members of the media just to start—and it wasn't until much later that McCarthy came in. The real story begins in 1938.

That year the House of Representatives created the Committee on Un-American Activities, a temporary investigative subcommittee that was the forerunner to the permanent HUAC, before which Elizabeth Bentley would testify ten years later. The committee would soon prove to be a one-man show, its leader Texas representative Martin Dies, a lawyer who carried on in the tradition of his father, himself a former congressman from Texas, blending his nativist views with an odd mix of economic conservatism and populism. Despite being a member of the same party as Franklin Delano Roosevelt, Dies considered himself a staunch foe of the president and most of the officials occupying the executive branch. But Dies didn't just think of himself as Roosevelt's enemy—he acted the part too. Within a few months of the committee's creation, Dies was warning of "Trojan horse" tactics of the communists and subversives who had infiltrated government service, accusing public school teachers of indoctrinating the American youth and calling on President Roosevelt's cabinet members to resign.

Other members of the committee, both Democrat and Republican alike, echoed Dies's claims. Representative Noah Mason, for example, a Republican from Illinois, would name a series of government officials as sponsors of communist front organizations, allegedly intending to use the government's resources to aid in the spread of socialism within the United States. And such statements were not lost on the American public. In a December 1938 Gallup poll, 74 percent of those who had heard of the committee wanted its investigations to continue.

This was just the beginning of the committee's smears, accusations, and guilt-by-association tactics, techniques that would be refined by McCarthy and his allies in the years to come. The following year, Dies released a list of the names of more than five hundred federal employees accused of belonging to the American League for Peace and Democracy, which he alleged to be a communist front organization. Taking to the radio to support his accusations, Dies would claim that "there are hundreds, yes thousands, of members of the Communist-controlled organizations scattered throughout the departments and agencies of our Federal Government and nothing will deter me from apprising the American people of this fact." Compared to other accusations made by Dies and the committee, these statements were rather tame. Dies soon disavowed organizations like the Boy Scouts, the Camp Fire Girls, and the American Society of International Law, going on to list the names of 1,121 subversive federal employees, all to great effect in both the pages of the nation's newspapers and on Capitol Hill.

Dies's accusations were, of course, completely unsubstantiated—by almost any standards. But that was not the point. Amidst the turmoil of the Great Depression, a band of representatives in the House had found a threat that seemed to resonate with much of the American public—even if the real threats, like Hitler and fascism, both of which the country would soon be fighting in World War II, were elsewhere. Indeed, the committee was originally set up to look into precisely *these* real threats, under the belief that agents of Hitler's Germany or Mussolini's Italy might be operating domestically. But Nazis and fascists did not keep Dies's attention for long. In one of the committee's first major reports, dated January 3, 1939, Dies spent roughly three times as much space tracking the communist menace than he did fascism or Nazism.

To Dies and his supporters, the so-called fifth column of secret communists in America was less about actual espionage and more about ideology. There were dark forces fighting a war, to be sure, but not with guns or secret meetings—this was about much more than the Elizabeth Bentleys of the world. The war was about the changes taking place within American society, most of which emanated from the minds of the elite bureaucrats who made up the Roosevelt Administration—Ivy League men, born and raised on the East Coast and educated at preparatory schools to attend Harvard or Yale, much like Franklin Roosevelt himself—men who had little in common with Dies. The war was about the rapid expansion of government authority, which Roosevelt directed in response to the Great Depression, and which placed large portions of the public welfare into the hands of the federal government and its bureaucrats. For the first time in the history of the country, the federal government now took responsibility for the economic security of the elderly and the unemployed through the Social Security Act, and it created large infrastructure projects to increase the number of citizens on its payroll through the Works Progress Administration.

Such changes were in fact revolutionary. If society is founded on a "political contract" between its citizens and their government, as many Enlightenment political philosophers believed, Roosevelt's policies, cumulatively known as the "New Deal," really did signal a new pact between American society and its government (hence the name "the new deal"). These policies constituted a shift away from a society in which individuals were largely left to their own accord, and pushed the country toward a society in which the government purported to act on its citizens' behalf. Even real American communists themselves jumped onto the New Deal bandwagon, lending its policies their full support. In 1938, one communist election pamphlet in Wisconsin read, "Elect Genuine New Dealers and Liberals. . . . Vote for Fred Bassett Blair, Communist Candidate for US Senator." Despite the fact that Roosevelt's policies were supported by a majority of Americans—most of them from Dies's own party—the New Deal was vehemently opposed by a small, though not insignificant, group that cut across party lines. Prominent among this group was Dies. The Soviets baited a "hook with a 'progressive' worm," Dies would proclaim, "and New Deal suckers swallowed bait, hook, line, and sinker." To be sure, Dies saw more in the communist threat than just communism alone.

Behind Dies's "communist menace" were broader forces at work in American society—forces that would help propel the nascent hysteria to new heights under McCarthy's stewardship later on. Indeed, the very timing of Dies's initial appointment to the Committee on Un-American Activities in 1938, and of the creation of the committee itself that year, is instructive. During the course of that same year, the US government became the purveyor of a new idea, one that was arguably as powerful as the New Deal itself, and one that would have profound effects on American society for years to come. That idea was multiculturalism.

Beginning on November 13, 1938, the US Office of Education began airing a series of radio broadcasts on CBS entitled "Americans All, Immigrants All." The twenty-six-week program covered everything from the Spanish influence on the American cowboy ("who inherited his horse, his outfit, his vocabulary, from Spanish America," according to one official pamphlet promoting the series), to Irish, Scandinavian, and African Americans' crucial roles in American history (the latter, "like most other ethnic groups, has been with us from the beginning"). The series was designed to give Americans a better sense of their shared history and culture, and was part of a broader trend in American society, beginning in the 1930s, to redefine national identity in newly inclusive ways. This new push was in part a reaction to racist political movements like Nazism that were sweeping across Europe, movements that served to highlight America's own racial intolerance as being at odds with the fundamental tenets of democracy. How could Americans claim moral superiority over Nazis, after all, if racism was tolerated at home? But this trend was also a corrective reaction to new prejudices that, spawned by the Great Depression, were growing within the United States. Anti-Semitism, for example, had been skyrocketing—as of 1941, 119 anti-Semitic organizations existed in the country, and all but five had been founded since 1933. At the same time, pro–German and Italian Americans, who noisily supported Hitler and Mussolini's tactics abroad, made Americans even more apprehensive about their own commitment to the nation's founding ideals. What distinguished Americans from their morally corrupt cousins in Europe? If racism across the Atlantic was clearly wrong, how could the bigotry that still existed in the United States be right? The answers were not as straightforward as most Americans would have liked.

When the time came to actually fight the Axis powers, beginning in December 1941 with the Japanese attack on Pearl Harbor, these questions became even more profound. The answer that Americans would slowly come to, prodded on by the US government through programs like "Americans All, Immigrants All," was multiculturalism—a new emphasis on *equality* as being the most important ingredient in the American recipe. It was America's tolerance for diversity that made the country exceptional, the argument went, and its ability to respect intergroup differences and minority rights. There were, of course, glaring contradictions to this general trend—the internment of Japanese Americans after Japan attacked Pearl Harbor in 1941, for example, or the continued existence of Jim Crow and other discriminatory laws. But by and large, beginning in the late 1930s and early 1940s, the country would take its first steps toward greater tolerance that would culminate with the civil rights movement a few decades later. One of the most lasting effects of World War II, writes historian Philip Gleason, "was that, by making the need for national unity more compelling, it intensified the efforts that were already under way to cut down prejudice, improve intergroup relations, and promote greater tolerance of diversity."

Historians like Gleason have described the changes that took place over this period as "a great ideological reawakening," a period in which Americans fundamentally altered the way they viewed their national identity. Soon, a host of organizations sprouted up to help make this awakening permanent. There was, for example, the Council for Democracy, created in 1940 by a group including media magnate Henry Luce, which held a conference that fall to "crystallize and instill in the minds of Americans the meaning, value, and workability of democracy as a dynamic, vital creed—just as Nazism, Fascism, and Communism are to their adherents." Groups like the Common Council for American Unity, which would subsequently contribute to a host of government educational programs, were created to foster "the acceptance, in fact as well as in law, of all citizens, whatever their national or racial origins, as equal partners in American society." Even the term "American identity" was itself a byproduct of these changes. Before the war people spoke of "American nationality" or "the American character," but it was only afterward that Americans had a unique "national identity."

Underpinning the dangerous communist revolution that Dies and his supporters spoke of were thus momentous changes taking place at all levels of American society, both before and during the war—these shifts were economic, ethnic, cultural. And though these changes weren't spawned by communism directly, men like Dies found it easier to paint the communist menace—in the form of its godless, utopian ideology and its intellectual supporters in the Roosevelt Administration—behind such fundamental shifts, rather than to talk about the actual threats many Americans were facing. The connection between Dies's witch hunts and multiculturalism was strong. Even with the nation plunged into World War II and confronting real threats in the Axis powers, the hunt for secret communists continued on the home front, spearheaded, of course, by Dies. His committee continued to publish its annual reports, and the Roosevelt Administration even took action in response to them. In 1944, for example, the committee specified that 245 communist front organizations were operating in the United States and used 344 pages of one report to list suspected communists—amounting to more than twenty thousand people, and naming Eleanor Roosevelt, the first lady, twenty times. In response to

Dies's agitations, President Roosevelt issued Executive Order 9300, setting up an official committee to handle complaints about subversive activity by government employees. Other Democrats in the House followed suit, creating a new subcommittee for the very same purposes.

Despite the fact that the Dies committee couldn't boast of any real accomplishments in the end—there were no actual "outings" of any communist spies, for example, like Elizabeth Bentley—it did provide a foundation for the anti-communist crusade that would intensify after the war. Indeed, some historians have identified the political movement Dies led as a "mini red scare," one that was ultimately dwarfed by the period of hysteria that took place under McCarthy. But the truth is that the two movements are connected, if not deeply entwined. Beginning in the late 1930s, a significant number of Americans whose view of their country was threatened by deep shifts in society began to project real threats onto symbolic ones, alleging that communists were "secretly undermining" all that was right with America from high inside the government. This is not to diminish the possibility that there was some truth to their claims— there were indeed some communists and communist sympathizers who really did favor the Soviet Union, or who even hoped for a communist revolution within America's shores. Documents declassified after the Cold War reveal that around five hundred Soviet agents were actually operating within the United States during the 1940s. But the threat was not even arguably close to the existential menace that Dies and his cohort claimed it to be. At root, Dies's anti-communist crusade was an argument about where the country was heading and who was to blame—as are all episodes of hysteria at their core. And though this argument would ultimately be drowned out by the actual threats Americans faced during World War II, the crusade did not go away during these years. It simply died down. In the years after the war, even with Dies deciding not to seek reelection—relinquishing, in effect, his national platform—Americans would quickly find more and more reasons to build on his legacy.

In February of 1945, something strange caught Kenneth Wells's eye. Wells was the chief of the South Asia division of the Office of Strategic

Services, known as the OSS, the wartime predecessor to the Central Intelligence Agency. He had been tipped off by a counterpart in British intelligence that the recent issue of a leftist American magazine known as *Amerasia* might be of more than routine interest. That British agent was right.

Wells picked up the January 26 issue only to read excerpts from a highly classified report that he himself had written for the OSS, circulated only to a select few among the highest levels of the government. The article, entitled "British Imperial Policy In Asia," plagiarized some fifteen points Wells had made about British-American relations in Southeast Asia, in addition to copying some sentences nearly verbatim from his original report. The good news was that some sections of Wells's report had been left out, like his overview of the top-secret anti-Japanese resistance movements operating from Thailand that were supported by the OSS. The bad news, however, was that the article's author clearly had access to this information. Three months before Germany's surrender, and seven months before Japan's official defeat, Wells had just discovered that the US government was leaking—and the leak was coming from the very top.

OSS security chief Archibald Van Beuren was deeply alarmed by Wells's revelation. Van Beuren quickly dispatched an OSS agent to *Amerasia*'s New York headquarters on 5th Avenue. After two weeks of surveillance, a five-man team broke into the *Amerasia* offices on March 11 during a winter storm. What they discovered inside was a nightmare scenario, far worse than what even Wells had imagined. Within one of the corridors, the team stumbled upon a darkroom used to develop photographs—an odd fact considering that the magazine had no photographic content. In the private offices of the publisher and his assistant, the OSS team discovered dozens of photographs that were still wet from the developing solution—someone, it turns out, had been using the darkroom that very day. Depicted in the photographs were pictures of US government documents, with the letterheads of various federal agencies and the moniker "Top Secret" stamped across the top of several of the pages. Nearby, the team discovered briefcases full of more classified documents from a host of government sources: Army and Navy intelligence, the State

Department, the OSS. Rather than a single leak, the OSS team had come across a torpedo hole.

But instead of confiscating all the documents on the spot, the OSS team quietly left the office and had the magazine placed under FBI surveillance, along with publisher Philip Jaffe and his assistant Kate Mitchell. By the time arrests of half a dozen *Amerasia* affiliates were made, more than two months later in June 1945, the FBI discovered what it believed were the foundations of a massive Soviet-run spy ring that had penetrated nearly every sensitive government agency. Almost two thousand government documents had been leaked to the magazine, compromising an untold number of government programs.

The only problem was that technically, *Amerasia's* employees had done nothing wrong. *Amerasia* was simply a magazine run by journalists engaged in journalism, attempting to shed light on the inner workings of the American government. And that is precisely what the magazine had done. There were First Amendment issues arising out of the freedom of the press and the right to free speech that made the government's case against the magazine questionable. And there were Fourth Amendment issues too—the FBI and the OSS had been a little too "enthusiastic," and had apparently overlooked basic constitutional requirements like the need to obtain a search warrant before breaking into an office or home. And even though the FBI would later discover that high-level government employees really did pass on some government documents to the *Amerasia* staff—officials such as John Stewart Service, a senior State Department employee and China expert—the only documents the FBI could prove were passed on were not sensitive. Despite the sensational FBI press release announcing the arrests, and a media firestorm focused on the case, the government ultimately backed down. Within six months, the chief prosecutor publicly admitted that all that could be proven about the defendants was that they were guilty of an "excess of journalistic zeal." The Department of Justice soon dropped the case.

Coinciding with the end of World War II, the *Amerasia* case became a symbol of the changes that the American public was facing—a threat that was so mysterious, so confounding, that even teams of investigators from the government's top agencies could not understand precisely what it was. The case would come to signify not only government incompetence—the leaked files were, after all, a massive security breach, and one that neither the Roosevelt nor Truman administrations were able to address—but also the undermining of public confidence in the government itself, giving rise to questions that would help buoy the anti-communist crusade for years to come. Why, for example, had the government simply dropped the case, with no apparent follow-up? Surely, there had to be a series of moles high inside the government who had leaked the classified documents—but who were they? And why had they done what they did? More importantly, were these moles still there? And if so, what type of treason were they engaged in now? What if they weren't simply leaking US government policies, but rather were *shaping* them? This long line of accusations, often veiled as inquiry, routinely took a kernel of reasonable suspicion (that there were, in fact, spies in the government), and stretched it to the extreme (that the government was being controlled by them). These questions would help feed many of the most rabid anti-communists' conspiracy theories, transforming concerns over the policies of the US government into accusations about its very legitimacy.

And if the deep changes that took place before the war helped to fuel Dies's anti-communist crusade, the turmoil that Americans confronted after the war would only intensify it. This was, in some senses, a delayed reaction to many of the same factors to which Dies had responded, factors that the public only really began to grapple with after the war. But in a larger sense, Americans confronted even greater changes as a result of the war itself. The United States's very role in the global order was flipped on its back—as was the global order itself. The British empire was officially in tatters, Europe was nearly destroyed, and the Soviet Iron Curtain descended over the eastern half of the continent, confirming deep-seated fears that the wartime alliance with the Soviet Union would soon transition to peacetime antagonism and even "cold war" (such suspicions were right). America, long the isolationist "city on the hill," separated from most of the world by two major oceans, was now thrust into the center of global geopolitics. The United States itself would remain on permanent war footing as a result, keeping its military draft in place until 1973 and the end of the Vietnam War. Suddenly, the Soviet menace loomed as large as ever, dwarfing nearly every other priority for the United States and standing as America's main rival for decades to come.

World War II also transformed America's economy at home, moving the country out of the Depression while exerting major changes on the workforce. In November of 1945, for example, when Congress ended the wartime price controls designed to stabilize the US economy, the country plummeted into short-term chaos. Nearly two million workers lost their jobs, and real incomes dropped considerably. As a result, the labor movement—long associated with socialism, as we learned in the previous chapter—engaged in the most dramatic series of strikes in US history up until that time. Between August of 1945 and August of 1946, more than five million workers engaged in 4,630 strikes, involving every major American industry—coal, auto, electrical, steel, and railroads. As with previous periods of labor unrest, many worried that the strikes were socialist in nature. Millions of workers were, after all, banding together to demand greater rights—the first step in the larger revolution, according to communist ideals. In this way, the changes brought about by the war compounded the crisis that Americans were already facing. In the span of just over a decade, the nation had undergone such profound changes that, to a large portion of Americans, it was no longer recognizable. It became increasingly clear that communism was to blame.

In the aftermath of the war, the "Red threat" quickly became jockeyed about by Democrats and Republicans alike. In July of 1946, shortly before the mid-term elections, the House Civil Service Committee created a subcommittee to investigate the loyalty of federal civil servants for suspected communist sympathies. Not to be outdone by congressional Republicans, in November Truman created the Temporary Commission on Employee Loyalty for the same purposes. During the 1946 election campaign, FBI director J. Edgar Hoover warned that over the last five years, "American Communists have made their deepest inroads upon our national life." The communist influence, he added, "has projected itself into some newspapers, books, radio and the screen, some churches, schools, colleges and even fraternal orders have been penetrated, not with the approval of the rank and file, but in spite of them."

Anti-communism of this sort was, of course, clearly nothing new, as Dies's "mini-crusade" had proven almost a decade before. What was new was the intensity and reach—nearly everyone now began to act as if they had to prove their anti-communist credentials, from elected politicians to conservative social clubs and even liberal groups like the American Civil Liberties Union. With memories of the war fading, politicians on both sides of the aisle were compelled to prove how "American" they were, and consequently how "un-American" communists had to be—and foremost among this group was the administration itself. In November of 1947, Commissioner of Education John W. Studebaker embarked on a national anti-communist speaking tour, and the government began a series of mass demonstrations at which its employees took a "loyalty oath" and sang "God Bless America." From September 1947 to January 1949, a red, white, and blue "freedom train" sponsored by Attorney General Tom Clark and the American Heritage Foundation toured the country. Inspired by the tour, the famous composer Irving Berlin wrote "The Freedom Train," which the noted singer Bing Crosby would then put to music and record, and which, by October, would rise to number twenty-one in the national Billboard charts.

The Republicans also sought to capitalize on Americans' insecurities, claiming that Democrats themselves were communistically inclined. During the 1948 presidential election, the issue of domestic communism even made its way into the Republican Party's platform, which endorsed new legislation to expose "the treasonable activities of Communists and defeat their objectives of establishing here a Godless dictatorship controlled from abroad." Representative Clare E. Hoffman, a Michigan Republican, made the point even more bluntly: "Every informed individual in Washington knows that from the day Mrs. Roosevelt appeared with a group of Communists before the Dies Committee, the New Deal, and more recently, the Truman Administration, has been coddling and encouraging Communists who, in federal positions, thrive on the taxpayers' dollar."

By 1948, groups and politicians of nearly every political stripe had consistently been making the case against communism, and warning the country of its deep-rooted domestic threat. For years, however, the *Amerasia* case was pretty much all the public had to go on. All that would change by the time the summer came to a close.

It started with Bentley, or the "Red Spy Queen" as she became known in the national press. Her revelations before the HUAC in July of 1948 set off a firestorm, the first hard proof that, draped behind the facade of real Americans—and elite New England ones to boot—hid the threat of communism. But Bentley's repentance from her communist ways, which she alternatively blamed on her love for the Russian spy who seduced her and on her liberal education, made her rise to national fame merely symbolic. Bentley was ultimately only an example of the greater threat—there was, after all, only one of her, and the leads she gave to investigators or to the Congress about secret agents operating within America's shores never materialized in any meaningful way.

The vast mystery behind the *Amerasia* leaks remained.

What the public needed was a saga—something that would draw Americans in, that would keep their attention, one that would expose networks of real spies while boosting the cause of domestic anti-communism. Political hysteria, after all, thrives on a scandal. And thanks to a lawsuit, a rare yellow bird, and a little-known California congressman named Richard M. Nixon, that is exactly what the public would get.

On Tuesday, August 3, just a few days after Bentley's testimony before the House Un-American Activities Committee, the HUAC called David Whittaker Chambers to the witness chair. Chambers was a forty-seven-year-old senior editor at *Time* magazine, a stout, disheveled man who contrasted with Bentley's image in every way. Where she was polished he was dingy; where she was polite he was muffled and indirect. He had spent the 1930s working as a member of the communist underground, a "true believer" who had served as a courier for actual Soviet spies, passing secrets between US government moles and their communist spymasters. At one point he had been a reporter for the communist newspaper the *Daily Worker*; at another, fearing for his life, he had gone into hiding. But now Chambers had come back into the public eye, sitting before reams of reporters in the nation's capital on a humid summer day, ready to air his secrets to the world. The members of the HUAC had hoped that Chambers's testimony would support Bentley's charges, helping to convince the nation that the government really was overrun with Soviet spies. And Chambers, now a rabid anti-communist himself, was all too happy to comply. All told, Chambers named eight members of what he alleged to be a secret group of communist officials working in the government. Some of the names were familiar to members of the committee: Henry Collins, Victor Perlo, John Abt. Other witnesses had made similar charges against these men before. But one name stood out. And that name was Alger Hiss.

If Elizabeth Bentley presented an elite facade, Alger Hiss was patrician through and through. Educated at John Hopkins and Harvard Law School, Hiss was exactly the type of New Deal bureaucrat that men like Dies had railed against for years. Hiss was a protégé of Felix Frankfurter, a Harvard Law School professor and future Supreme Court justice. Tall, clean-cut, and handsome, Hiss had clerked for Supreme Court justice Oliver Wendell Holmes Jr., then moved on to a high-profile career in the State Department, accompanying Roosevelt to the Yalta Conference, during which arrangements were made for the postwar division of Europe. He had later served as secretary-general of the San Francisco–based international conference that gave birth to the United Nations. At the time of Chambers's accusation, Hiss was the president of the Carnegie Endowment for International Peace, one of the most prestigious think tanks in the country, and he counted some of the most high-echelon members of the Washington upper crust as his friends. Hiss, in short, was not someone who took his reputation lightly.

Hiss quickly demanded an opportunity to refute the charges. Two days later, he sat before the HUAC indignantly, denying ever knowing any man by the name of Whittaker Chambers, and marshaling all of his gravitas as proof to that end. Chambers had accused Hiss of being a one-time secret communist. Hiss swore that this was patently untrue. Hiss was a patriot with a sterling record of public service. He loved his country, and his track record proved it.

Hiss's attempt to clear his name worked—at least in the short term. Several HUAC members quickly favored backing off Chambers's charges.

But one member in particular, a wily Republican congressman by the name of Richard M. Nixon, remained unconvinced. Nixon, an ambitious young lawyer and Navy veteran, was new to Congress, having only been elected by his California district two years before. But he understood the power of Chambers's accusations. In his 1946 campaign, Nixon had unseated a popular congressman by repeatedly calling him a communist. There was little substance to the claims, but Nixon had been unapologetic, linking his rival to "a socialist-dominated group and its 'gigantic slush fund'" at every opportunity. And his ploy had worked—so great was the fear of communism that Nixon won the election resoundingly. When he came to Washington, Nixon operated with the same mindset. The more he could associate Democrats and the administration with communists, he believed, the higher he and his party would rise. To that end, Nixon cultivated relationships with a number of "experts" in anti-communism, a ragtag group of conspiracy theorists and legitimate investigators alike who saw communist spies in every corner. Among this group was Father John Cronin, a rabid anti-communist employed by the National Catholic Welfare Conference, who had received inside information from the FBI about Hiss and had passed along what he knew to the California congressman. When it came to Alger Hiss, then, Nixon was operating on more than just a hunch.

In the days following Hiss's testimony, Nixon led a subcommittee to investigate Chambers's allegations further. And though it was publicly obvious that Nixon was no disinterested party—he clearly favored Chambers's credibility over Hiss's, believed that the administration harbored communists, and had a past that demonstrated how the communist issue was beneficial to his own career—Nixon's efforts ultimately prevailed. In the coming days, more and more Americans would share his point of view.

Shortly after Hiss's testimony, Nixon brought Chambers back before his own subcommittee to recount the details of his relationship with Hiss. Chambers responded by providing intimate descriptions of Hiss and his wife's private lives, hobbies, and social circles, and of their interactions with fellow communists and Soviet agents—anything he could say to keep his accusations alive. Chambers explained how he had lived in an apartment owned by Hiss, staying rent-free as "part of the Communist pattern," and of an old car that Hiss had donated to the Communist Party. At one point, Chambers even recounted how Hiss, an avid bird-watcher, had once seen a prothonotary warbler—a rare bird with blue-gray wings and a bright yellow belly. And it was on account of this last little detail that a national scandal would soon unfold.

A few days after Chambers's testimony, Hiss was called back before the committee, ostensibly to defend himself again from Chambers's new accusations. What Hiss did not know was that Nixon and the members of the committee had hatched a plan to test whether the two men did, in fact, know each other, and thus whether Chambers's claims were true. The test was based on Chambers's story of that strange bird with the yellow belly. On Monday, August 16, Nixon and another representative from Pennsylvania, Republican John McDowell, himself an amateur bird-watcher, or ornithologist, jointly laid the trap:

Mr. Nixon: What hobby, if any, do you have, Mr. Hiss?
Mr. Hiss: Tennis and amateur ornithology.
Mr. Nixon: Is your wife interested in ornithology?
Mr. Hiss: I also like to swim and also like to sail. My wife is interested in ornithology, as I am, through my interest. . . . I think anybody who knows me would know that.
Mr. McDowell: Did you ever see a prothonotary warbler?
Mr. Hiss: I have right here on the Potomac.

Hiss's fate was sealed. The bird was rare enough, and knowledge of his sighting was so detailed and so intimate that it proved the two men did in fact know each other, despite Hiss's repeated denials—at least to the congressmen on the HUAC and to the press at large. Hiss himself had confirmed that anyone who knew him well enough would know that he was an avid bird-watcher. Knowing the names of the birds he had actually spotted? That must have made him and Chambers close. The committee members, now convinced that Hiss was lying about his non-relationship with Chambers, began to believe that whatever the substance of Chambers's accusations, they bore some truth. "Never in the investigation of espionage have so many placed so much reliance upon such an apparently minor fact," wrote one historian, "upon a solitary twit of a bird."

The conflict between Chambers and Hiss soon gathered steam. With each accusation, the men lay more and more of their reputation on the line. Consequently, each new charge raised the stakes of the game. The two men finally confronted each other face-to-face in a dramatic hearing on August 17. After listening to Chambers talk and inspecting his teeth—to verify, apparently, that he was who he said he was—Hiss suddenly admitted to having known Chambers under the assumed name "George Crosley." Hiss, however, denied most of the other charges, and even dared Chambers to repeat his accusations outside of Congress, where Chambers would lack congressional immunity and where he could be sued for slander.

Chambers quickly complied.

A few days later Chambers appeared on the popular news show *Meet the Press* and accused Hiss of being a communist on the air. Hiss then filed suit. Now there was not only a congressional investigation, but a living, breathing lawsuit to be played out in the courts—over the course of months, if not years. And not only that, but the administration itself appeared to come to Hiss's aid. In one press conference, President Truman called the accusations against Hiss "a red herring" designed to distract the public, a charge that Truman would repeat in the months to come—doubling down, in effect, on Hiss's sterling reputation. Even former first lady Eleanor Roosevelt publicly defended "the word of a man, who for many years has had a good record of service to his government." This was exactly what men like Dies had been waiting for—a scandal that would catapult the hysteria from a mid-level episode to one of the most intense, far-reaching in American history, one that would take an isolated dispute between two men and link it to three presidential administrations.

Thurlow Weed himself would have been proud.

With the stakes now sufficiently raised, the pressure was on for Chambers to prove his claims. Otherwise he could be convicted of slander, or even worse, indicted for perjury for lying to Congress. Chambers himself had now upped the charges. Hiss hadn't simply been a communist, he now alleged, he had been a real-life spy, passing secrets from the government into the hands of Soviet agents. At one point, the weight of the accusations was so intense that Chambers reportedly attempted suicide—but to no avail. As Chambers recovered, the investigations into both him and Hiss kept on rolling.

Chambers's "life preserver," in his own words, came in the form of a packet of materials he had hidden in 1939 in the dumbwaiter shaft of his cousin's Brooklyn apartment. Consisting of a few dozen typed copies of State Department cables, he had kept the materials as "insurance" against any members of the communist underground seeking to do him harm. In November of 1948, during a pretrial deposition in Baltimore in connection with Hiss's slander suit, Chambers offered the papers as proof that Hiss was spying for the Soviets. Hiss, Chambers claimed, had given him the documents to pass along to his Soviet handlers, and had even typed them on his own typewriter. Here, at long last, was hard evidence to back up Chambers's claims. The only problem was that none of the evidence was definitive. The typewriter that the documents had been printed on, for example, was nowhere to be found—though that didn't stop a massive effort to uncover the instrument. At one point, thirty of the 263 FBI agents working on the Hiss case were assigned *solely* to look for the missing machine.

Nixon and the HUAC, meanwhile, pressed Chambers for even more hard evidence—anything he could muster that might tilt the case in favor of his accusations. As always, Chambers complied. On the night of December 2, Chambers took two HUAC investigators out to his Westminster, Maryland, farm, where he directed them to a hollowed out pumpkin hidden within a strawberry patch on the property. (So careful was Chambers, who was concerned about a communist raid, that he had concealed his evidence where no one would think of looking.) Within the pumpkin were five 35-millimeter rolls of film that he had also removed from his cousin's Brooklyn apartment. Rather than turn them in with other documents in November, however, Chambers had apparently kept them to himself because he did not know their true contents, though he suspected they might further implicate Hiss. The timing and motivations of Chambers were doubtless confusing—why hadn't he simply turned over everything the month before? In the scheme of things, however, his motivations mattered little, if at all. The so-called Pumpkin Papers, as the rolls of film later became known, consisted of a series of photographed State Department documents from the very place where Hiss once worked. Chambers turned the film over to the HUAC, where they were quickly developed, and just as quickly used as ultimate proof of Hiss's guilt. According to one press statement issued by the committee, the Pumpkin Papers collectively provided "definite proof of one of the most extensive espionage rings in the history of the United States." Karl Mundt, a Republican representative from South Dakota and one of the most vocal members of the HUAC, declared that the documents were "of such startling and significant importance, and reveal such a vast network of Communist espionage within the State Department, that they far exceed anything yet brought before the Committee in its ten-year history."

Less than two weeks later, Hiss was formally charged with perjury. Since the statute of limitations had passed on his alleged espionage activities, Hiss was charged with lying before Congress when he said that he had never turned over any of the State Department documents to Chambers. The defense's case would rest on the contradictory details that formed Chambers's accusations—the dates Chambers offered did not neatly match up, and there were a host of discrepancies that indicated his memory was less than reliable. Hiss's lawyers also hammered away at Chambers's past drinking habits and mental instability, citing both as evidence that none of what he said could be trusted. Perhaps most importantly, the Hiss defense team marshaled an all-star list of witnesses to attest to his good character, including two sitting Supreme Court justices (Felix Frankfurter and Stanley Reed), along with a former Democratic presidential candidate (John W. Davis) and a future Democratic presidential nominee (Adlai Stevenson). The roster of Hiss's high-profile defenders turned the case into even more of a national spectacle. The public could be forgiven for connecting the liberal establishment with Hiss—some of its most prominent members, after all, were associating their fates with his. Something much bigger than Alger Hiss was now on trial.

Ultimately, however, it was Hiss's own actions that sealed his fate. Before of the trial, Hiss had located and volunteered the long-sought-after typewriter himself—a Woodstock typewriter with the series number N230,099—which the prosecution was able to prove was the same machine that Chambers's State Department cables were typed on. Although the first trial culminated in July of 1949 with a hung jury, when the second trial began later that year, the fact that Hiss's own typewriter had been used to produce the State Department documents was too much to bear. Hiss was found guilty of perjury on January 21, 1950. On January 25, he was sentenced to five years in prison.

Convicted with Hiss was an era and a political style, signaling that the connection between the New Deal Democrats and communism was more than just rhetorical. And it did not help that Democrats as a whole had come to Hiss's aid, and with great assurance too. Even after Hiss's conviction, the Democratic secretary of state, Dean Acheson, the very official who was accused of harboring communists within his own department, refused to condemn Hiss as a traitor. "Whatever the outcome of any appeal which Mr. Hiss or his lawyers may take," said Acheson on the day of Hiss's sentencing, "I do not intend to turn my back upon Alger Hiss." The Hiss scandal thus served as a vindication of the decade-long attack on the liberal bureaucrat—the elites who since the 1930s had administered the New Deal and who, after the war, suddenly found themselves the stewards of a new world order. Hiss became the vital link connecting the domestic anti-communist crusade to the international one.

But Hiss's conviction did not take place in a vacuum. Heightening the significance of his sentence was the fact that, throughout his trial, a series of events suggested that communism was spreading throughout the world, and that it was becoming increasingly lethal. In August of 1949, the State Department issued a white paper describing the failure of American foreign policy in China. Within a few months, the pro-American government there led by Chiang Kai-shek fell to communist revolutionaries, placing more than half a billion people under Mao Tse-tung's communist rule. In September, Truman confirmed to reporters that the Soviet Union had successfully tested its first atomic bomb, ending the American monopoly on nuclear weapons and thrusting upon the American public the fear of a nuclear holocaust. In October, eleven leaders of the American Communist Party were convicted for conspiracy to attempt to overthrow the government by force. By the end of January 1950, when Hiss was finally convicted, the American public was on high alert. And within two days of Hiss's sentencing, the next major shoe dropped. This time the revelation took place in England, where British scientist Klaus Fuchs, a man who had been intimately involved in the top-secret Manhattan Project, which led to the United States's development of the atomic bomb, and who had worked in Los Alamos National Laboratory, confessed that he had been engaged in espionage for the Soviets. The questions became more frightening: Was there no United States program the Soviets hadn't managed to penetrate? And why, in the midst of all of this, had the administration not cracked down on the communists harder? Indeed, why did it seem to be defending them? The American public's growing confusion, and its increasing fear, was more and more palpable by the day. Just as Alger Hiss was being sentenced to a federal penitentiary at Lewisburg, Pennsylvania, in the early months of 1950, an unknown senator from Wisconsin spotted a major political opportunity, and he began readying himself for the national stage.

In February of 1950, most Americans didn't know much about Senator Joseph McCarthy. Born to an Irish-American family in northeastern Wisconsin's Outagamie County, the forty-one-year-old senator had risen from an obscure political career in Wisconsin to a slightly less obscure one in the Senate, thanks mainly to an ambition that was driven more by intensity than by intellect. Indeed, McCarthy's very life and personality had been defined by extremity from an early age. He moved in and out of school throughout his childhood, at one point working sixty hours a week to put himself through college, then cramming "a year's work into a few days of study" to pass his courses, according to one friend. He was a rough-and-tumble student, an Irishman who liked to fight and drink and gamble—the latter activity being a major source of income. He once earned enough money from gambling to pay for an entire semester of college. His style? Reckless bluffing. So reckless, in fact, that his opponents would end up doubting their own cards. But McCarthy wasn't all brashness all the time. He was fiercely loyal too. He'd lend money to whoever needed it, beg for forgiveness if he wronged any of his friends. "He couldn't stand to have people stay mad at him," recalled one associate. "It upset him to no end."

By 1935, he had received his law degree and moved to Waupaca, a small town near Appleton, Wisconsin, to become a practicing attorney. By 1939, he had gotten himself elected circuit judge for Langlade, Shawano, and Outagamie Counties. When war came after the Japanese attack on Pearl Harbor in December of 1941, McCarthy signed up for the Marine Corps. Soon McCarthy became a statewide celebrity, known as "Tail Gunner Joe," routinely sending dispatches to Wisconsin newspapers from his station in the Pacific, where he served as an intelligence officer, to enhance his image of a "fighting judge" back home. It didn't take long, however, before reporters learned that most of McCarthy's stories were grossly exaggerated, if not flatly fabricated. They learned, for example, that when McCarthy claimed to be a tail gunner engaged in Japanese bombing raids, he was really firing at coconut trees during danger-free joyrides. And yet, in a lesson that would stay with him for the rest of his career, McCarthy's supporters back home wanted to hear of his exploits much more than they wanted to know that they were fake, and the image he crafted for himself would ultimately endure in the public mind. Sure, some reporters attempted to correct McCarthy's distortions, but such reports were by and large overlooked. McCarthy's falsehoods never seemed to catch up with him, even from the earliest days of his life in the public sphere.

When McCarthy returned to the States after the war, he had his sights set on the US Senate. Through a combination of bluster and politicking, McCarthy got himself onto the Republican ticket for the 1946 campaign, where he slung all the mud he could against his opponent, including allegations that his challenger was "communistically inclined." McCarthy's tactics bore fruit—he won the election by 5,000 votes. By the end of 1946, McCarthy was a newly elected senator with a bright future. The *Saturday Evening Post* called him the "Senate's remarkable upstart," and *US News* praised his "hustling, whirlwind" style. The hype quickly got to his head. When McCarthy arrived in the nation's capital in December, for example, he promptly telephoned the White House to arrange a one-on-one meeting with the president (the White House politely declined the breach of protocol). Undeterred, McCarthy called a press conference from his hotel room, where instead of announcing news—the purpose that press conferences generally serve—he simply opined on current events.

But despite McCarthy's high ambitions and his audacious behavior, the Wisconsin senator didn't do much with his first few years on Capitol Hill, aside from generating a handful of sensational headlines and earning the contempt of Washington's elite. His disdain for rules and procedure quickly got him into trouble with his Republican colleagues in the Senate, who came to view him as a liability and pushed him into unfavorable committee assignments. At first, however, McCarthy's failures didn't sink in. He continued to gamble, drink, and carouse in DC, living in rented rooms and sleeping wherever he passed out, frequently offending the more mannered around him. One witness, for example, described him arriving at an upscale dinner party with a "buxom young woman," where he quickly "disappeared upstairs and screwed her on the hostess' bed." What's more, as McCarthy was losing allies in Washington, his popularity was tanking back home, his constituents growing hostile with his inaction. By 1949, isolated, constantly criticized, and increasingly alone, McCarthy watched the Hiss scandal unfold. Disrespected by his peers, his career prospects uncertain, the fate of his 1952 reelection was now in jeopardy. McCarthy began to realize that he needed an issue to resuscitate his political career. It is not hard to imagine the major political opportunity he saw.

—◆—

McCarthy's official entry into the national spotlight came on February 9, 1950, in the unlikely town of Wheeling, West Virginia, during a dinner speech to the Ohio County Women's Republican Club—an even more unlikely choice for a politician seeking to rise from obscurity. Nearly three weeks after Alger Hiss's conviction, it was here that McCarthy would attempt to turn himself into a single-issue politician. The Wisconsin senator began his now-infamous speech by rehashing standard anti-communist claims—projecting class resentments onto the New Deal elites, blaming the "pompous diplomat in striped pants" for America's failures around the world, decrying the dangers of subversion and an alien ideology. At one point, he even repeated verbatim parts of an earlier speech Richard Nixon had delivered on the House floor. But then the junior senator from Wisconsin offered the audience something that no politician had offered them before: details.

"I have here in my hand a list of 205" communist agents, McCarthy declared, "a list of names that were made known to the Secretary of State as being members of the Communist Party and who nevertheless are still working and shaping policy in the State Department." There were more Alger Hisses out there, he proclaimed, ingrained in the State Department, hiding within the administration and covertly working to sabotage the United States. This was a dangerous, treasonous state of affairs, one that had continued inexplicably for years and years. But finally one man was willing to take on this grand conspiracy, to put his own health and safety on the line and take the threat head on. And that man was standing on a podium in Wheeling, West Virginia, ready for the fight.

In the aftermath of the speech, reporters scrambled to learn just what evidence McCarthy could really provide. Whose names were on the list? How had McCarthy gotten it? How reliable was his information? The Wheeling speech kicked off a larger cross-country tour, in which McCarthy doubled down on his outrageous claims. When he changed planes in Denver the next day, en route to Salt Lake City, a group of journalists mobbed him for more details and asked to see his list. The senator assured the reporters that he had nothing to hide—he even had the list right there with him. But when he reached for the roster in his suitcase he "discovered he had left it in his baggage on the plane," according to one newspaper report, which took the senator at his word, printing McCarthy's allegations with a photo of him looking into his briefcase. Below the photo read a caption: "Solon Left Commie List in Other Bag."

By the time McCarthy made it to Salt Lake City, more "details" emerged, though the number of agents in the State Department had changed from 205 to fifty-seven. The communist agents were "no ordinary espionage agents," he now claimed, but rather were "men in the $5,300 or higher income bracket—the shapers of American foreign policy." Time and time again, it was exactly this kind of extraneous detail that McCarthy would provide to sway the skeptics. If he were lying, how would he know such a fact? And why would he go out on a limb to provide it? It was like the case of the prothonotary warbler all over again—a detail so intimate, so easily contradicted, that no one in his right mind would make it up. To Joe McCarthy, of course, it was bluffing at its finest.

Over the next few days, McCarthy repeated his charges again and again, causing the administration itself to wonder whether the senator had access to information that it did not. On February 20, now back in Washington, McCarthy recited many of the claims from his Wheeling speech on the Senate floor in a spectacle that lasted nearly six hours. This time, however, McCarthy was willing to add more details, stating that he had a new list of eighty-one "loyalty risks." The Democrats in the chamber were alternately dumbfounded and enraged by McCarthy's speech, and by the support fellow Republicans now seemed to show for him. Shouting matches and political slurs erupted from the Senate floor. In the aftermath of McCarthy's performance, both parties immediately called for an investigation. And both quickly agreed to create a committee to examine McCarthy's accusations, known formally as the Subcommittee on the Investigation of Loyalty of State Department Employees, and soon called the "Tydings Committee," after its chairman, Millard E. Tydings, the long-respected Democratic senator from Maryland. Republicans viewed an official inquiry as an opportunity to turn the heat on the administration after the Hiss case. The Democrats, meanwhile, hoped a bipartisan study would speedily expose McCarthy's outrageous charges for exactly what they were—bogus lies. Regardless of each party's motivations, the communists-in-government issue was now squarely at the center of partisan politics. Two weeks earlier, McCarthy had had nothing to do with the topic. And now he was at its core.

In the lead-up to the hearings, set to begin March 8, all eyes in Washington were focused on Senator Tydings and his committee. For the first time in his career, McCarthy was at the middle of a national controversy, and he took the honor seriously. He prepared furiously for the proceedings, enlisting all the support he could get from conservative supporters, including the use of Nixon's own files to supplement his research. But if

McCarthy ever had the upper hand with the Tydings Committee, he lost it pretty quickly—the Democrats were out for blood. At one point early in the hearings, McCarthy dropped onto the hearing table a folder filled with "evidence" about security risks in the State Department, one of them a State Department official named Dorothy Kenyon. Without missing a beat, the Democrats brought her in to testify. Yes, she had been a member of a few controversial organizations, Kenyon said, but that was a decade ago, and as soon as she discovered their true objectives she had resigned. Now thanks to McCarthy's baseless accusations, however, her reputation was "seriously jeopardized, if not destroyed." Kenyon's appearance accomplished exactly what the Democrats had hoped—it made McCarthy look bad. In fact, it made him look terrible. Here was a smart, well-spoken, and dignified public servant whose character had been sullied by McCarthy's lies, and for no apparent reason. *Life* magazine called Kenyon "impressive"; *Time* referred to McCarthy as "loudmouthed" and "irresponsible."

But where others might have halted, McCarthy was just getting going. It didn't matter that the Kenyon accusation fell flat. There were plenty more like her, and perhaps one charge would stick. For McCarthy, this was all just a game of high-stakes poker, and the only way to lose in the game of bluffing was to stop.

He was all in.

On March 21, McCarthy informed the press that he was about to name the top Soviet agent in the State Department, the "boss" of Alger Hiss himself. "I am willing to stand or fall on this one," he said. The man's name was Owen Lattimore, and despite the fact that he was not a State Department employee—he was a professor of international relations at Johns Hopkins University who specialized in Chinese studies—McCarthy was sure that he was at the epicenter of anti-American subversion in the government. Indeed, McCarthy hurled all the invective he could at Lattimore, turning him into a household name and blaming the fall of China to the communists on the professor and his like-minded friends. Again, there wasn't much real evidence to back up McCarthy's claims. For McCarthy, however, all of this was standard fare.

McCarthy thrived on conflict, for with it came confusion. In the end it was the conflict between his own party and the Democrats that saved him from the wrath of Tydings and his committee—and ultimately from the hollowness of his wild accusations themselves. By the time the committee submitted the report to the Senate, on July 20, 1950, the investigation was fully tainted by partisan politics. The Democrats on the committee insisted on condemning McCarthy in the harshest language possible, while the Republican members refused to sign on as a result, wanting to preserve the larger issue that McCarthy touched upon as legitimate, and thus removing any traces of moderation from the report. Indeed, by the Senate's own standards, the outcome of the Tydings Committee was unusually vicious. The report called McCarthy's charges "a hoax perpetrated on the Senate of the United States and the American people," representing "perhaps the most nefarious campaign of half-truths and untruth in the history of the Republic." In this way, the investigation that was ultimately supposed to settle McCarthy's charges ended up fueling them. And though the GOP did not officially endorse his accusations, its failure to condemn them gave McCarthy a perverse sense of credibility, making it seem like it was the veracity of his claims that was actually up for dispute.

Soon, cries of "whitewash" came from McCarthy's lips, who now announced that the report constituted a "green light to the Red Fifth Column in the United States." The investigation had been a diversion, he claimed, meant to trick the American public into believing that the communist issue was being taken care of, when in reality it was getting worse. Far from removing McCarthy's personal brand from the communist issue, as the Democrats had hoped, the Tydings Report legitimized his claim to it. McCarthy emerged from the conflict more powerful and popular than before. The junior senator, it seemed, was just getting started.

By the fall of 1950, McCarthy was a verified national celebrity. Hated by liberals and Democrats, praised by many Republicans, and adored by those who despised communism and the New Deal, the Wisconsin senator was now a symbol of conflict and controversy, resentment and fear. By October, he had two thousand requests for speaking engagements, more than every other senator combined. But McCarthy owed his sudden fame to more than his knack for political manipulation alone. Coinciding with McCarthy's rise to prominence were also deep troubles abroad, ones that exacerbated the fear of communism at home. As the Tydings investigation had come to a close that summer, the United States began fighting and killing communists abroad, entering the Korean War after the communist North Koreans attacked the pro-western government in South Korea. Terrified by the Red assault, the American public initially supported the war. It was, after all, being waged to defeat communists, and this was an objective everyone could support. But the public also expected the fighting to come to a quick conclusion. America was now a superpower, and General Douglas MacArthur, the commanding general of the United Nations forces in Korea, assured the American public that the troops would be "home by Christmas," a sentiment that the Truman Administration shared. Winning the war, however, would prove far more complicated than it at first seemed. In late November, the Chinese entered the fighting on a scale that few in the West had imagined, sending hundreds of thousands of troops to support the North Koreans, and raising the specter of an American military defeat for the first time in history. Christmas came and passed, and yet the fighting in Korea dragged on. From a political perspective, the war was proving to be a disaster for the Truman Administration.

But bad news abroad was not necessarily bad news at home. In McCarthy's eyes, America's perceived failures overseas offered clear prospects for his own advancement. "I am inclined to think," McCarthy wrote to a friend, "that as the casualty lists mount and the attention of the people is focused on what actually has happened in the Far East, they can't help but realize there was something rotten in the State Department." Indeed, as the fighting raged on across the Pacific, McCarthy spotted a new political opportunity. This time, however, it would take McCarthy nearly a year to capitalize on what he saw.

On June 14, 1951, nearly twelve months after the US invasion of Korea, McCarthy took to the Senate to deliver his boldest anti-communist speech since Wheeling. There on the chamber floor, McCarthy declared the existence of "a conspiracy on a scale so immense as to dwarf any previous such venture in the history of man," one that explained all of

America's foreign policy missteps since the end of World War II: the Soviet expansion in Europe, the loss of China to the communists, the failing Korean War. These were not mere accidents, he claimed, but were direct results of a "great conspiracy" perpetrated upon the American public by one man.

His name? General George Catlett Marshall.

By even McCarthy's standards, these were bold claims. Marshall was an American war hero, one of the most important military leaders in US history. He had planned the US invasion of Europe in World War II, served as chief of staff of the Army, secretary of state, and was then serving as the secretary of defense. Marshall's military bona fides trumped those of nearly every other living military figure at the time. And now McCarthy was accusing him of executing a conspiracy "spun from Moscow," of manipulating an American president, of ruling "by disloyalty." To put it simply, McCarthy was calling George Marshall a traitor and a Soviet spy.

Just what evidence did McCarthy have to support his latest accusations? None, of course. But the substance of his claims was far less important than the political fallout he expected his accusations to generate. McCarthy knew that the administration looked weak on account of the Korean War, and that the American public was confused and distraught by the communist advances overseas. He knew that the public's fear that more Alger Hisses were hiding within the administration was still very much alive, thanks in no small part to his own efforts. And he knew that the bigger the target of his accusations, the bigger the reaction would be. Next to the president, Marshall was perhaps the biggest target of them all.

McCarthy's ploy worked, and quickly too. Sure, most Democrats, and even now some Republicans, were enraged at McCarthy's attack on a living icon, and many in the national press now condemned the senator as an outright liar in ways that were new. But McCarthy understood his audience. His latest accusations would help to keep the communist issue alive, and for that he still had many Republicans' support. To the Americans around the country who wanted to see domestic communism attacked, McCarthy was quite simply fighting their fight. They knew it wouldn't be pretty. Indeed, they hoped for as much, and the condemnation McCarthy received from the elites in the government and the media made it look like the senator was doing exactly what he claimed. The patriotic group the American Legion compared McCarthy's tactics to a shotgun loaded with rock salt, "bound to bring down several important Reds and spies even though a few comparatively innocent people may get some rock-salt in their hides." McCarthy was David taking on Goliath; the more vigorously he was denounced, the more he could fall back on this claim.

By the 1952 campaign, McCarthy was riding high. In a nationally televised address during the GOP convention, McCarthy assailed the Truman Administration as having been in bed with the Russians for years. The convention chairman, introducing McCarthy over the gathering's noise, proclaimed that Republicans would never "turn our backs at any time on that fighting Irish Marine," daring McCarthy's critics "to name just one" innocent man he had accused. Throughout the course of that fall's campaign, he spoke in thirteen states in aid of other Republican candidates, barely even touring his home state of Wisconsin, where he would win reelection with 54 percent of the vote. Said one Wisconsin voter to John B. Oakes, a reporter for the *New York Times*: "I guess almost everybody in this part of the country is for McCarthy. He's against Communism—and we're against Communism."

But to millions of Americans baffled by McCarthy's success, was *that* all there was to McCarthy's support? Could one senator, so clearly full of lies, rise to national prominence based on an ill-founded and frenzied sense of anti-communism alone? The answers are, of course, complicated. On the one hand, governing institutions, business organizations, and members of the elite were partly to blame. The Democrats' own deep fear of taking on McCarthy, combined with their attempts to claim the communist issue for themselves, helped legitimize the underlying anti-communist fear upon which McCarthy capitalized. Indeed, by offering his own made-up details, McCarthy was beating other anti-communists—from all parties—at their own game. And the widespread failure of the media and the GOP to effectively counter McCarthy's mistruths played an even greater role in propelling McCarthy to fame.

Through a combination of masterful manipulation on McCarthy's part, and self-interest on the part of profiting institutions, neither group was willing to debunk his claims with enough forcefulness to stop McCarthy in his tracks—the media, after all, knew that their audience loved a good story, and the GOP was reluctant to place in jeopardy an issue that resonated so strongly at the polls. In the end, no one was willing to condemn McCarthy, claim by unfounded claim.

But in broader terms, McCarthy's success was about much more than self-interest, political manipulation, or communism alone. This meant that to support his crusade did not equate to believing his every assertion. Contrary to what some have argued, McCarthy's supporters were not fooled; they were not mentally ill; and they were not stupid. Their struggle was, at root, a revolt against the growing power of the elites—a group whose bold ideals began to encroach into every aspect of American life, beginning with the New Deal in the 1930s, and continuing with twenty years of Democratic control of the White House. It was the same struggle that men like Dies had waged the decade before, but now in different circumstances—the economic, cultural, and social changes that had begun in American society before the war were exacerbated after it ended. Indeed, polling data show that many of McCarthy's most fervent supporters hailed from groups whose social status and economic role in American society were among the most vulnerable to these changes. They were conservative Irish, German, and Italian Catholics, many of them second-generation Americans, who were neither at the top nor at the bottom of the nation's economic classes—groups with much to gain from America's postwar prosperity but with just as much to lose. "Far from being aggrieved," wrote one historian, McCarthy's supporters "found fresh opportunities and prosperity in postwar America," but they were also "anxious about whether those opportunities could continue." Sure, communist agents posed a real threat to the US government, and this played a part in driving the hysteria, but McCarthyism was at root about something much more profound.

Indeed, the fact that McCarthyism wasn't really about communism helps to explain a striking mystery: the fact that European countries like France or Italy—which possessed far larger populations of *actual* communists, and which were much more vulnerable to an actual Soviet attack—did not suffer comparable anti-communist movements after World War II. Among the Allied powers, it was only the United States that reacted so strongly to the threat of communism in the early 1950s. As the French philosopher Jean-Paul Sartre once told a group of Americans, McCarthyism in the United States was unlike anti-communism anywhere else, "for a strange reason: that you have no communists." The hysteria was never really about communists at all.

In the course of the 1952 election, McCarthy cemented his status as a leading voice in the Republican Party, the nation's foremost anti-communist crusader. He battered and smeared the Democratic presidential candidate, Adlai Stevenson, at every opportunity, repeatedly referring to him as "Alger," purposefully confusing him with Alger Hiss—a sore spot for most Democrats as a whole, but especially for Stevenson, who had publicly testified on behalf of Hiss during the trials. In November, the Republican ticket edged out in the polls, sending Dwight Eisenhower to the White House and capturing control of Congress for the first time in years. It was a big win for the GOP, and for McCarthy too.

But problems lay ahead for the Wisconsin senator. With no Democratic president in the White House, and no Democratic majority on Capitol Hill, McCarthy suddenly lost the mantle of the opposition. He could no longer claim that the government was harboring communists without sabotaging his own party. Yet to dial down his crusade would be to forgo his position in the limelight. A decision like this might have haunted an ordinary politician: isolation and fame on the one hand, stability and party approval on the other. But McCarthy was no ordinary politician. For anyone who knew him, including the members of the GOP leadership, there wasn't much doubt about which path he would choose.

By early 1953, with Congress back in session, Republicans now had two items on their agenda: reclaim the communist issue for themselves and marginalize McCarthy. The first came easily. The second did not. When it came to the first, the Republicans had always excelled at sounding the alarm, with or without McCarthy. Republican chairman of the

HUAC, Harold Velde of Illinois, now declared that communists "are foreign to our nation and to our God," launching a subsequent crusade to rid them from America's schools and its churches. Loyal partisan that he was, however, he did not look for communists in the Republican-controlled government. In the Senate side of the Congress, meanwhile, the Republicans thought they had a handle on McCarthy, to whom they awarded the dubious honor of chairing the Committee on Government Operations, an obscure assignment meant to keep him far from the issue of communists in government. "We've got McCarthy where he can't do any harm," boasted Senate majority leader Robert Taft.

But Taft could not have been more wrong.

Under the power of McCarthy's new committee fell an even more obscure Senate body known as the Subcommittee on Investigations, with the vague but little-used authority of "studying the operation of Government activities at all levels." No previous chairman had ever done much with the subcommittee. The former chairman, for example, had investigated subjects like the sale of a government-owned aluminum plant in California. But then again, no previous chairman had been Joseph McCarthy.

Taken together, McCarthy's own party had slapped him with one hand, and given him a weapon with another. They just didn't know it yet. "No one can push me out of anything," boasted McCarthy. "I am not retiring from the field of exposing Communists."

McCarthy would soon put his subcommittee to work, installing himself as chairman and using his new powers to hold hearings and call witnesses, issue subpoenas and publish reports, cementing his image as grand inquisitor—the very image he still holds in the public mind to this day. But first he needed to hire a staff. And so McCarthy went looking for talent, recruiting bright young men like Robert F. Kennedy, a former lawyer for the Justice Department, future presidential candidate, and the brother of then-Senator John F. Kennedy of Massachusetts (McCarthy would later serve as the godfather for Robert Kennedy's first child). But perhaps McCarthy's most important hire was a twenty-five-year-old prodigy named Roy Marcus Cohn, appointed to the position of chief counsel, and who soon became one of McCarthy's closest confidantes. Cohn had all the right credentials: He graduated from Columbia University and its law school before the age of twenty, and then served as an upstart assistant US attorney in New York, helping to prosecute some of the government's highest-profile spy cases. By the time he was twenty-four years old, Cohn was working as a special assistant to the attorney general in Washington, DC. Short and abrasive, Cohn possessed a brilliant mind, no doubt. But he also had the ego to match. He acted like he was a celebrity, and he expected to be treated as such. When he began his job at the Justice Department in the nation's capital, for example, he rankled colleagues by staging a swearing in ceremony in the attorney general's private office— when no swearing in ceremony was necessary in the first place. And when Cohn came to the subcommittee, he did not leave this king-sized ego behind—a fact that would ultimately get him into serious trouble, and for the first time in his political career, McCarthy too. With Cohn now by his side, all the ingredients of McCarthy's downfall were coming together. All except for one.

———

His name was G. David Schine, and he was Roy Cohn's best friend. At twenty-five years old, age was about all that both men had in common. Where Cohn was dark, slight, and unattractive, Schine was smooth, tall, and handsome, with features that were often compared to a Greek god's. The heir of a hotel tycoon, Schine didn't just look like a Hollywood star, he lived like one too. At Harvard, where he had graduated a few years before, Schine was best known for his over-the-top lifestyle. "Wealth, of course, is not out of place here," wrote the *Harvard Crimson*, "but Schine, certainly one of the richest men in his class, made it so." He dated starlets, wore only the most expensive clothes, and made use of his own personal valet and two-way phone-radio. After a stint as the president of the hotel chain that his father owned, Schine came to the subcommittee to fill the unpaid position of "chief consultant," created by McCarthy at Cohn's request. Schine's credentials were, to put it mildly, less than impressive. His sole qualification was a pamphlet he had written for his father's hotel chain denouncing the evils of communism, and which was offered in every room alongside the Gideon bible as a "public service." Lasting all of six pages, Schine's pamphlet misspelled Lenin's first name and misdated the Russian Revolution. But McCarthy did not hire Schine for his intellect; he hired him out of loyalty to Cohn. "He had little use for Dave Schine," said one reporter. But he kept him on figuring that "one more guy around the office wasn't going to kill him." For the first time in his political career, McCarthy's instincts were wrong.

But in early 1953, neither the senator nor Cohn knew what was in store, and at first their work on the subcommittee proved a success. McCarthy's popularity and his influence soared. By its own count, the subcommittee initiated 445 "preliminary inquiries" and 157 "investigations" into the communist issue, seventeen of which reached the stage of public hearings. Though roughly two dozen staffers formally worked for McCarthy, he boasted a network of hundreds of government workers, known informally as the "Loyal American Underground," who fed him information to keep his investigations going.

McCarthy's status was reflected in his growing approval numbers. Polls throughout the summer of 1953 would record roughly one in three Americans in support of the senator, with that number rising to 50 percent by the end of the year.

There was much more activity within the hysteria, however, than McCarthy's own. In some senses, what McCarthy said and did was trivial; it was the public's reaction to the threat of domestic communism that showed how profound a phenomenon McCarthyism really was. By the following year, more than three hundred federal, state, and local laws prohibiting "subversive activities" were on the books in the United States. Tennessee now punished "unlawful advocacy" with the death penalty, and Virginia proposed executing anyone caught "lurking with intent to spy." Free speech itself came under attack. Police in Houston were once summoned to a restaurant because two diners were "talking communist." In Indiana, one woman crusaded to get *The Adventures of Robin Hood* removed from public libraries for its "subversive" message—the actual sheriff of Nottingham, Indiana, however, protested the move. The crusade was reflected vigorously in the private sector, with businesses of all sorts using blacklists and loyalty oaths to keep their workforce communist free. Perhaps no sector was more high profile in its anti-communism than the

entertainment industry, which had spent the war years patriotically portraying America's allies as heroic partners in defeating the Nazis, only to
watch the Soviet Union transition from grand ally to primal foe at the
end of the war. Producers and studio executives in Hollywood whiplashed
back to portraying communists as evil villains, aware of the confusion this
caused, and increasingly sensitive to accusations that the industry was
un-American. As McCarthyism took hold, members of the entertainment industry began vigorously policing themselves, spreading fear and
paralysis throughout Hollywood in the process.

By the early 1950s, the idea that one could be both American and
communist seemed heretical to some, and absurd to many more. In
one poll, 77 percent of Americans advocated stripping American communists of their citizenship, while 51 percent wanted to throw them in
jail. National columnist Drew Pearson, perhaps McCarthy's most hated
member of the press, and a man whom McCarthy once kneed in the
groin at a press club dinner, diagnosed the country as being plagued with
"a disease of fear." But Pearson was wrong. This was more than a disease—
it was a pandemic. And McCarthy, meanwhile, was doing everything in
his power to help it spread.

With his staff hired and ready to go, McCarthy would soon give his Subcommittee on Investigations a starring role in American politics. His first
target? The Voice of America, a State Department propaganda program
created the decade before to spread positive news about the West. By
most accounts, the campaign had done well, becoming the third-largest
communications network in the world and reaching an estimated three
hundred million people in forty-six languages and dialects. But where
others saw success, McCarthy saw an organization crawling with communists. His charges focused on the location of major transmitter sites
that broadcasted the Voice of America programming overseas, alleging that the sites had been surreptitiously placed in North Carolina and
Washington State so as to be rendered ineffective by their vulnerability to magnetic storms—a surprisingly technical allegation, but one that
McCarthy would ride for all that it was worth. During the subcommittee's

investigation, which lasted throughout February and into March of 1953, McCarthy questioned the loyalty and integrity of nearly every engineer involved in setting up the transmitters. Some of them lost their jobs. One young engineer by the name of Raymond Kaplan threw himself under a speeding truck. "I have not done anything in my job which I did not think was in the best interest of this country," he wrote in a suicide note to his wife. "When the dogs are set on you, everything you have done since the beginning of time is suspect."

McCarthy's next subject of investigation was the selection of books used in the State Department's overseas libraries. He accused the department of using taxpayer dollars to purchase books by communists and to help spread communism abroad. In preparation for the subcommittee's investigation, Cohn and Schine took an eighteen-day "fact finding mission" throughout Europe. Among other stops on their whirlwind tour, the duo spent forty hours in Paris, sixteen in Bonn, twenty-three in Belgrade, and six in London, at least once racking up exorbitant bills at their hotel and having the American embassy pick up the tab. At one point in Frankfurt, Cohn charged Theodore Kaghan, the deputy director of public affairs for the US High Commission in Germany, of having once signed a Communist Party petition. Kaghan laughed off the charges, publicly jeering that Cohn and Schine were "junketeering gumshoes." Two weeks later, Kaghan was called home by the State Department and fired. This constituted only one of many other episodes in the pair's drama of the absurd, which generated headlines in Europe and at home. Everywhere Cohn and Schine went, dozens of reporters and photographers followed, publishing their exploits and, as a regretful Cohn later put it, handing "McCarthy's enemies a perfect opportunity to spread the tale that a couple of young, inexperienced clowns were hustling about Europe." Indeed, many reports embellished the most negative aspects of the trip, with some insinuating that the two men were homosexuals. One London article even made the claim outright, publishing an article with the headline, "COHN AND SCHINE, THE TWO LONDON LOVERS."

But the truth was that the duo's antics were nothing new. In the United States, their weekly routine was marked by the carelessness of extreme power and wealth. They would fly down to Washington from

New York every Monday, take adjoining rooms at the Statler Hotel for the week, and then fly back to New York to spend the weekend hobnobbing at the most exclusive clubs in the city. They were an inseparable team, Cohn and Schine, riding high on McCarthy's fame and on their own spectacular riches, in the United States and beyond.

The immediate fallout from the pair's trip to Europe, negative though it was, barely touched McCarthy, but that was not the point. The tour served as a symbol of something much greater. For the first time, McCarthy's political power was warping his judgment, and now it started to show, providing new opportunities for his enemies to pounce, as Cohn later recognized. He began to act more erratic than in the past, lashing out at both his critics and at the Republican administration, which had silently tolerated his crusade up until that point. Over the summer, for example, he held a one-day hearing on a bogus "plot" to assassinate him. Then he threatened to subpoena former president Truman to testify about a hidden super-secret list of spy suspects. In November, McCarthy delivered an address on national television directly accusing the Eisenhower Administration of harboring communists. In the words of one Eisenhower aide, the speech served as "a declaration of war against the president"—and against McCarthy's own party too. McCarthy may have been as powerful as ever on the outside, but on the inside he was losing control.

Big changes were in store for Cohn and Schine. That fall, Schine received unexpected news from Uncle Sam: He was being drafted. Even with the war in Korea near its conclusion, the military was still requiring Americans to serve involuntarily. The Army now wanted Schine. This was a personal slap in the face not just to Schine, but also to Cohn. The pair claimed the authority of the most feared man in Washington; they could practically bark an order and any branch of the government would comply. And now the chain of command had shifted. Now it was the government that was telling Schine what to do.

Cohn took this as a personal challenge, and he began working to get the Army to change its mind. First, he enlisted McCarthy's help to get Schine a commission—if Schine had to enter the military, he could at the very least serve as an officer, holding a title with the perks and honor befit for a man of his dignity. McCarthy quickly placed a personal call to the Army's top lawyer, John G. Adams, to intervene on Schine's behalf. But apparently his heart was not in it. According to Adams's later account of the conversation, McCarthy told him that he had no use for Schine. Sure, McCarthy would have moved heaven and earth to save Cohn if he had been drafted. "He's a brilliant fellow," McCarthy once said of Cohn. "He works his butt off and he's loyal to me. I don't think I could make it without him." But McCarthy had no such esteem for Cohn's best friend. The Wisconsin senator told Adams to keep his true feelings about Schine to himself.

Before long Schine was drafted into the Army as a lowly private, and in November he began his training at Fort Dix, in New Jersey. But Cohn was far from giving up on his friend. He called Adams himself and demanded that Schine be given special treatment, that he be made available nights and weekends so that he could complete his work for the committee. Adams, evidently terrified by the prospect of Cohn's fury, complied with the young aide's request. Schine received passes for seventeen of the next thirty-one days of training, and word came down in the base that Private Schine was a VIP. Every weekend a chauffeur-driven Cadillac would whisk Schine away from the base, carrying him to Cohn and their extravagant life in New York City.

On December 8, however, the Army brass, upset over the disturbing amount of time it had spent dealing with Schine, decided that enough was enough. When Adams broke the news to Cohn, Cohn was reportedly enraged, warning Adams that there would be big consequences for what the Army had done.

"Is that a threat?" Adams asked.

"No," Cohn replied, "that is a promise."

In the end, Cohn was right. There would indeed be big consequences for what just occurred. But they would be much worse for Cohn and McCarthy than for anyone else.

In January of 1954, after repeatedly harassing military leaders in the Pentagon, Cohn learned that Schine would be leaving New Jersey for Camp

Gordon, Georgia, and perhaps even a station overseas. As a result, Cohn began pestering Adams with such frequency that the Schine issue came to monopolize his life. Higher-ups in the Eisenhower Administration were now worried about Cohn's wrath, including the attorney general, the UN ambassador, and even the president himself. The administration decided that this was the chance they had been waiting for. The senator's right-hand man was threatening an entire military branch over the fate of one unpaid assistant on a Senate subcommittee. This was reckless by even McCarthy's standards, and it bore the mark of extremely poor political judgment too. If Cohn's abuse of power became public, it just might ruin him—and if it could be proved that McCarthy was complicit in it, it might ruin the Wisconsin senator too.

Soon, the Army began compiling a record of all of Cohn's requests, detailing the improprieties of his influence peddling and of his back-channel threats. In March of 1954, a report on Cohn was leaked to the press, alleging that McCarthy's top aide had threatened to "wreck the Army" if he did not get his way with Schine, and listing forty-four counts of improper pressure over a period of eight months to secure preferential treatment for his friend. On orders from the White House, a copy of the report was delivered to every member of McCarthy's subcommittee.

But there was much more at play in the now-public dispute between the administration and McCarthy than Roy Cohn's poor judgment. During the eight-month period in which Cohn harassed the Army about Schine, it just so happened that McCarthy was also investigating the Army for harboring communists at one of its signal laboratories in Fort Kilmer, New Jersey. In one hearing, McCarthy had publicly berated the service's leaders, telling Brigadier General Ralph Zwicker that he was "shielding communist conspirators" and declaring that "you should be removed from any command . . . you are not fit to wear that uniform." Sure, the administration had been threatened by McCarthy before. But now the Wisconsin senator was assailing the very dignity of the Army itself. Now was the time to strike.

The Eisenhower Administration and others would come to the same conclusion independently: The time was ripe for an attack. On March 9, for example, two days before the release of the Army report, Senator

Ralph Flanders, a seventy-three-year-old Republican from Vermont, took to the chamber floor in one of the most vigorous public denunciations of McCarthy by a member of his own party. The Wisconsin senator, Flanders would declare, was inflicting immeasurable harm to the country, and at the same time "doing his best to shatter that party whose label he wears." Later that same evening, famed journalist Edward R. Murrow aired an exposé on McCarthy aimed at showing the American public just how much hypocrisy it had tolerated under McCarthy's dominion. "The actions of the junior senator from Wisconsin have caused alarm and dismay amongst our allies abroad," Murrow declared. But "he didn't create this situation of fear; he merely exploited it—and rather successfully." That night, Murrow held a mirror up to the face of the public. For the millions of Americans watching on television, they did not like what they saw.

But McCarthy was not one to take shots from the administration, or from anyone else, sitting down. "I don't answer charges, I make them," he boasted. He and Cohn quickly fired back with accusations that the Army was using Schine to "blackmail" the subcommittee into calling off its investigation. Of all McCarthy's reckless attacks, this was perhaps his biggest mistake. McCarthy could have fired Cohn immediately, declared he had nothing to do with his young aide's improprieties and attempted to move on—and this was exactly what his remaining Republican allies advocated. In that way, McCarthy would have shifted the focus of the administration's attack to another issue, perhaps to one that was more favorable, or perhaps the administration might have backed down altogether. But that would have meant betraying Cohn, and when it came to McCarthy's closest friends, he was steadfast. Cohn was indispensible to McCarthy—"as indispensible," the senator once said in defense of his young aide, "as I am." McCarthy was loyal to a fault.

By mid-March, an examination into the charges and the countercharges was inevitable. Was McCarthy attempting to blackmail the Army? Or was it the Army that was attempting to blackmail McCarthy? How far would the Eisenhower Administration really go to discredit the Wisconsin senator? At first glance, the answers did not look too good for McCarthy, and spectators in the national press and on Capitol Hill sensed as much. But if one thing was true about the senator, it was that no one knew what he was capable of achieving from one moment to the next—not even McCarthy himself. The unpredictable senator might have more tricks up his sleeve.

Soon McCarthy's own subcommittee began an investigation into the charges, with McCarthy agreeing to step down from the subcommittee for the duration of the inquiry. It was clear that the senator himself was now on trial, and McCarthy's enemies in the Eisenhower Administration understood exactly what was at stake. The Army needed a legal heavy-weight, someone smarter, faster, and more convincing than McCarthy, someone who could get into McCarthy's mud pit and yet remain clean. The administration found exactly these qualities in Joseph Nye Welch. At sixty-three years old, Welch was a graceful man, tall and erudite with a background similar to McCarthy's own. Both came from big Midwestern families with little means, both had risen to become prominent lawyers, with Welch attending Harvard Law School and becoming a partner at the Boston law firm of Hale and Dorr. But where McCarthy was brash and self-centered, Welch was elegant and self-effacing. He was the Wisconsin senator's perfect foil.

By the time the hearings began airing on television, on April 22, 1954, the investigation was already a national obsession. During the first week alone, roughly two-thirds of all Americans with television sets tuned in for the proceedings. Department stores reported decreased daytime sales while the hearings were on, and the *New York Times* reprinted a dozen pages of testimony every day. For the first time, the nation had a front row view into McCarthy and his antics. Sure, Americans had watched the senator before, but never so closely, and never with so much at stake. And McCarthy, for his part, did not disappoint. He hurled baseless accusations left and right, interrupted and rambled on; he was reckless and he was loud and he was disrespectful. This was Joe McCarthy at his best—or at his worst, depending on where you stood.

Perhaps the most dramatic point in the proceedings came on June 9, more than one month into the hearings, with Cohn on the stand. In the midst of one particularly heated exchange between Welch and Cohn, McCarthy interrupted with an attempt to shift the focus of the proceedings to an unknown lawyer named Fred Fisher. Fisher, a thirty-three-year-old associate at Welch's firm, turned out to have been a member of an organization listed as "subversive" by the House Un-American Activities Committee in the 1940s. His connection to Welch and the Army was so tenuous that few would have considered him a liability. Indeed, the association was a decade old. But Welch knew better. Two months before, Welch had made a deal with McCarthy and Cohn to keep Fisher out of the hearings. In return, Welch would not raise the issue of how Schine managed to avoid military service during World War II. But here McCarthy was, blatantly violating these terms.

Welch "has in his law firm a young man named Fisher," proclaimed McCarthy, "who has been for a number of years a member of an organization which was named, oh, years and years ago, as the legal bulwark of the Communist Party."

Welch, keeping his anger in check, explained that Fisher was innocent of any wrongdoing, that he had nothing to do with the hearings, and that he should be kept out of them. "Little did I dream you could be so reckless and cruel as to do an injury to that lad," he said. "It is true that he will continue to be with Hale and Dorr. It is, I regret to say, equally true that, I fear, he shall always bear a scar needlessly inflicted by you."

The old McCarthy, the master manipulator, would have moved on at this point, aware that to dwell on the subject would make him look sinister, heartless, cruel. The old McCarthy was reckless up to a point, and he knew when to back down. But this was not the old McCarthy, and he was not done with Fisher yet.

"I just give this man's record," protested McCarthy, "and I want to say Mr. Welch, that it has been labeled long before he became a member—"

Here Welch himself barged in.

"Let us not assassinate this lad further, Senator. You have done enough. Have you no sense of decency, sir, at long last? Have you left no sense of decency?"

Welch spoke in a slow, accusatory staccato, as if to prolong this moment for the millions of viewers tuning in at home—McCarthy disheveled and vicious, Welch eloquent and morally outraged. Here was a symbol of McCarthy's reign of terror, captured in one instant and in stark contrast. The hearing room soon erupted in applause. If there was one moment when America turned on McCarthy, when his crusade was exposed for the sham that it was, this was it. Soon, the chairman hit his gavel, and the proceedings were adjourned. Welch stormed out, still visibly near tears, while McCarthy looked at those around him, turning his palms up, asking out loud, "What did I do?"

By the time the hearings ended later that month, it was clear McCarthy's political career was nearing its end. The Wisconsin senator's approval ratings began to drop precipitously, and he was soon openly shunned by his party. At the beginning of the year, 50 percent of Americans had viewed McCarthy favorably. Now, that number sank to one in three, and would only continue to fall. Once the most sought-after speaker for Republican candidates, by the time of the 1954 congressional campaign, McCarthy became persona non grata. There was growing talk of censure in the Senate too, a measure that would serve as a formal denunciation of McCarthy—one of the harshest available to the chamber short of impeachment. On December 2, 1954, by a vote of 67–22, the Senate moved in favor of the measure, officially denouncing the Wisconsin senator. And with that, McCarthy became an object of pity rather than fear, one of only nine US senators in history to be censured by the Senate. Eisenhower himself now stopped referring to McCarthyism and instead called the movement "McCarthywasism"—a clear indication that the senator's time had come and gone. The following year, the administration made it known that McCarthy was no longer welcome at White House functions.

McCarthy did his best to hit on his old themes and to keep up the attack—dogged fighter that he was, he refused to give up, and he continued to proclaim the growing threat of domestic communism with increasing alarm. This was, after all, his one card, and he played it for all that it was worth. After four years in the national spotlight, however, it wasn't worth much. Languishing in obscurity, McCarthy turned to alcohol, and he began to drink more and more. By 1956, with two years remaining in his Senate term, he hit rock bottom. At one Milwaukee event for Nixon's vice presidential campaign that year, the Wisconsin senator attempted to sit next to his old Senate ally when an aide asked him to leave. A reporter found McCarthy weeping at curbside shortly afterward. On May 2, 1957, at the age of forty-eight, McCarthy passed away in Bethesda, Maryland, with his wife and a priest by his side. His cause of death: inflammation of the liver. McCarthy drank himself to death.

But the hysteria did not vanish with McCarthy's passing, or even his national disgrace. The fear that communist agents had infiltrated American society, and were secretly subverting the nation from within, lingered on. In January of 1955, the month after officially condemning McCarthy, the Senate voted 84–0 in favor of a resolution affirming that the Communist Party of the United States was part of an "international Communist conspiracy," and resolving that the chamber should continue "to investigate, expose, and combat this conspiracy." The threat of domestic communists continued to retain a role in the national discourse, but it featured less and less prominently as time wore on. By the 1960 presidential election, at the height of the Cold War, neither candidate would even mention the threat of domestic communist subversion. After nearly two decades in and out of the limelight, the movement we refer to as McCarthyism made its way back to the fringes of American politics, right where it belonged.

As for the others who contributed to the hysteria, their influence did not die with McCarthy either. Whittaker Chambers, the man who publicly outed Alger Hiss, went on to write a bestselling memoir credited with turning one young Hollywood actor from a Democrat into a Republican. That actor's name was Ronald Reagan, and four years into his presidency, in 1984, he posthumously awarded Chambers the Medal of Freedom, the highest civilian honor a president can bestow on an American. Roy Cohn, for his part, left the subcommittee shortly after the Army hearings, returning to New York as a prominent socialite and as a personal lawyer to the rich and powerful, representing men like Donald Trump and members of the Mafia too. Cohn would continue to live a life of extravagance and confusion to his dying day, believed to be homosexual and yet, at one point, dating a soon-to-be-famous journalist named Barbara Walters, who once described herself as his beard. But so too would Cohn ultimately die in disgrace. Deeply in debt, disbarred and widely hated, Cohn passed away on August 2, 1986, in Bethesda, Maryland, officially sick with AIDS but publicly insisting that he was ill with liver cancer. As for David Schine, he found success on his own. Three years after the hearings, he married the 1955 Miss Universe, a Swedish actress by the name of Hillevi Rombin, and went on to start a successful Hollywood production company, eventually producing the Oscar-winning best picture of 1972, *The French Connection*, starring a young Gene Hackman. On June 19, 1996, however, Schine's life would also end in tragedy. He would die alongside his wife and son when their private plane crashed in Burbank, California. Schine was sixty-eight years old.

CHAPTER 6

The United States after 9/11

The American Right and the Threat of Sharia Law

The June 13, 2011, Republican presidential debate began like most GOP presidential debates do—the seven candidates took the stage at Saint Anselm College in Manchester, New Hampshire, to champion cutting taxes, castigate bloated government bureaucracy, and to criticize the Democratic administration in Washington. But halfway through the evening's events, meant to help determine who would challenge President Barack Obama the following year, the debate turned abruptly to a new topic, briefly illuminating an issue that most Americans weren't aware of then, and many still aren't today.

That topic was Sharia law, Islam's legal code.

In response to a question about the role of Muslims in government, Herman Cain, a Georgia businessman and the number two GOP candidate in the polls at that time, held out the threat of Muslims who "are trying to kill us," saying that he would not be comfortable with such a person serving in his administration. Then he went on to answer a very different question.

"I do not believe in Sharia law in American courts," said Cain. "I believe in American laws in American courts, period."

Given the raucous atmosphere of the night, with the television lights and the live audience and the jarring cuts to commercial breaks, these comments failed to garner much attention. But they revealed a nascent political movement's entrance onto the national political stage—one whose energy many of the Republican presidential candidates would, at one time or another, attempt to harness during the course of that year's campaign. Newt Gingrich, for example, the former speaker of the House of Representatives and the one-time front-runner in the primary, would declare that, "Sharia is a mortal threat to the survival of freedom in the United States and in the world as we know it." Michele Bachmann also joined the chorus, becoming the first candidate to sign an official pledge committing herself to the "rejection of Sharia Islam." Rick Santorum, the former senator from Pennsylvania and the winner of the first GOP contest in Iowa, would call Sharia "evil," declaring Islamic law "incompatible with American jurisprudence and our Constitution."

For all the lip service Republican candidates gave to the Anti-Sharia movement that year, however, it would only gain steam in the months and years ahead.

Spawned by the belief that there are two enemy offensives in the war on terror—physical acts of aggression like the violent attacks of September 11 on the one hand, and a secret attempt to subvert America from within through Islamic law on the other—the movement has made surprising inroads into American culture and politics, far deeper than even an ardent follower of the news would expect. Like the episodes of hysteria before it, it is largely based on familiar themes—spies in high places throughout the government, murders and betrayals, and a global conspiracy so sinister that denying its existence is akin to participating in its plans. Unlike previous episodes, however, we do not have the luxury of decades worth of hindsight to assess the movement's accusations—many of its claims are hard to parse, harder to place in context, and, as we're about to see, some will even seem real. After all, the movement capitalizes upon legitimate threats—there really are radical jihadists who want to harm western civilization, using both violent and nonviolent means. And there really are facets of modern Islam that are troubling, from issues ranging from women's rights to free speech. But just as with McCarthyism and the dangers posed by communist spies, today's threat is not as menacing as it first appears.

And yet for all its obvious flaws, the Anti-Sharia movement has gained serious traction at a national level and zealous adherents around the country. This relative success is driven by a potent combination of Islamophobia and general apprehensions over America's future—a toxic mix that blurs the real threat of Islamic extremists with the symbolic fear of the Muslim next door. More than thirty state legislatures have introduced measures to ban the use of Islamic law. In nine states, these measures have actually passed, in some cases garnering more than 70 percent of the public's support. One such bill was even introduced into the US Congress, with ninety-one co-sponsors.

Anti-Sharia sentiment may not be as widespread as support for McCarthyism or the other episodes of hysteria, and it certainly has been much less reported on in the national press. But the movement is far from over—indeed, by some accounts it has just begun. And that summer night in New Hampshire, on the cusp of the nation's most important political contest, the GOP's leading contenders proved that, after a decade in the shadows of American politics, the Anti-Sharia movement was no longer a fringe phenomenon.

The Anti-Sharia movement traces its roots to the period immediately following the terrorist attacks of September 11. Just as President Bush was assuring Americans that "the face of terror is not the true faith of Islam," in an effort to distance the religion from the violent jihadists who had attacked the United States on 9/11, a small group of four eccentric, isolated Americans were coming to the opposite conclusion. They were slowly waking up not just to the threat of Islamic extremism, but to the religion of Islam as a whole. It was thanks to this cast of characters that the Anti-Sharia movement would emerge half a decade later. The group included a Hasidic Jew in his mid-forties named David Yerushalmi, then living in the Jewish settlement of Ma'ale Adumim in the Israeli-occupied West Bank. A Floridian by birth, Yerushalmi would move back to the States the following year, where he began to study Islam—the attacks on the World Trade Center, he would argue, made him realize the radical dangers of the world's second-largest religion. There was Pamela Geller, a self-proclaimed fashionista and blogger, and a former associate publisher at the *New York Observer*, whose ignorance about Al Qaeda led the New Yorker on a journey to "learn everything about the enemy who vowed to destroy America." That journey quickly led her to conclude that there was no such thing as a "moderate" Muslim, that Islam itself was synonymous with militant extremism, and that all the world's 1.6 billion Muslims were in essence "spies" to a foreign cause. All moderate Muslims, she would write, were simply not real Muslims at all. "There is nothing moderate in Islam, and this is the deception that must be unveiled."

Then there was Brigitte Gabriel, a Lebanese-born Christian who had immigrated to the United States during the Lebanese civil war, and who saw in the 9/11 attacks an opportunity to educate Americans about the universal threat of Islam. "On September 11, 2001, as I looked into the frightened eyes of my young daughters, I pledged to devote the rest of my life to doing all that I can to protect my newly-adopted country, the United States," she would later write. "That day I was reborn as an activist." For Gabriel, however, the word "crusader" would be more fitting than "activist," and her target would become the entire world of Islam.

There was Robert Spencer too, a stocky Melkite Greek Catholic living in New England, whose suspicions of Islam were also rooted in his family history—his own grandparents were forced to leave Turkey for refusing to convert to Islam—and who saw in 9/11 the same opportunities as Gabriel. Soon publishing books with titles like *Islam Unveiled: Disturbing Questions About the World's Fastest-Growing Faith*, Spencer was on his way to becoming the preeminent voice for scholarly-sounding denigrations of the entire religion of Islam.

In the years immediately after the attacks of September 11, however, this group was about as obscure as it was unorganized. For one thing, the members of this motley cast were not only unaware of the movement they were helping to create, they weren't even aware of each other—on the fringes of American politics, the loudest cries tend to arise in isolation. In addition, the George W. Bush Administration's efforts to disassociate the war on terror from an attack on Islam were, by and large, successful. Those who feared a McCarthyist-type movement against Muslims in the United States were relieved to find just the opposite, at least for the time being. The American public was, on the whole, able to separate the wars it was fighting against Islamic extremism overseas from life on American shores—with the exception of a few anti-Islamic acts around the country, Jews, Christians, atheists, and

Muslims all rallied around the American flag as the Bush Administration inaugurated a new era. Islam itself seemed to remain largely untarnished in the post-9/11 world.

Disorganized and out of the mainstream, this four-person movement was left to spread its message on its own. In 2002, for example, Gabriel founded the American Congress for Truth, a grassroots organization meant to provide local venues for anti-Islamic lectures and book talks, soon sprouting chapters across the country. In 2003, Robert Spencer created a news website known as Jihad Watch, juxtaposing daily reports of Muslim violence around the world with citations of Islamic texts—attempting to equate Islam directly with terrorism. Pamela Geller's campaign took the form of a popular blog as well, created in 2004 and entitled Atlas Shrugs, and soon devoted to, among other things, the demonization of Islam (and eventually, the demonization of Barack Obama, who she would later suggest had slept with "a crack whore" and was a secret Muslim). As for David Yerushalmi, the activist lawyer would wait until 2006 before finally taking action, when he founded an organization known as the Society of Americans for National Existence. One of the organization's first efforts would be an attempt to criminalize Islam. According to one early bill Yerushalmi proposed, devout Muslims were to receive sentences of twenty years in prison for practicing Islam.

Over the following years, Gabriel, Spencer, Geller, and Yerushalmi would each do their best to justify and to help spread their new brand of Islamophobia—each in his or her own way, according to his or her own strengths. Despite all their conviction, it would be many years before their efforts resulted in a movement, before their conspiracy theories about Islam would be taken up and treated seriously at grassroots Tea Party meetings and even, for one brief moment in the summer of 2011, a New Hampshire presidential debate. This group needed a message first, beyond the mere vilification of Islam, that would resonate with the American public. They needed compelling arguments about the declining state of modern America and persuasive evidence for how Islam was to blame. Perhaps most importantly, the early leaders of the Anti-Sharia movement needed to meet each other, to find an opportunity to get organized—a national event, for example, that could serve as a rallying cry for their cause. They would find all this and more in 2007.

—◆—

Six years after 9/11 marked a strange time in American politics, one that would prove seminal in the history of the Anti-Sharia movement. Just before the financial crisis and the election of Barack Obama in 2008, Americans were slowly losing faith in the Bush Administration. News from the wars in Afghanistan and Iraq was grim, the economy was in decline, and the president's approval ratings had dropped below 30 percent for the first time. Americans' confidence in the direction the country was headed was at some of the lowest levels in over a decade—deep insecurities in the country's sense of national identity were beginning to arise. And just as confidence in the United States was diminishing, a new movement of hysteria would emerge from the public's newfound lack of faith. Almost at once, in separate incidents across the country, large groups of Americans suddenly began to awake to the purported dangers of Islam, just like Geller, Yerushalmi, Spencer, and Gabriel had warned.

It began in Brooklyn, New York. On February 12, 2007, the New York City Department of Education announced its plan to open a new public school, to be named the Khalil Gibran International Academy, after the famous Christian Lebanese poet. Spanning grades six through twelve, the school would offer programs in both English and Arabic, just like the sixty-plus other schools in the city that already offered instruction in languages like Spanish, Russian, or Chinese. The goal of the school was to offer American children the opportunity to learn about Arabic language and culture, and to help better equip the city's students to be "citizens of the world"—noble aims, surely, and ones that might have succeeded in another time and place.

One of the first to publicly reject the school was Daniel Pipes, a Harvard PhD with a well-honed suspicion of Islam. In an April 24 article for the *New York Sun*, Pipes wrote that the school appears to be a "marvelous idea," but that in reality the school would serve as nothing more than a recruiting tool for Islamists attempting to convert Christian and Jewish students. "Muslims," he wrote, "tend to see non-Muslims learning Arabic as a step toward an eventual conversion to Islam." For Pipes, global education and foreign recruitment were one and the same. One week later, conservative columnist Alicia Colon expanded on Pipes's themes in the same paper. "How delighted Osama bin Laden and Al Qaeda must have been to hear the news—that New York City, the site of the worst terrorist attack in our history, is bowing down in homage to accommodate and perhaps groom future radicals." Far from being dismissed, such language found widespread support. Jeffrey Wiesenfeld, for example, a trustee of the City University of New York, would publicly call the school's plan a "soft jihad" carried out by Islamists. The controversy would soon stand for a whole range of concerns over the Middle East and Islam itself—quickly becoming a beacon for those around the country who had been waiting since the days of 9/11 to express their anti-Islamic views.

Public condemnation of the school rapidly transformed into a formal organization, created by a retired Spanish teacher from Queens, Irene Alter, who called the group the Stop the Madrassa Coalition, referencing the Arabic word for "school" in an effort to make the project seem as alien as possible. The Coalition quickly got to work, holding public rallies and stoking up fear over the potential school, with much of its efforts focusing on the school's Muslim-American principal, Debbie Almontaser, implying that she was a covert radical. One website, for example, noted that Almontaser wore a Muslim headscarf that usually covered nearly every body part above her shoulders, but that more recently she had begun exposing her neck and jawline as part of a "PR makeover" to disguise her Islamist agenda. Accusations like this abounded.

David Yerushalmi would join the effort by serving as the organization's general counsel, leading a series of legal actions aimed at stoking the controversy, soon calling the school a "radical experiment" and attempting to sue the city and even threatening legal action against Almontaser herself. Pamela Geller came to the Coalition's aid as its unofficial media arm, cheerleading the organization's every move from her popular blog. Brigitte Gabriel joined in too, warning the Coalition's members that the threat of Islam was extending much more widely than in New York City alone. "They are very well organized and have been orchestrating this comprehensive educational plan for many years with great success," cautioned Gabriel in reference to the grand Islamist conspiracy. "This must be monitored and stopped." The Brooklyn school was just the tip of the Islamist iceberg. The Coalition would, in short, bring together for the first time a group of voices who found unity and meaning in the demonization of Islam.

And that was just for starters. When the Khalil Gibran International Academy ultimately opened its doors in Brooklyn on September 4, 2007, the Coalition held a rally across the East River on the steps of city hall, attracting even more prominent supporters from around the country to its cause. In attendance, for example, was Brian Rooney, an attorney with the Thomas More Law Center, a Michigan-based conservative public interest law firm. Bill Donohue, president of the conservative Catholic League for Religious and Civil Rights, was there as well. Perhaps most importantly, Frank Gaffney, a former defense official in the Reagan Administration and the head of the Center for Security Policy, an ultra-conservative Washington think tank, spoke on behalf of the Coalition (Gaffney would later become known for labeling Obama as "America's first Muslim president").

"We're here to oppose this action," Gaffney told CNN during the rally. "Our efforts to oppose it in this school are only beginning and they will be redoubled to ensure that in fact this model is not allowed to replicate like a cancer across America."

Gaffney, with his apparent credibility and his Washington connections, would soon become a core member of the fledgling Anti-Sharia movement, lending the group a newfound veneer of respect. And while the controversy at this point may have been local, for those who cared to pay attention, it drew national attention, both on cable news and in the mainstream press. The Coalition would, in the end, lose the fight against Islam, at least in the near term. The Khalil Gibran International Academy remained open, though Debbie Almontaser was forced to step down—the New York City public school system, apparently, did not have the stomach for the publicity her presence soon elicited as a result of the Coalition's work. But at a larger level, the group's efforts were a resounding success, for the Stop the Madrassa Coalition had proven that there was an appetite, in New York City and across the country, for broad-based denunciations of Islam. Indeed, by stirring up public apprehensions over Islam at a time of growing national insecurity, the early leaders of the Anti-Sharia movement discovered a deep power in the fight against the Khalil Gibran International Academy. And this would only mark the beginning of their efforts. For the group had brought together a country-wide network of leaders who, in the aftermath of the Stop the Madrassa campaign, would soon begin to organize a national crusade to spread their message. "It's a battle," Daniel Pipes told the *New York Times*, "that's really just begun."

In 2007, just as they were organizing the Stop the Madrassa Coalition against the Brooklyn school, the early leaders of the movement would find their own real-life equivalent of the Alger Hiss case—receiving the first pieces of seemingly persuasive evidence that they could harness in support of their cause. The new evidence came to light in a Dallas, Texas, courtroom during the trial of five key leaders of a charity known as the Holy Land Foundation for Relief and Development. Shut down by the US government in 2001, the Holy Land Foundation was accused of serving as a front organization for the Palestinian terrorist organization Hamas, secretly channeling money to the group in support of its violent, anti-Israel activities. Money raised by the Holy Land Foundation was being "used by Hamas to recruit suicide bombers and to support their families," President Bush himself declared in December of 2001, detailing the government's initial high-profile crackdown on the organization. Trials stemming from the raids of the Holy Land Foundation in the US would take place over the course of the next decade, eventually sending five of the charity's top leaders to jail on sentences ranging from fifteen to sixty-five years.

And like the trials that gave rise to previous episodes of hysteria, the prosecution of the Holy Land Foundation would be no different, providing an ample source of evidence to further the Anti-Sharia movement's false sense of alarm. Over the summer of 2007, for example, with the trial against the foundation's top leaders just beginning, government prosecutors would introduce into evidence an eighteen-page document written in

1991 and entitled "An Explanatory Memorandum On the General Strategic Goal for the Group in North America," meant to illustrate that the Holy Land Foundation had far more sinister aims than simply supporting charities in the Middle East. The document implied that the charity itself was a front for a global organization known as the Muslim Brotherhood.

Referred to as the "Ikhwan" in Arabic, the Brotherhood had been founded in 1928 by an Egyptian schoolteacher named Hassan al-Banna, adopting the goal of subjugating secular government and society to strict interpretations of Islamic law, an ideology known as Islamism. The group would soon spread throughout the Middle East in small, and at times secretive, units. Up until the Holy Land trial, however, little was publicly known about the Brotherhood's existence in the United States—other than the fact that it had a presence, likely made up of a minor network of supporters who were incapable of doing much harm. But the memorandum brought to light at the trial, penned by a member of the Muslim Brotherhood named Mohamed Akram, suggested differently—it gave the impression that, in the eyes of Akram and his cohorts, the Brotherhood in the United States had a far loftier self-image, and aspired to far-reaching goals.

According to Akram, the objectives of the Brotherhood were to replace western civilization with a society dedicated to a pure version of Islam, and to convert as many nonbelievers as possible. In one key passage—one of the most frequently cited within the Anti-Sharia movement today, and one of the most bizarre—Akram would describe just what such an ideological war against western civilization entailed. "The process of settlement is a 'Civilization-Jihadist Process' with all the word means," he wrote. "The Ikhwan must understand that their work in America is a kind of grand Jihad in eliminating and destroying the Western civilization from within and 'sabotaging' its miserable house by their hands."

Akram would go on to describe the various stages of this process, beginning with the peaceful spread of Islam and the creation of Islamic centers in every city, along with fake charities like the Holy Land Foundation. It was only later, once a devout Islamic community had been established, that the Muslim Brotherhood would "activate" its true plan to overthrow American society from within, when front organizations would emerge across America to reveal their true intentions.

By introducing Akram's memorandum as evidence, the prosecutors' aims were to equate the Holy Land Foundation's intentions with the Muslim Brotherhood's own motives—suggesting that men like Mohamed Akram were the driving force behind the charity, and thus making the trial about a threat much larger than one bogus charity alone. The more sinister the Holy Land Foundation's intentions, after all, the tougher the sentencing. This was, in other words, a legal tactic that made sense in the context of the case, and not new intelligence to indicate the existence of an existential threat to the US government.

But by connecting the Holy Land Foundation to Akram's plans, the prosecutors made it seem as if Akram's far-reaching conspiracy theory, staged by the Brotherhood, with front organizations like the Holy Land Foundation at its core, was more than an Islamist fantasy, but was a vision actually capable of being carried out—exactly the type of evidence the Anti-Sharia movement's leaders had been waiting for. The prosecutors would, without knowing it, end up providing ammunition to the Anti-Sharia movement for years to come.

———

Over the course of the trial, government prosecutors would go on make Akram's Islamist fantasies seem more ambitious still. The prosecutors would, for example, publish a list citing more than three hundred persons and organizations as "unindicted co-conspirators" in the case, containing the names of many major Muslim-American organizations in the United States. Although the co-conspirators were not being prosecuted themselves, the list enabled the government to introduce statements from any member of the list into the court proceedings without their statements being dismissed as hearsay—this was, in short, a legal technicality that had very little to do with the actual organizations, and the real reason behind the list. The National Association of Muslim Lawyers and the National Association of Criminal Defense Lawyers, in a letter condemning the prosecutors' move, would together call the list "overreaching," and the government itself would later admit that the list "was simply a 'legal tactic' intended to allow the government to introduce hearsay evidence." But the list also had the effect of associating almost the entire American Islamic community with the Holy Land Foundation, implying that Akram's plans somehow connected to not just the one charity on trial, but to *all* the unindicted co-conspirators as well. In the months and years to come, the leaders of the Anti-Sharia movement would use the prosecutors' list for all it was worth, labeling American Muslim organizations as "unindicted co-conspirators" at nearly every turn, and suggesting that every mainstream Islamic organization in the United States was nothing more than a front for the Muslim Brotherhood's global conspiracies.

Thanks to both Akram's memorandum and the prosecutors' list, then, the Anti-Sharia movement's leaders now finally had facts, or what they believed were facts, to suggest that their concerns were indeed legitimate, and that even the US government supported their conspiracy theories. For those who knew better, these facts did not carry much weight beyond the trial of the Holy Land Foundation. But knowing better also required an understanding of the details of the case—a perspective that could only come with reflection and research, something that most busy Americans do not have the time to allow. The Holy Land Foundation trial would thus serve as a catalyst for the Anti-Sharia movement, granting its leaders' claims the facade of legitimacy they had long been waiting for.

Before moving on to describe how the trial furthered the efforts of the early Anti-Sharia movement, however, two key insights are worth noting. The first is that, if anything stands out about Akram's memorandum, it is how perfectly it conforms to the model established by previous symbolic threats, from the Illuminati to the Masons to the Bolsheviks. Indeed, Akram's plans were almost cookie-cutter in their approach, as if they had been copied and pasted from the conspiracy-laden documents of earlier episodes. Whether in the 1790s, the 1830s, or the twentieth century, the perceived threat always begins with small ideological inroads into American society—in the Anti-Sharia movement's case, the creation of seemingly legitimate Muslim community centers—and it is only later that these centers are said to be publicly enlisted in the global conspiracy's schemes.

In this way, Akram's plans ended up aligning his own perverse motives with those of the Anti-Sharia movement as a whole: Both normal Muslims and Muslim organizations suddenly became pawns in a bigger game. The idea that Islamic groups or individuals could ever make decisions according to their own ideologies or beliefs, or that those preferences might diverge, was simply out of the question. For Akram, as for the members of the Anti-Sharia movement, Muslims as a whole were little more than instruments of grander plans, incapable of exercising their own free will.

The second insight is that, as scary as Akram's plans might have sounded, a little historical perspective reveals that his goals were nothing new—indeed, though the jihadist element and the connection to Islam might seem novel at first, the fears stoked by the Anti-Sharia movement were merely a new variation on a very old theme. Even if Akram's memorandum had been in the initial stages of being carried out, for example, and even if the Holy Land Foundation represented one among a handful of front organizations for the Muslim Brotherhood, small groups of radicals have plotted the downfall of the US government throughout American history. Compared to the threat of the Soviet Union during the Cold War, for example, with its billions of dollars and its teams of well-trained spies, the plotting behind the Holy Land Foundation was mere child's play. The very fact that the foundation's efforts had been exposed, and that the charity's leaders had been caught and successfully prosecuted, should have given comfort to the Americans who were newly alarmed by the threat of a domestic conspiracy.

Indeed, despite the vigor with which the members of the Anti-Sharia movement might sound the alarm, the threat of "civilization jihad" in America is small on just about every scale. Polls of American Muslims, for example, consistently reveal a group that mirrors other religious communities in the United States. According to one 2013 poll, for example, 63 percent of US Muslims believe there is no inherent tension between being devout and living in a modern society, compared to 64 percent of

American Christians who feel the same way. When it comes to tolerance for other religions, nearly 60 percent of US Muslims agree with
the view that many religions can lead to heaven, compared to the US
average of 65 percent. The vast majority of American Muslims, in short,
espouse modern values that parallel other mainstream religious groups in
the United States today. Men like Mohamed Akram may pose a threat,
surely, but that threat is simply not that compelling.

In the long history of political hysteria, however, what should be cause
for comfort is regularly cause for alarm. And as we will see, the evidence
that emerged from the Holy Land Foundation trials would be interpreted
no differently. Soon, the Holy Land Foundation trial would become less
about one charity, or even about supporting Hamas, and more about a
true global Islamist conspiracy. In time, the trial would come to symbolize
an indictment of the Muslim-American community as a whole.

Mohamed Akram's memorandum was quickly taken up by the early
leaders of the Anti-Sharia movement and viewed as confirmation of
all their worst fears. The memorandum served as proof that the bigger
threat to America wasn't simply violent Muslim extremists—the United
States could simply declare war upon and kill the members of that group,
as the government was actually in the process of doing. Instead, the real
threat lay in the nonviolent, ideological extremists—men and women
who lived in the United States and who called themselves Americans,
perhaps serving in civic or political roles, or even the armed forces
themselves, only to conceal far deeper and darker aims. These were men
and women just like Akram, who came to the United States from the
Middle East to study at its universities, to build families and careers, but
who had secretly declared a "civilization jihad" against the United States.
Their mosques, their schools, even their newspapers and magazines were
all just front organizations in a larger ideological struggle between Islam
and the West.

In the months after Akram's memorandum was made public, his language began to make its way into the rhetoric of the leaders of the Anti-
Sharia movement, which increasingly resembled McCarthyism with an

anti-Muslim hue. The following year, for example, Robert Spencer would publish *Stealth Jihad: How Radical Islam Is Subverting America Without Guns or Bombs*, a treatise on the secret threat of Islam—or, as the title of its first chapter elucidated, an attempt to prove that "Muslims [Are] Trying to Take Over the USA." Men and women like Akram, Spencer declared, "envision not only a Muslim president, but that the United States Constitution be replaced or amended so as to comply in all particulars with Islamic sharia law." The subtext of Spencer's claims, of course, was that radical Islam wasn't all that radical—that most of the world's 1.6 billion Muslims were, deep down, just like Akram. Indeed, Spencer would imply that Akram himself couldn't have been an outlier in the American Islamic community—it was the peace-loving, patriotic American Muslims who were the anomalies. Armed with such arguments, as preposterous as they might sound, the early leaders of the Anti-Sharia movement finally had the evidence they needed to start making their case.

In the wake of the Brooklyn school controversy, this group began to make its case more vigorously than ever. By the end of 2007, for example, Yerushalmi would team up with Gaffney, the former Defense Department official, in an attempt to win mainstream support in Washington, and to foster a movement at a national level from the top down. The movement's leaders, however, would soon realize that Akram's memorandum, on its own, was not enough. Sure, the document looked like proof of an Islamist conspiracy, but his words were nearly two decades old. How could they prove that Akram's writings were more than the ranting of one lone Islamic extremist? How could they show that his goals for a "grand jihad" were, in fact, being carried out today? Akram's memorandum may have laid the foundation for the Anti-Sharia movement. But that foundation—as flimsy as one manifesto written by one man—would not be enough on its own.

And so Yerushalmi and Gaffney attempted to document, for the first time, the actual perils of Islam in the United States. If they could illustrate that the Islamist threat wasn't limited to one public school in Brooklyn, but was lurking in mosques and Muslim community centers throughout the country, exactly as Akram had written, there was no limit to where their nascent movement might go—or so, at least, they hoped. The pair's ambition, Gaffney once explained, was to "engender a national debate about the nature of Sharia and the need to protect our Constitution and country from it." In his eyes, this was about nothing less than the very survival of the United States.

And so Yerushalmi, with funding from Gaffney's think tank, began a project designed to win real supporters for the movement, to turn those fearful of Islam into ideological warriors convinced of its depravity. The mission amounted to a nationwide study, referred to as the "Mapping Sharia" project, attempting to document the number of mosques in the United States that advocated violence, in an effort to conflate violent Islamic ideology with Muslims as a whole. Ultimately published in a journal run by Daniel Pipes, the survey concluded that 81 percent of mosques in the United States advocated some form of violence in pursuit of institutionalizing Sharia law. Writing in the *Washington Times*, Gaffney declared the study proof that American Muslims "are using our tolerance of religion to create an infrastructure of mosques here that incubate the Islamic holy war called jihad."

The study was quickly condemned, and just as quickly discredited, but such rejection was beside the point. For when it comes to building a mass movement, putting forth "facts" in support of your case is far more important than ensuring that those "facts" are correct. The ability to cite a study or a figure in an argument, no matter how outlandish, is often enough to get a talking head on cable news—or in Gaffney's case, an article into print—and from there it was just a matter of finding supporters sympathetic to the cause. Indeed, this was just the first of many similar studies, all designed to provide ammunition for those organizing against worldwide Islam.

By the spring of 2008, Gaffney thought their efforts were ready for prime time: They were ready to enlist federal officials in their crusade against Islam. Through his connections in Washington, Gaffney was able to set up meetings between Yerushalmi and some of the most senior officials in government, including the number two official in the Treasury Department, Deputy Secretary Robert M. Kimmitt. In the series of high-level briefings that followed, Yerushalmi warned of the dire threat of Islam in "sweeping and, ultimately, unconvincing" language, according to Stuart A. Levey, the under secretary for terrorism and financial intelligence, who participated in the meetings.

In the end, Yerushalmi and Gaffney's efforts in DC fell flat. There was simply no appetite in the Bush Administration for demonizations of Islam—a setback surely, but merely a temporary one, for it marked a turning point in the brief life of the movement that Gaffney and Yerushalmi were helping to create. After being rejected by federal officials, the pair decided to take a different track.

"If you can't move policy at the federal level, well, where do you go?" Yerushalmi once explained to the *New York Times*. The answer was clear, he said: "You go to the states."

—◁▷—

By 2009, Yerushalmi and Gaffney had settled on a grand plan to get anti-Muslim laws passed in state legislatures around the country, constructing support for the movement from the ground up. Over the course of that summer, Yerushalmi began drafting a model law to pitch to state officials. Entitled "American Laws for American Courts," the legislation would formally prohibit Islamic law from being recognized in the United States. Specifically, the law banned American courtrooms from relying upon any legal system that did not guarantee "the same fundamental liberties, rights, and privileges granted under the US and state Constitutions"—specifically targeting Sharia law.

On its face, the law was both extremely odd and seemingly reasonable. It was a far cry from the type of sweeping claims Yerushalmi and Gaffney made about the efforts of the Muslim Brotherhood in the United States. Stopping judges from recognizing foreign laws in American courtrooms would, in reality, do little to prevent a global Islamist takeover. But the effort seemed reasonable in the sense that laws based on foreign traditions, Islamic or otherwise, do not ordinarily have a place in American courtrooms. Indeed, when foreign laws would undermine fundamental privileges guaranteed by the Constitution—in, for example, legal judgments relating to foreign divorce and marriage contracts—such laws are never held up in US courts as a matter of public policy. Yerushalmi's measure was entirely unnecessary in the view of its actual legal aims.

But the aims of the draft law were not exactly legal. This was about symbolism. Yerushalmi's measure was packaged as one small step—a first step—to countering the influence of Islam. By preventing American judges from recognizing foreign laws in the courts, the theory went, devout Muslims would be formally excluded from a key sector of American life, the legal sphere. After that, support would build for more drastic measures—such as criminalizing the observance of Islam, declaring non-US Muslims enemies of the state, or even deporting them from the country, as Yerushalmi had once advocated. Indeed, if there were any similarities between this measure and the team's previous anti-Islamic efforts, they were all under the surface—in fact, the draft bill never mentioned Islam by name. If the bill could be proven to be directly discriminatory against Muslims, the measure would be overturned as unconstitutional. In this respect, the pair was exceedingly careful not to single out Islam overtly as the object of their efforts. Gaffney and Yerushalmi needed to walk a fine line, to appear as defending American society from a group of foreign invaders, but without specifying which group they believed the invaders to be. They needed to peddle a worldwide conspiracy theory to the public, in other words, and keep the profundity of their paranoia hidden at the same time.

Appearing to address an issue much larger than Sharia was a brilliant strategic move. The pair's newfound focus on *all* foreign law helped them to win the support of another, ready-made constituency—those who have long opposed the influence of international laws in the United States. Increasingly worried about foreign encroachments into US sovereignty, this largely conservative group has made a handful of attempts to undermine the legitimacy of international law in American courts, introducing measures in nearly two dozen states over the last decade. As a testament to just how vocal, and how popular, this constituency really was, in 2004 and 2005 legislators introduced into both chambers of Congress bills that would have impeached federal judges for any citation to international law when interpreting the US Constitution, attracting five co-sponsors in the Senate and thirty-four in the House. The fact that Yerushalmi's legislation immediately appealed to this group would be a key factor in its success.

And success was an understatement. The measure would soon take off in legislatures around the country, spearheaded by a lobbying campaign

directed by Gaffney. With the draft law written, Gaffney organized conference calls with a nationwide network of grassroots activists in the fall
of 2009, calling on Brigitte Gabriel and her organization for help. Indeed,
just as the Anti-Sharia movement's early leaders were organizing against
the Arabic school in 2007, Gabriel was expanding her own American
Congress for Truth, the organization she had created in 2002, and to
great effect. Under a newly launched sister organization called ACT! for
America, Gabriel's goal was to form "a nationwide citizen action network
so formidable that no elected official anywhere will feel it is politically wise
to ignore our concerns." To that end, she hired Guy Rodgers, a prominent
Evangelical political strategist, who quickly proved to be a good choice:
The organization would soon boast an astonishing 180,000 members,
organized into 573 chapters across the nation. The group would come to
function like a well-oiled political campaign, recruiting activists and then
training them on messaging techniques and political outreach, holding
annual conferences to introduce its members to Anti-Sharia celebrities
like Gaffney and eventually even some members of Congress.

By the time Gaffney reached out to Gabriel in the fall of 2009, she
was more than ready to help. Gabriel enlisted local chapters of her organization to sponsor the bill, pouring money and time into the effort in what
Gaffney would later describe as a "force multiplier," drawing on grassroots
support that Gaffney and Yerushalmi could not have leveraged on their
own. Lawmakers in Tennessee and Louisiana were some of the first to
sign on. By May of 2010, for example, just under a year after the ink had
dried on Yerushalmi's draft of the bill, Tennessee became the first state to
enact the law. The following month, Louisiana joined in, passing a nearly
identical version of the law. Around the same time, the movement would
begin its highest-profile effort yet. More than thirteen hundred miles
away from the site of the attack on the World Trade Center, that fight
would ultimately take place in Oklahoma—a most unlikely crossroads in
the nation's growing battle against Islam.

Rex Duncan was no stranger to the political power of Islamophobia.
The Oklahoma state representative's introduction into the fray came in

October of 2007, when a woman by the name of Marjan Seirafi-Pour, the head of the Governor's Ethnic American Advisory Council, e-mailed Oklahoma state legislators to notify them that they would be receiving free copies of the Koran, the Muslim holy book, to commemorate the state's hundred-year anniversary. Duncan had other ideas. The state representative rejected Seirafi-Pour's gift, explaining that "Most Oklahomans do not endorse the idea of killing innocent women and children in the name of ideology."

Duncan was the leading edge of a trend. Soon, sixteen other state legislators came to his side, publicly rejecting the Koran as un-American and generating national headlines in the process. Initially, Duncan feigned surprise at all the attention—this wasn't a political stunt designed to win publicity or supporters, at least not at first. "I just didn't want the thing," Duncan told one reporter shortly after refusing the Koran. But in the weeks and months ahead, Duncan would become much more outspoken—slowly recognizing the political value in condemning Islam. In no time at all, Duncan would warn of an ideological clash between civilizations and an Islamist conspiracy on American soil, eventually spearheading one of the nation's most prominent efforts to ban Sharia law in his home state.

Just as Tennessee and Louisiana were enacting Yerushalmi's bill, Duncan was drumming up support for an even more drastic measure, one that would overtly single out Sharia as the object of the legislator's aims. Entitled State Question 755, and known as the "Save Our State Amendment," Duncan sponsored an amendment to Oklahoma's constitution in early 2010 that would directly ban Sharia law, placing the measure in the hands of state voters in the form of a referendum. Mixing language from Yerushalmi's bill with more directly anti-Islamic language of his own, Duncan's bill sailed through by a whopping 82–10 vote in the Oklahoma House of Representatives and a 41–2 vote in the state's Senate. With the measure now firmly on the ballot, all it would take next was the approval of the voters in the November elections to enact it into law, and that was where national leaders like Brigitte Gabriel stepped in. ACT! for America would pour sixty thousand dollars into promoting the effort, staging a campaign that included six hundred thousand robocalls featuring James

Woolsey, former director of the Central Intelligence Agency and himself a convert to the Anti-Sharia movement. There was already a "major campaign in Europe to impose Sharia law," Woolsey warned in the phone messages, cautioning that Islamic law was even now "beginning to be cited in a few US courts." Only by banning Sharia in Oklahoma, his message was, could voters prevent whatever apocalyptic scenario was next. Rex Duncan himself illustrated just how high the stakes really were. "This is a war for the survival of America," he proclaimed on national television. "It's a cultural war, it's a social war, it's a war for the survival of our country."

By November 2, 2010, Oklahomans had come to side with Duncan, and rather drastically. Despite the fact that only an estimated fifteen thousand Muslims lived in the state, out of a population of 3.7 million at the time, more than 70 percent of the electorate voted to ban Sharia law. The measure became a national talking point, baffling most Americans—who had not previously considered Oklahoma to be on the front lines of the war on terror—while motivating many others to join the cause. In the meantime, the Save Our State amendment would prove to politicians and the press what Rex Duncan had learned years before: that almost a decade after 9/11, a profound shift had occurred in public opinion. Something deep, and hard to pinpoint, had changed in the American electorate. Finally, at long last, there was real political power in demonizing Islam.

The Save Our State amendment, however, was soon blocked by a federal judge, exactly as Gaffney and Yerushalmi had feared. On November 29, Vicki Miles-LaGrange of the Federal District Court in Oklahoma City ruled that the amendment "may be viewed as specifically singling out Shariah law, conveying a message of disapproval of [the Muslim] faith," and thus violating constitutional protections on religious freedom. A setback for the Anti-Sharia movement? Surely. But in the scheme of things, Duncan's measure itself was not the point. The real victory had come during the campaign for the ban, and in the support that campaign received. Indeed, the Oklahoma initiative would count as a major win for the Anti-Sharia movement. Its leaders would soon sponsor more laws, in even more states, carefully designed to skirt the Oklahoma judge's ruling, drumming up even more support for their growing war on Islam. This was only the beginning of a longer fight, and the movement's leaders were learning their lessons early on.

~ ~

But there was much more to the Anti-Sharia movement than the fight to keep Sharia out of American courtrooms alone. Just as Gaffney, Yerushalmi, and Gabriel were campaigning for state legislatures to ban Sharia, two other members of the movement's inner core, Pamela Geller and Robert Spencer, were busy turning the spotlight on Islam at the national level, attempting to create a symbol that their newfound followers could rally around. Indeed, if Yerushalmi and Gabriel were the movement's early political strategists, Geller and Spencer would become its early directors of PR. The pair would spend the years after 2007 looking for an example to symbolize the dangers of Islam, a national event that Americans could, at a profound level, latch on to—something much bigger than a public school or the Holy Land Foundation trials alone. And it would take them just over two years to find it.

The duo's quest began on a trip to Europe in the wake of the controversy over the Khalil Gibran International Academy. In the fall of 2007, Spencer and Geller traveled to Belgium for an event known as the Counter-Jihad Conference, in which "warriors, bloggers, scholars, politicians, from across the globe converged in Brussels . . . to strategize against the onslaught of the Islamization of the West," as Geller described the event on her blog. In attendance were anti-Islam activists from all over Europe, such as Filip Dewinter of the Belgian nationalist Vlaams Belang party, an offshoot of a group allegedly founded by Nazi sympathizers. While in Brussels, Geller and Spencer would learn from these kinds of activists how Muslims had infiltrated European society, and how they had done so under the protection of western legal norms. Europeans, they were told, had been bullied into submitting to Islam by their fears of appearing politically incorrect. Perhaps most importantly, the activists confirmed to the two Americans that radical Islam was about to cross the Atlantic, to invade American shores. Spencer and Geller would return home to the United States with new energy for their cause.

The following year, the two began their first informal collaboration by working to publicize the death of Aqsa Parvez, a sixteen-year-old Canadian girl brutally murdered by her father and brother. The details of Parvez's murder were heinous, but Geller and Spencer would soon proclaim the act an Islamic "honor killing," arguing that it was motivated by the core tenets of Islam. In that way, the pair would seek to portray Aqsa as much more than a victim—in time, she would become a symbol of Islam's "barbarity," a tragic icon who would help more people rally to the nascent movement's cause. Geller began a fundraising drive to buy the slain teenager a headstone, campaigning relentlessly for a memorial to stand in place of the unmarked grave that initially identified her burial site. "Islam will not win and this gentle soul will not have died in vain," wrote Geller on her blog. The efforts quickly paid off: Donations poured in, articles were written about their campaign, and all the while both Geller and Spencer's public profile grew. Ultimately, however, the cemetery where the girl was buried saw these efforts for what they were and refused the gift, forcing the creation of a memorial site elsewhere. As one popular conservative blogger declared at the time, the campaign was "one of the most disgusting publicity stunts I think I've ever heard of." Aqsa Parvez made a compelling symbol, but in the end her story was not compelling enough. As Spencer would later admit to the *New York Times*, the plight of a Muslim immigrant girl was simply too abstract to resonate with most Americans.

But that did not stop the pair from searching for another symbol, doing all they could to dig up new reasons to rally against Islam, and seeking new allies in the process. The following year, in 2009, Spencer and Geller would attempt to connect their crusade formally to the right wing of American politics, hosting an unofficial talk at the Conservative Political Action Conference, also known as CPAC, the largest annual gathering of conservative activists, on the dangers of Islam. Headlining the talk was none other than Geert Wilders, a Dutch anti-Islam activist who had, among other efforts, attempted to ban the Koran from his home country. The talk would prove to be a turning point in Spencer and Geller's journey, one small step forward in their growing crusade against Islam. Not long after Wilders's talk, for example, the two were asked to take over the American affiliate of an organization known as Stop Islamization of Europe, a European organization whose motto was, "Racism is the lowest form of human stupidity, but Islamophobia is the height of common sense."

Spencer and Geller reacted enthusiastically. In April of 2010, the duo founded a nonprofit group known as the American Freedom Defense Initiative, also known by the name Stop Islamization of America, in a nod to the connection to its European counterpart. Among their first acts was to take out bus ads offering to help Muslims who were converting away from their religion—"Is your family or community threatening you," the ads asked, for "leaving Islam? Got questions? Get answers!" The campaign proved so provocative that the pair was forced to litigate their constitutional right to display the ads, with the help, of course, of their lawyer—none other than David Yerushalmi. Indeed, the campaign and the subsequent lawsuits to defend it would generate so much publicity that it formed a model for the pair's organization in the years ahead: They would pour money into a public marketing campaign designed to illustrate the dangers of Islam, placing ads on public buses, taxis, and billboards in cities from Miami to Washington, DC, to San Francisco, galvanizing local citizens and garnering headlines in the process. At one point, the group would sponsor ads in New York stating, "19,250 deadly Islamic attacks since 9/11/01. It's not Islamophobia, it's Islamorealism." Below the ad, of course, were the addresses of both Spencer and Geller's websites.

Controversial? Surely. Highly provocative? No doubt. The pair continued with such campaigns, stirring up attention, condemnation, and outrage everywhere they went. By 2009, however, Spencer and Geller had yet to find a lasting way to get their message across, beyond the transitory indignation and publicity they were able to generate. Images and advertising campaigns, fundraising drives and memorial sites—these were all simply not enough. And that's when the pair came to a realization. "Most people are only concerned with their families and friends and their immediate circle," Spencer would later explain. But "there is a visceral connection that Americans have with 9/11 that is not felt about other issues." If the pair could connect their fight against Islam directly to the attacks of September 11, there was no limit to where their fight might take them.

On May 5, 2010, Sharif El-Gamal and Feisal Abdul Rauf made a modest presentation to a lower Manhattan community zoning board. Gamal, a

New York City developer, and Rauf, a New York City imam, or Muslim cleric, hoped to build a Muslim community center in the neighborhood, at that time the fastest-growing area of the city. "There are Jewish Community Centers all over the city," Gamal would explain, but no Muslim one in lower Manhattan. "I see a Muslim Community Center as a way of giving back to the people." After scouring the neighborhood for locations, Rauf and Gamal settled on the site of a former Burlington Coat Factory retail space, located at 45-51 Park Place. The two decided to name the center the Cordoba House, in homage to the tolerance thought to have reigned in medieval Spain, where Muslims, Jews, and Christians had coexisted in peace. "We want to push back against the extremists," Rauf had explained while announcing the plan for the project, five months before. The plan quickly won the backing of the city's Jewish and Christian leaders, and when the two men presented their project to the local zoning board on May 5, all fifteen members approved without objection.

But on May 6, the morning after the presentation, the *New York Daily News* ran an article describing the community center as a "13-story mosque" to be located "steps from Ground Zero," including a quote from the father of a 9/11 victim and firefighter describing Islam as a "religion of hate." Retired FDNY deputy chief Jim Riches, whose son, himself a firefighter, was killed during the attacks, was quoted as saying, "I don't want to have to go down to a memorial where my son died on 9/11 and look at a mosque." And this was only the first of many more such profiles of the community center, filled with negative, emotional rhetoric, soon stirring a controversy that few at the time could have predicted. Rauf and Gamal had simply wanted to bring a community center to lower Manhattan. But soon, it appeared, they had unleashed a storm.

The Cordoba House was, in short, the perfect symbol for Spencer and Geller—and the pair reacted quickly, mixing Americans' apprehensions over Islam with far-reaching conspiracy theories about the secret threat of Sharia law. That same day, Geller lambasted the plans for the community center on her blog, calling it "Islamic domination and expansionism," a "stab in [the] eye of America," and a demonstration of "the territorial nature" of Islam. "What could be more insulting and humiliating," she asked, "than a monster mosque in the shadow of the World Trade Center buildings brought down by Islamic attack?" But Geller's assault would not be limited to her own blog. A week later, Geller and Spencer had already planned a rally at Ground Zero against the center—which was now widely referred to simply as the "Ground Zero mosque"—set to take place in early June, with another rally to be held on September 10, under the auspices of their organization. Gaffney's think tank and Brigitte Gabriel's ACT! for America were quick to join the cause. For the Anti-Sharia movement as a whole, this was too good an opportunity to miss. "We can't undo 9/11," Geller would proclaim. "But we can stop the jihadis from marking their territory."

By June 6, on the day of the first rally, both Spencer and Geller had ridden the wave of controversy to the national spotlight. Thousands were in attendance—defiant, sure of their patriotism, and emotionally charged. Standing before the crowd, Robert Spencer mirrored their sentiments with a rallying cry that was short and straight to the point. "They say it will be different," he said, referring to the community center's leaders, "but they will be reading the same Koran and teaching the same Islamic law that led those nineteen hijackers to destroy the World Trade Center and murder three thousand Americans." The crowd cheered on, holding up placards proclaiming "All I Need To Know About Islam, I Learned On 9/11" and labeling the community center a "symbol of conquest of [the] West."

With a Spencer and Geller co-authored book set for publication the next month—entitled *The Post-American Presidency: The Obama Administration's War on America*, and with a foreword by John Bolton, the right-wing former US ambassador to the United Nations—the timing of the controversy could not have been more perfect. The pair gave interviews to a host of international news outlets about the rally, and about their larger project of demonizing Islam. Their national profile rose to monumental proportions, most notably for Geller, who would soon appear on numerous cable talk and radio shows to oppose the Islamic center. So omnipresent was Geller over those summer months that the liberal watchdog group Media Matters for America would warn news networks against hosting her, ultimately to no avail, stating that her views on Islam "demonstrate that she cannot be expected to make accurate statements and should not be rewarded with a platform on national television." In the end, the denouncement served as a symbol of her newfound success.

If the pair was at the forefront of the opposition to the Muslim center, however, their broader vision was not shared by everyone who opposed it. Abraham Foxman, for example, the director of the Anti-Defamation League, a national civil rights group that has labeled Spencer and Geller's own organization a "hate group," came out against the center himself, saying that the organizers should "find another place." Americans' "anguish entitles them to positions that others would categorize as irrational or bigoted," he explained. John Boehner, then Republican House minority leader, would join the fray, stating that, "This is not an issue of law, whether religious freedom or local zoning. This is a basic issue of respect." So too did many families of 9/11 victims object to the center for reasons beyond fears of Islam alone. "It's not really about a mosque and Islamic center in Manhattan," described Rosaleen Tallon, whose brother, Sean Tallon, was a firefighter who died in the north tower. "It's about a mosque and Islamic center at Ground Zero. And that's where the real insensitivity is."

And this was, of course, exactly what the leaders of the Anti-Sharia movement had been hoping for. They had found a symbol that resonated with the American public, one that conflated the public's apprehensions of Islamic extremism—which, with the wars in Iraq and Afghanistan, had dominated Americans' perceptions of Islam for years—with Islam itself, mixing legitimate grievances and personalities with irrational ones. No longer were they fighting in the shadows, easily cast as "bigots" and dismissed. They were now fighting alongside major figures like the House minority leader and the head of the Anti-Defamation League. When, for example, President Obama eventually weighed in on the subject that August, stating that "Muslims have the same right to practice their religion as anyone else in this country" and siding with the developers, Geller would appear on mainstream talk shows to counter the president's arguments. It seemed, at times, as if she were speaking for the opposition to the community center as a whole. The "Ground Zero mosque" controversy lent the Anti-Sharia movement a share of the limelight and a national platform that made its views appear less extreme than they really were. The movement's PR directors had found a symbolic fight worthy of their cause.

In the wake of that summer's controversy, the Anti-Sharia movement would gain even more steam—as would the plans for the community center, which eventually opened its doors the following year (ironically, without much fanfare). In September of 2010, Gaffney and Yerushalmi, along with a host of other converts to the Anti-Sharia movement, released their largest study yet, a nearly two-hundred-page tome entitled "Shariah: The Threat To America," devoted to proving that Sharia was a "totalitarian socio-political doctrine" akin to the communist menace Americans faced during the Cold War. The study soon found its way into talking points for some of the nation's leading figures on the right, including former speaker of the House Newt Gingrich, who just one week after the study's release would state that, "we should have a federal law that says Sharia law cannot be recognized by any court in the United States." Sensing a political opportunity, other national leaders soon jumped in. The next month, former Alaska governor and vice presidential candidate Sarah Palin would warn that "Americans are smart enough to know Sharia law, if that were to be adopted," would "be the downfall of America."

More importantly for the grassroots growth of the movement, local political leaders sought to capitalize on the same opportunity—just as Gaffney and Yerushalmi had hoped. The year 2011 would see more state legislatures pick up on the Sharia law bans. In April, Texas Republican state representative Leo Berman introduced a measure to ban foreign laws, explaining that Sharia is already spreading "all over Europe" and that "it could spread throughout the United States." In Florida, two legislators penned a similar ban, despite the fact that, as the *Tampa Bay Times* reported, neither legislator "could name a Florida case where international law or Islamic law has caused a problem in a state court." The South Carolina legislature also followed suit—a sponsor of the bill, State Senator Mike Fair, would go so far as to declare that, "there are some localities around the country that have imposed Sharia law in lieu of local laws."

Whispering into the ears of all these legislators, of course, were Anti-Sharia movement leaders like Yerushalmi, Gaffney, and Gabriel. All told, fifty-one bills were proposed in twenty-three states seeking to ban Sharia law in 2011, and the effort would continue to grow the following year. In the first half of 2013 alone, at least thirty-six measures were introduced in fifteen states.

In the months since, the push to ban Sharia has, if anything, showed little signs of stopping. In May of 2014, Florida governor Rick Scott would become one of the latest governors to sign the ban into law. And in November of that same year, 72 percent of voters in Alabama would vote to ban Sharia in their state as well. As of this writing, nine states have enacted the bans into law—almost one in five states in the union.

And yet for all the success of the Anti-Sharia movement, its momentum has largely stalled. Unlike past episodes of hysteria, this one has not yet peaked, nor is it clear that it has begun to fade away. As with past movements, it has expertly drawn on national fears, mixing concerns over terrorism with harder to pin down worries, like demographic tensions, economic anxieties, and resentment of the elites. It is no coincidence, for example, that the movement's true origins began in 2007, just when the Republican electorate was beginning to turn on the Bush Administration. And when Bush presided over the largest government intervention in the economy since the Great Depression the following year, huge numbers of conservatives took this as proof that the Republican Party, long opposed to government interference in the economy, had lost its soul—exacerbating a rift within the conservative wing of American politics that would soon lead to the rise of the Tea Party. It was out of this rift that, ultimately, the Anti-Sharia movement arose.

Feeding on the resentments of mostly white, aging conservatives, based largely in the South and Midwest, the Anti-Sharia movement claims to be defending America against far more than Islam. Peppering the rhetoric of its leaders and supporters are profound lamentations about the decline of "traditional" American values. The American public, they claim, has been consistently betrayed by those purporting to represent them, by Democrats and Republicans alike, and by the mainstream media. These are many of the same Americans who watched their pensions vanish during the recession, and who are watching now as America becomes blacker and browner, more economically divided, and less religious than ever before. "Our institutions are beyond infiltration—the enemy is in charge," wrote Geller and Spencer in their 2010 book. "America's 44th president and America's enemies have a common dream," proclaims another central tome in the movement's cannon, the *New York Times* bestseller *The Grand Jihad*, written by former federal prosecutor Andrew C. McCarthy, which equates Barack Obama's "totalitarian, collectivist" policies like healthcare reform with the Islamists' goals for societal domination. The Anti-Sharia movement, at root, has always been about much more than the symbolic threat of Sharia alone.

The movement's enemies, of course, are not just men like Mohamed Akram. The Islamists are just the most visible symbols of the threat posed by more powerful enemies—men like Barack Obama, whose foreign-sounding middle name and liberal agenda underscore his true intentions to "preside over the destruction of America," and who, to quote Brigitte Gabriel, is "transforming the country right before our own eyes." They are public servants and politicians, Democrats and Republicans alike, who purportedly "bow to the forces of political correctness" when refusing to condemn a religion with more than one billion adherents. Ultimately, they are also authors like this one, who believe that attempts to ban Sharia law from American courtrooms are ill advised and extreme. When crusading against a symbolic threat, enemies are, in short, very easy to find.

But if the movement has stalled in recent years, this is not for lack of trying. In 2012, for example, Gaffney's think tank released a report ominously entitled, "The Muslim Brotherhood In America: The Enemy Within." The report outlined the vast scope of the Islamist conspiracy within the United States, including new details on how the Obama Administration had been penetrated by Muslim Brotherhood operatives. A few months later, five members of the US House of Representatives picked up on the think tank's allegations. In June, Republican representatives Michele Bachmann of Minnesota, Trent Franks of Arizona, Louie Gohmert of Texas, Tom Rooney of Florida, and Lynn Westmoreland of Georgia publicly alleged that the State Department had been infiltrated by members of the Muslim Brotherhood. Singling out a longtime aide to Secretary of State Hillary Clinton, Huma Abedin, the representatives cited Gaffney's report as evidence that Abedin had somehow steered US policy in the Middle East to aid the Muslim Brotherhood in "destroying Western civilization from within." The accusations sparked immediate outrage, as the representatives must have predicted. The former manager of Bachmann's 2012 presidential campaign, for example, would call the allegations "extreme," "dishonest," and reminiscent of "the late Senator Joe McCarthy," as would numerous other Republicans, such as former presidential candidate Senator John McCain, who labeled the accusations "an unwarranted and unfounded attack on an honorable woman, a dedicated American, and a loyal public servant." But the charges revealed that the Anti-Sharia movement remained strong as a national political force—strong enough, at least, for five members of the House of Representatives to seemingly risk their reputations in a crude bid for its members' support. While somewhat adrift in 2012, the Anti-Sharia movement was certainly far from dead.

And so it remains today. The leaders of the movement have continued to repeat the same tactics that brought them into the spotlight to begin with—hoping that something, anything, will bring their cause back to center stage. Robert Spencer and Pamela Geller continue to churn out anti-Islamic posts on their websites, and they have kept up their public ad campaigns around the country, paying for billboards and signs demonizing Islam, while generating higher and higher levels of condemnation in the process. By 2013, the government of England would officially ban Spencer and Geller from entering the country, condemning the duo's activities as extremist.

As for Brigitte Gabriel, she has continued her grassroots campaign of organizing Americans against Islam, though below the radar and with increasing success. By early 2014, for example, ACT! for America claimed an astounding 270,000 members and supporters nationwide. While Gabriel has shied away from the limelight in recent years, she has quietly built an army of anti-Muslim political warriors—and her army shows no signs of dispersing.

So too have Gaffney and Yerushalmi pressed on, testifying in state legislatures and slowly advancing their battle against Sharia law. In

Yerushalmi's case, this has meant serving as the go-to lawyer for the Anti-Sharia movement as a whole, defending defamation lawsuits when they arise and bringing suits in individual cities each time municipalities attempt to stop anti-Muslim ad campaigns. But they have also pressed on with other, more mystifying battles. Among Gaffney's prime targets has become Grover Norquist, the prominent Republican anti-tax activist whom Washington insiders have called "the most powerful man in America," and whom Gaffney has come to regard as a prime agent of the Muslim Brotherhood in America. In the fall of 2013, for example, Gaffney took to the set of popular right-wing TV host Glenn Beck's program to accuse Norquist of directly working for the Islamists. "I saw *terrorists* in his office space," said Gaffney of Norquist. "I had colleagues come to me and say, 'You know there's a Muslim Brotherhood front operating out of his office suite?'" Gaffney's attacks would not decrease Norquist's power inside Washington, but neither would they discredit Gaffney, who would, until early 2014, maintain a column in the *Washington Times*, a prominent newspaper, and who continues to appear as a talking head on mainstream cable news outlets like CNN and Fox News. In February of 2014, Gaffney would escalate his attack on Norquist by publishing a report entitled, "Agent Of Influence: Grover Norquist and the Assault on the Right," signed by, among other notable figures, former attorney general Michael Mukasey.

What will become of the Anti-Sharia movement? Will new political leaders rise to national prominence based on the demonization of Islam? Are the movement's best days behind us, or do they lie ahead? The fact is that we do not know. The underlying grievances that gave rise to the movement all remain—the economic, racial, and religious shifts that gripped the United States toward the end of the Bush presidency show few signs of reversing, causing a large number of Americans to feel, in some instances accurately, that their assumed role in American society is being diminished. Extreme polarization within the electorate has only served to magnify these grievances, further fracturing our shared sense of national identity. All of these trends have served as contributing factors to the rise of the Anti-Sharia movement; indeed, the timing of the movement itself, beginning in 2007, right when Americans' confidence began eroding, demonstrates the phenomenon is about much more than 9/11, or even Islam. Similarly, Americans' views of Islam as a whole have been increasingly negative in recent years, especially among older Republicans. A year after the attacks of 9/11, for example, just 33 percent of Republicans believed that Islam was more violent than other world religions, compared to 22 percent of Democrats, according to research by the Pew Center for the People and the Press. By 2013, however, that number had skyrocketed to 62 percent of Republicans and 29 percent for Democrats. The fact that the United States has been fighting wars in Muslim countries for more than a decade has certainly not helped to reverse this trend.

What the Anti-Sharia movement has managed to achieve so far suggests we are in for a long-lasting episode of political hysteria. And yet, unlike the previous episodes of hysteria we have catalogued in this book, the rationale that the movement's leaders have drummed up is, at root, simply not that compelling. Arguments about the threat of Sharia and the Muslim Brotherhood do not resonate across the American public like the arguments and accusations forged by the McCarthys, the Palmers, or the Weeds of American history. Grover Norquist is just not that menacing of a symbol, nor is Huma Abedin, the longtime aide to Hillary Clinton—a message the Anti-Sharia movement's leaders appear not to have received. Indeed, the very demographic underpinnings of the movement—the fact that its aging, white supporters will become increasingly marginal as America becomes younger and more diverse in future years—suggests that while the movement's political power may remain for some time to come, it will not be long-lasting.

Or so it seems in the early months of 2015. Perhaps all it would take is another tragic attack by violent Islamic extremists—another Boston Marathon bombing, for example—to win the movement new converts, to forge a sufficiently compelling case that Islam is the root cause of modern America's ills, placing the movement on par with McCarthyism and the other episodes of hysteria we examined in the preceding pages.

Ultimately, this is a book about history, not about predictions. And that means that the next chapter in the story of the Anti-Sharia movement remains untold.

CHAPTER 7

The Way Forward

A Practical Guide to Confronting Political Hysteria

Political hysteria is, in the end, an essential part of the American story. And hysteria's tale is far from over—as long as there is an American identity, so too will the threat of political hysteria linger. New changes in America's societal fabric will produce threats to newly vulnerable groups. Conspiracies will arise that give these groups the false promise of regaining their lost social prestige. Real threats will be projected onto symbolic ones.

But as new movements will arise, so too will they fade away. For just as political hysteria presents a reoccurring force in American history, it has always been a transient one, strong enough to emerge but ultimately too weak to stay. The hope, and the past, suggests that it will remain that way.

And yet larger questions remain. What does the story of political hysteria have to teach us about ourselves, and about our future? What concrete lessons can we draw from the stories this book recounts? More practically, how do we—the American public, its academics, journalists, and politicians—respond to the next episode of political hysteria when it arises? The answers are threefold: In times of hysteria, we must *accept*, *affirm*, and *attack*.

First, we must *accept* that, irrational as the movement might seem, there is an intrinsic power to political hysteria, built upon a deep appeal during times of profound change in America's national identity. Such movements will undoubtedly arise, again and again, and the idea that they can be prevented, or simply dismissed, is neither helpful nor practical. If anything, attempting to minimize the attractiveness and power of such movements only gives them the space to linger, and to grow. Second, we must realize that political hysteria arises from insecurities in American national identity, and as such, *affirming* an inclusive version of our national identity—both before such movements arise, and in the midst of each episode—can serve to lessen their sway. Lastly, we must *attack* the assertions made by each movement's adherents, exposing their wild theories for what they are: unjustifiable demonizations and wildly exaggerated readings of the facts at hand.

Hysteria is a deeply perilous phenomenon, and its episodes are, as Supreme Court justice William Brennan once reflected, "all so baseless that they would be comical were it not for the serious hardship that they cause during the times of crisis." The story of political hysteria, while offering a fascinating view into American history, also illustrates a deep danger to our freedoms and to the rule of law. What follows in this short, final chapter is a practical guide to facing such movements head on. Ultimately, political hysteria is not only worth comprehending for its own sake, but it is worth understanding so that it might be practically confronted as well.

———

Before outlining the three specific ways to confront political hysteria, there is a more general point that's worth noting at the outset.

That point: Audience matters.

We must be conscious of tailoring our approach to the specific audience to whom we are speaking. It is much easier, for example, to convince a room full of Muslims how mistaken the Anti-Sharia movement is than it is a group of people who know nothing more about Islam than the stories of Islamic extremism they see on TV. Similarly, a room made up of Americans of every color might be more receptive to inclusive notions of American identity than would a room composed of elderly white men. *How we make our case to each audience*, to put it simply, *can matter as much as the arguments we actually make.*

The key question, then, lies in how best to relate to skeptical or even antagonistic groups—those that may sympathize with the arguments made by the Anti-Sharia movement, for example, or those that may simply harbor suspicions of Islam. And here the research of Dan Kahan, a professor of law and psychology at Yale Law School, offers us some basic guidance. In researching the debate over climate change, Kahan has come up with insights as to why certain groups hold the beliefs that they do, sometimes in the face of overwhelming evidence to the contrary. Oddly, Kahan found that the more informed some people are, the more unwilling they are to take into account new evidence that might contradict their views. And it is here where Kahan's research points to two important conclusions.

Kahan's first lesson is that trust matters. If an audience does not trust you, it is not going to listen to what you have to say. The easiest way to convey trust is to convey membership, to demonstrate that you are part of the community. Being a member of the tribe, so to speak, opens the door for the logic of your arguments to do its work. This means that the best way to confront the actual supporters of an episode of hysteria is to emphasize their ability to trust you, and that you belong to the same overarching clan. For some of us, this is impossible to do—there is, frankly, nothing a headscarf-wearing Muslim woman could say to the supporters of the Anti-Sharia movement to convey her status as a member of their community. But for some of us, the case is easier to make. Those of us with deep American roots, who are harder to typecast as out of touch or alien, may find it easier to approach many of the audiences that may support or sympathize with movements of hysteria. In instances where we cannot win over an audience's trust, seeking the endorsements of people whom the audience does trust may also do the trick.

Secondly, values matter more than facts. Kahan found that the best way to approach skeptical audiences is to argue through values rather than through reasoning—that is, to demonstrate how the audience's goals converge with your own, irrespective of the facts involved with your argument. In the case of hysteria and its supporters, such movements are based largely upon the fear of loss of prestige, and the coinciding need for reassurance and belonging. If we can convince supporters of hysteria that their movement is actually contributing to instability, that it is undercutting the American values they seek to protect, then our need to rely on actual facts about communist propaganda or Muslim conspiracies will diminish.

Integrating each of Kahan's two lessons into the ways we confront movements of hysteria is certainly complex—the way we demonstrate our trustworthiness and the way we tailor our arguments to each movement's values will change over time, just as they will adapt to each specific audience. But as we outline the broader guidelines for confronting episodes of hysteria below—*accepting, affirming,* and *attacking*—it is important to keep these points in mind.

Now, to the guidelines themselves.

<hr />

Accept. This is perhaps the simplest, and the most intuitive, approach to hysteria, in that hysteria cannot simply be ignored or wished away. The loss of prestige among one or more groups within society, and the projection of loss from a real to a symbolic threat, feeds a profound need within certain sectors of the American public—the need to belong, to feel superior, to protect each group's role and vision for American society. Once such movements begin, it is easy for those on the outside to dismiss their relevance or their power, just as it is easy for such movements to gain steam. And thus arises the disconnect that marks episodes of political hysteria: On the one hand, supporters of the movement act like they are engaged in a life-and-death struggle for the soul of the country; on the other, those outside the movement shrug its theories off as little more than pure craziness.

Yet it is also this separation that gives movements the space to grow unchallenged—space that allows new supporters to approach each movement without adequate skepticism and caution. And it is this disconnect that presents those outside the movement with the false sense that each episode poses no risk, that it doesn't draw on motivations and insecurities that may be both widespread and profound. Indeed, we see exactly this approach to today's Anti-Sharia movement and its leaders, men and women who are often branded as nothing more than "whackos" too crazy to affect real political change.

The first rule of hand in approaching movements of hysteria is thus to accept them for what they are, rather than dismissing them outright, as is so often the temptation. Each episode presents powerful arguments about the destruction of American values and the direction of the changes taking place within American society. As crazy as these arguments may sound, they tap into understandable longings to belong and be recognized, and should at the very least be acknowledged.

—◦—

Affirm. Because hysteria arises from changes to America's national identity, civic affirmation—that is, attempts to strengthen our national sense of self—can help to lessen the appeal of each movement as it arises, and to prevent future episodes before they occur. When confronting episodes of political hysteria, we should thus seek to affirm our national identity, making powerful arguments about what it means to be an American by appealing to the most compelling ideological aspects of the American Creed. The proper response to McCarthyism was thus not simply to correct each of McCarthy's wild assertions (on this approach, see below), but also to invoke grander ideas about equality and tolerance, to appeal to the ideals at the heart of such founding documents as the Declaration of Independence and the Bill of Rights. The proper response would have been to combat his vision of what it meant to be an American with a grander, more inclusive one.

Indeed, it is crucial that civic affirmation focus on an *inclusive* vision of our national identity—one that emphasizes the equality of every individual, despite his or her color or creed. Hysteria, after all, is about exclusion—it is the story of groups of men and women, like McCarthy and his supporters, confronting profound changes within American society and then excluding other groups as a result. It is the story of Americans telling each other, in so many words, "You do not belong." The antidote to this vision of American identity, to a society where we know who we are by virtue of who we are not, is inclusion. Given our history, the case for inclusion is an easy one to make. We can appeal to narratives no less powerful than the story of America itself—a history made up of waves of immigrants migrating to American shores, each generation more diverse than the last, each becoming more politically and economically integrated than the previous, and the country growing stronger, decade after decade, as a result.

To be sure, such appeals would not have prevented McCarthyism from arising, just as they would not have dissuaded McCarthy from launching more tirades about the secret communist menace, as he went on doing until his eventual death. But addressing hysteria through appeals to American national identity would have rooted the movement in the language of its core concerns, reminding its supporters that communists weren't the real focus, for example, of the House Un-American Activities Committee. The idea that Americans could agree upon what constituted an actual "American activity" formed the committee's real concern.

This type of civic affirmation can take place on multiple levels. At a minimum, it means responding to the arguments of leaders and supporters of each episode with even stronger arguments about American national identity—in newspapers, in public debates, and in our living rooms. But it also means initiating larger-scale efforts aimed at unifying the American public behind a more inclusive sense of self. There is room for government involvement, for renewed emphasis on civics in education, and for organizations ranging from youth groups to sports leagues, each emphasizing the importance of an inclusive sense of national identity. Such civic affirmation can help to lessen the appeal of movements of hysteria, strengthening America's sense of self, and thereby making the public less vulnerable to such movements in the future.

Appeals of this kind, however, are far from a cure-all. Indeed, some of these exact methods of shoring up America's national identity actually did take place before McCarthyism arose, and in some senses, actually helped contribute to the movement's ascendance. Think, for example, of the "Americans All, Immigrants All" effort described in chapter 5, promoted by the US government in the late 1930s as a way of unifying the population in the face of a splintering Europe and America's entry into World War II. It was precisely this new, pluralist conception of American identity that highlighted the weaknesses in the country's older sense of self, giving rise to the crusades of men like Martin Dies, and ultimately, over a decade later, to Joseph McCarthy himself. In that sense, the medicine of civic affirmation may actually make the disease of hysteria worse, at least in the short term. In the long term, however, the "Americans All, Immigrants All" effort, and those like it, were a resounding success, creating a new and more pluralistic sense of national identity that unified the country for decades afterward.

The importance of civic affirmation is a timely message. The rise of the Anti-Sharia movement highlights the growing factionalism within the American public, and along with it an emerging crisis in the realm of national identity. Beginning with the second term of the George W. Bush Administration, Americans began to realize the magnitude of the changes confronting our country, and since then we seem to have lost our way. Among such changes are a deep decline in religiosity amongst the American public, unprecedented political polarization, and radical transformations along racial and ethnic lines—in 2011, for example, more nonwhite children were born than white children for the first time in the country's history, and the United States is projected to be a majority-minority nation in less than three decades. Polls in recent years illustrate a growing segment of Americans who appear to have lost faith in the American system as well. For almost the entirety of the last decade, two-thirds or more of Americans have described themselves as dissatisfied with the way things are going. Levels of mistrust in institutions have also shot up in recent years. According to one 2011 poll, roughly 80 percent of Americans have less trust in politics, the government, big business, and corporations than they did ten or fifteen years ago. Andrew Kohut, the longtime pollster and founding director of the Pew Research Center, now refers to this wide-ranging loss of faith as "chronic disillusionment." The examples of such rampant cynicism go on. Today's America, in short, is not a society confident in the bonds that unite it.

At the same time, civics education—the time and effort we spend teaching our children what it means to be an American—has undergone a deep decline. This means that just as America's adults are losing faith in the American system, its children are not being equipped with the tools and the knowledge to undermine that skepticism. To take just one example, in a 2006 nationally administered civics test, more than two-thirds of students scored below even the minimal levels of proficiency—not even a third of eighth graders could identify the purpose of the Declaration of Independence, for example, and less than a fifth of twelfth graders could answer how citizen participation benefits democracy. When the same test was administered in 2010, the performance of the nation's twelfth graders actually declined from its 2006 low.

Given the time that the nation's students now spend learning civics, such poor results are no wonder, as former Florida Democratic senator Bob Graham has pointed out. By the time Graham graduated from high school in 1955, for example, he had spent three years studying civics in accordance with national standards; when his granddaughter graduated in 2009, she had spent only one semester learning about civics. "In less than sixty years," laments Graham, "American students lost 450 school days of civics instruction."

The case for civic affirmation, then, has never been easier to make, both in our schools and outside of them. And it is in conjunction with this need that we should view the modern, exclusionary Anti-Sharia movement. Each time a member of the movement decries the all-powerful threat of the Muslim Brotherhood, or the dangers of Islamic "civilization jihad," we should call to mind the clear national need for a stronger, more inclusive sense of self.

—◦—

Attack. Lastly is the need to attack episodes of hysteria where it matters—not simply using the language of the American Creed, but also marshaling all the available facts to demonstrate that the movement's accusations are patently false. To return to McCarthyism, this would have meant correcting each of McCarthy's wild assertions, placing them in context, and illustrating how quickly and conveniently the details of his accusations changed. It would have required the courage to stand up to McCarthy and his supporters, early and often, to reveal what the actual facts were.

As with civic affirmation, however, attacking is not a cure-all. There were some—a precious few—who did indeed take this approach to McCarthy and to his acolytes, and they did not stop the movement from arising, nor did they stop McCarthy from continuing to level his baseless charges. But if such efforts were more widespread, they would have made it more difficult for McCarthy to continue to generate his characteristically unruly accusations for so long. Perhaps more importantly, a concerted effort to correct McCarthy's so-called facts would have increased the skepticism of his audience, limiting his ability to win new supporters.

In looking for a model of this type of factual assault, we can do no better than to turn to Louis F. Post, the assistant secretary of labor, who, three decades before McCarthyism arose, used precisely this method to turn Americans against Attorney General A. Mitchell Palmer, and who helped to end the period of anti-Bolshevik hysteria as a result.

— ◆ —

I described in chapter 4 how Louis F. Post, the elderly civil servant, lawyer, and former journalist, testified before Congress in the last days of the anti-Bolshevik hysteria, questioning the tactics of A. Mitchell Palmer and the assumptions upon which the hysteria was based. I quoted newspapers that described his performance in May of 1920 as flaying the attorney general, and as an old man "full of fight." But I did not describe his methods, nor did I delve into his precise words before a skeptical Congress and an angry nation. Indeed, he was brought before the very House Rules Committee that was considering impeaching him from his post as assistant secretary of labor, a committee whose members viewed his unwillingness to deport hundreds of immigrant radicals rounded up in the Palmer raids as nothing less than treason. I have saved this exposition for the end.

For ultimately, Louis Post is one of the heroes of this book, a quiet, calm, and collected public servant who deeply opposed the tactics of A. Mitchell Palmer and what he would later call the "deportation delirium of 1920," and who stood up to protect the rights of the many accused of radicalism, in spite of the prevailing national mood. When questioned by a hostile Congress, he defended both his actions and the greater principles upon which they were based, helping to change the disposition of that great deliberative body, and the American public as well. It was not Post alone who turned the tide against the hysteria, but he played a major role. Louis Post's performance before Congress thus offers deep and lasting lessons about how best to confront hysteria.

The transcript of Post's testimony, which commenced the Friday morning of May 7, 1920, and lasted throughout the following Saturday afternoon, stands at just over two hundred pages, and contains the type of back-and-forth one would expect of an extremely antagonistic hearing—congressmen reading highly charged press statements, pulling obscure facts from reports prepared by their aides, attempting anything and everything that would goad Post into making a statement that would turn the nation against him, a slip-up that would show him to be the communist-lover everyone suspected he was. And in that sense, the first lesson of Post's testimony lies in what he did not say. Even while defending the rights of the accused immigrants, many of whom he had failed to deport as acting secretary of labor, and many of whom did harbor radical beliefs, he did not give his enemies any one-liners that they could use against him. Nor did he utter any incriminating quotes the newspapers could reduce to a headline or a caption. Instead he used technical, lawyerly language, relying only on the facts he knew to be true and pointing out the facts he did not, sticking to the details of each deportation case and refusing to be goaded off topic. In one hostile exchange, for example, Post simply refused to be drawn into an argument where no real facts existed. Here, for example, is Philip Campbell, Republican of Kansas and chairman of the House Rules Committee, asking for Post's stand on the worst of all symbolic threats: the radical intellectual.

Rep. Campbell: As a matter of fact, Mr. Post, don't you think these high-brow anarchists, these college professors, these Harvard and Yale anarchists . . . who weep in articles about the laboring man but never labored a day in their lives . . . are more dangerous than the poor ignorant fellow who is willing to take his hatchet and go out and break up the government or any of its representatives that he can reach—don't you think that the high brow, the high-brow philosophical anarchist, is the more dangerous of the two?

Mr. Post: I have no opinion about that. . . . You of course are using newspaper epithets, Mr. Chairman, and I must ask to be excused from giving an opinion upon mere epithets.

Rep. Campbell: You understand what a high-brow anarchist is; he is the millionaire type of anarchist, the college professor type of anarchist.

Mr. Post: Suppose you give me names; I can answer better if you give names?

Rep. Campbell: I do not think that is necessary.

Mr. Post: I think that is necessary. I am not going to decide against an unknown man because you call him a high-brow anarchist.

And so the exchange went, with Campbell getting nowhere and Post standing his ground, appearing more and more dignified for sticking to the facts, and exposing the chairman's tactics for the baseless posturing that they were.

But Post's reliance on the facts also helped to undermine the dignity of his antagonists in another way, for in so doing Post was able to place a human face on each accusation. These weren't simply high- or low-brow anarchists who were being accused of sabotaging the country and threatened with deportation, as Campbell insisted, these were real men and women with families and careers and ties to their communities. And at each available moment Post tried to point that out. "I was not keen, in the cases of persons who had good moral character, and who had children born here who were Americans citizens," declared Post, "to break up their families, send them away, and turn their wives and children upon the community." Added Post, "I think that some humanity should come into the trial of these cases when there is doubt as to the guilt."

Once the humanity of the accused had been established, any reservations about their actual guilt helped to swing their ultimate status the other way—it no longer seemed "soft" to empathize with the accused; it seemed humane. In one case, for example, Post described a man with clear radical beliefs, one who had published a paper advocating the violent overthrow of the government and its replacement with representatives of the working class. Based on these facts alone, members of the media and of Congress were furious with Post—here the evidence suggested an enemy of constitutional democracy, of capitalism itself. And yet here was also a man that Post had allowed to remain in the United States, whose warrant for deportation Post himself had cancelled. How could Post stand by his actions?

The man's name was Enrique Flores Magon, and Post began the defense of his decision by providing details about Magon's life. Magon was married to a woman named Teresa. Together they had six children—the oldest, Esperanya, was fifteen years old, and the youngest, Enrique Jr., was only three. The family lived together in a house at 1120 East 28th Street in Los Angeles. A staunch opponent of the corrupt Mexican government, Magon had been granted political asylum in the United States, as his opposition to the government in his home country had placed his life in danger. In context, Post explained, Magon's radicalism only pertained to Mexico—the articles he had published, the statements he had made, were never about the United States, the country that had saved him, but about his home government in Mexico. The evidence that incriminated him as a radical, Post thus asserted, proved only that he harbored violent views toward the Mexican government. And given that no one could prove that Magon felt the same way about the US government—not the media, not the government, not A. Mitchell Palmer himself—it was only humane to refrain from deporting him back to Mexico, where he would certainly face death. "It was a question of doubt," explained Post, "and the man to whom that doubt attached had six American children dependent upon him, American citizens, in this country."

Post's defense of the Magon case might not have won over all the congressmen on the committee—Magon, after all, still held radical beliefs—but Post's testimony provided nuance to a case where, at least in the public's eye, there were only anti-communist slurs. Post's defense thus gave onlookers a sense of the gravity of the hysteria—that accusations led to deportations and deportations ruined lives. How many more Magons were there, whose cases were far from clear-cut? Where reasonable arbiters of the facts might disagree? How many more instances existed where the evidence was far from complete?

Once it was clear that each case was far from black and white, far from the Manichean world of good versus evil that the hysteria portrayed, it wasn't too much of a mental leap to conclude that the hysteria itself was unfounded. And from there that the so-called conspiracy against the United States was far from all-powerful, but was rather nothing more than a radical ideology shared, in varying degrees, by fallible and flawed individuals, who combined to form a movement with much less sway than many in the public feared. Post's introduction of humanity first, and then nuance, into the debate would provide the key to unraveling the hysteria.

But Post didn't just stop there. Once the details of each case had been laid bare, and the humanity of each accused individual displayed, Post would reaffirm his decisions by appealing directly to American values, using the powerful language of the American Creed—this was civic affirmation at its best. "Now I shall quote one clause in article 5—the Fifth Amendment of the Constitution—that 'no person shall be deprived of life, liberty, or property without due process of law,'" he declared. His treatment of the men and women accused of being radicals and threatened with deportation was in accordance with nothing less than those same standards. "If I am to be impeached for that, Mr. Chairman," Post added indignantly, "I am willing to be impeached."

And with that the hearings would soon end, Post's adversaries now in disarray and the actions and outlook of the elderly assistant secretary of labor clearly vindicated, and so clearly worthy of admiration. Accounts of Post's performance would win him new acolytes by the day, just as support for A. Mitchell Palmer began to weaken. By insisting that the proponents of the hysteria stick to the facts, and by using the language of the American Creed, Post was able to deal a decisive blow to the anti-Bolshevik movement, helping the public to decompose each wild accusation, piece by unfounded piece.

And so what, in the end, are we to make of Post's example, and of the wider story of political hysteria in the United States? The first answer lies in the deep and abiding struggle that marks American identity—a struggle that has required, at its most trying moments, men and women like Post to stand up before the nation, vulnerable and alone, to remind its citizens and elected officials of the values embodied in America's laws and institutions. Values that dictate that no one—no matter his or her color or creed, is to be excluded—and that there is strength in diversity. Though this country has not always been faithful to such ideals, America's evolution has been defined by a singular commitment to inclusion, by an evolving faith that, at a fundamental level, every individual is created equal, and entitled the same unalienable rights.

The second lesson of this story is the importance of all segments of society struggling to forge a national identity together—that this is not a game that should be left to only the most vocal, or only to those with much to lose. Rather, each one of us has a role to play; we need not be a high-ranking government official, or be sitting in front of a congressional panel, to make a difference. What it means to be an American is affirmed and reaffirmed in our daily interactions, both in our homes and outside of them—in discussions with family and friends, in restaurants and around the dinner table. We need merely assert our fundamental values, frequently and often, and to defend them at every opportunity, attacking, affirming, and ultimately accepting movements of hysteria for what they are, all while relying on the language and ideals of the American Creed. For the more united we are in our national sense of self, and the more inclusive that sense of self is, the harder it will be for hysteria to take root, and to thrive.

As for the actual danger each episode arose to confront, the lesson is just as clear. We should approach supposed threats to our way of life with deep skepticism, just as we should remain wary of figures who seek to capitalize upon such risks—the Weeds and the Palmers and the McCarthys of this world. During the course of our two-hundred-plus years of existence, this country has faced numerous perils, imagined and real, and yet American society and its government remains. For as Thomas Jefferson once wisely declared, "If there be any among us who would wish to dissolve this Union or to change its republican form, let them stand undisturbed as monuments of the safety with which error of opinion may be tolerated where reason is left free to combat it." The best way to protect the freedoms we cherish, our third president asserted, is to leave them untouched—not just in times of normalcy, but in periods of crisis as well.

Acknowledgments

This book is dedicated to the memory of my grandfather, Millard Cass, who taught me what it means to be an American, and to my parents, who first taught me to cherish books, and inspired me to write this one.

The preceding pages would not have come into being without the love and support of countless others, and the first among them is my wife, Claudia, whose enduring patience gave me the time and space to write this book (she is, and always has been, my best editor). Any success this book has, I owe directly to her.

Next in line comes Jack Balkin who, along with countless members of the faculty of Yale Law School, encouraged me to spend my time writing about political hysteria instead of undertaking more traditional law school activities (such as studying). I relied heavily on Professor Balkin's unparalleled understanding of American history, and am deeply grateful for the time he devoted.

My agent, Deirdre Mullane, also helped to shape this project from its earliest conception. Both Deirdre and my editor, Keith Wallman, took a chance on a first-time author, and I am profoundly indebted to both of them. I am also grateful to Sarah Yager for the relentless fact-checking abilities she applied to my research, and for the whole team at Lyons Press, who helped turn this book into a physical reality and who helped get it into the hands of readers.

I also had support from a first-rate team of friends, editors, and mentors, from Moisés Naím and Byron Tau, to Robert Schlesinger, Jordan Chandler Hirsch, and Corinna Barsan, to name just a few. Moisés's example and guidance, in particular, gave me the confidence to continue working on this project when I could have moved on to other, easier endeavors. These friends, along with many others, provided the intellectual and moral encouragement that allowed me to believe in this project, and challenged me to improve it.

Lastly, to all my friends and family, I owe this book and much more to your constant support.

Notes

CHAPTER 1

1. . . . something much deeper was at work.: *Murray v. Geithner*, 763 F. Supp. 2d 860 (E.D. Mich. 2011).

1. . . . are unwittingly complicit in it.": See "Lawsuit Filed Against Treasury Dept: Stop AIG Bailout Financing Terrorism," Thomas More Law Center, December 15, 2008, www.thomasmore.org/news/lawsuit-filed-against-treasury-dept-stop-aig-bailout-financing-terrorism.

2. . . . began echoing versions of Beck's accusations.: Massimo Calabresi, "Why Harold Koh Is Dividing the GOP," *Time*, April 24, 2009, http://content.time.com/time/politics/article/0,8599,1893857,00.html#ixzz2tJMHlnSs.

2. . . . world's second-largest religion.: States that have banned Sharia include North Carolina, Arizona, Kansas, Louisiana, Oklahoma, South Dakota, Tennessee, Florida, and Alabama. This list excludes states such as Missouri, in which a Sharia law ban made its way through the state legislature but was vetoed by Governor Jay Nixon in 2013.

3. . . . that they start away in fear.: Samuel F. B. Morse, *Foreign Conspiracy Against the Liberties of the United States*, seventh edition (New York: American and Foreign Christian Union, 1855), 129.

3. . . . establishment of an absolute despotism.: "Populist Party: The Omaha Platform," 1892, historymatters.gmu.edu/d/5361.

3. . . . conspirators are banking on it.: Andrew C. McCarthy, *The Grand Jihad* (New York: Encounter Books, 2010), 330. Note that I've replaced "Grand Jihad" with "conspirators" in the quote above to remove any movement-specific identifiable features and in order to fully emphasize my point.

5. . . . international dimensions of this analysis to others.: Note I use the term "hysteria" fully aware of the risks in doing so—for the term is a slippery one, equally fitted for dismissal as for careful analysis. Despite my best attempts, however, I have not been able to come up with a term that is equally descriptive or equally compelling.

7. . . . human beings' most animalistic desires.: See generally Gustave Le Bon, *The Crowd: A Study of the Popular Mind*, 1895 (Kitchener: Batoche Books, 2001).

7. . . . characteristics of our epoch of transition.": Ibid., 8.

8. . . . intrigued him as much as it stung.: As Hofstadter student Eric Foner would remember, Hofstadter found it "hard to resist the conclusion that Stevenson's smashing defeat was . . . a repudiation by plebiscite of American intellectuals and of intellect itself." See Sam Tanenhaus, "The Education of Richard Hofstadter," *New York Times*, August 6, 2006, www.nytimes.com/2006/08/06/books/review/06tanenhaus.html?pagewanted=all&_r=0.

9.... movements outlined in the pages to come.: See Joseph R. Gusfield, *Symbolic Crusade: Status Politics and the American Temperance Movement* (Urbana: University of Illinois Press, 1986), 14.

9.... that characterized periods like McCarthyism.: See generally Richard Hofstadter, *The Paranoid Style in American Politics* (New York: Vintage, 2008), 52 *et seq.*

9.... in a book by that same name.: Note that Hofstadter would likely disagree with my analysis of his work, as he explicitly attempted to resist setting forth a "psychological" theory in *The Paranoid Style*. Nevertheless, I do not think his actual analysis met his ambitions.

9.... Nothing but complete victory will do.": Hofstadter, 31.

10.... mob mentality among the declining classes.: For simplicity's sake, I refer to other scholars' account of political hysteria with my terminology, even though the precise wording might have been foreign to them.

10.... analyzed as if they had a collective mind.: Quoted in Maggie Koerth-Baker, "Crowds Are Not People, My Friend," *New York Times Magazine*, December 18, 2012, www.nytimes.com/2012/12/23/magazine/crowds-are-not-people-my-friend.html?smid=tw-nytimes&pagewanted=all&_r=0.

12.... visiting the White House to go back to Africa.: Samuel P. Huntington, *Who Are We? The Challenges to America's National Identity* (New York: Simon & Schuster, 2004), 55, citing John Patrick Doggins, *On Hallowed Ground: Abraham Lincoln and the Foundations of American History* (New Haven: Yale University Press, 2000), 175–76.

13.... body of principles, to a great hope.": Rogers Smith, "The 'American Creed' and American Identity," *Western Political Quarterly* (1998), 225.

14.... by the sociologist Gunnar Myrdal in the 1940s.: See Gunnar Myrdal, *An American Dilemma: The Negro Problem and Modern Democracy* (New York: Harper, 1944).

15.... process of cultural and social change.": Gusfield, 9.

18.... supported the senator's witch hunts.: David M. Oshinsky, *A Conspiracy So Immense: The World of Joe McCarthy* (New York: The Free Press, 1983), 356.

19.... it just "takes a little time.": Quoted in Merle Miller, *Plain Speaking: An Oral Autobiography of Harry S. Truman* (New York: Berkeley Medallion Books, 1974).

CHAPTER 2

22.... are yet stigmatized continually.": Jedidiah Morse, Fast Day Sermon, May 9, 1798.

22.... threatens to overwhelm the world.": Ibid.

22.... members of the *Illuminati* as well.: Paine's own *The Age of Reason*, a bestseller in its day, "proceeded from the fountain head of *Illumination*," said Morse. Morse, Fast Day Sermon, 1798.

23.... for an academic in those days.: Vernon Stauffer, *New England and the Bavarian Illuminati* (New York: Columbia University Press, 1918), 200, Fn. 2.

23.... Masonic lodges he had been exposed to.: Ibid., 201, Fn. 2.

24.... in the University of Ingolstadt, and abolished in 1786.: Ibid., 202–3, quoting John Robison, *Proofs of A Conspiracy Against All the Religions and Governments of Europe* (Philadelphia: 1798).

24.... of one indistinguishable chaotic mass.": Ibid., 209, citing Robison 209 *et seq.*

24. . . . open to the public to wield significant influence.: Ibid., 150.

25. . . . mutual associations and forgotten bylaws.: Ibid., 183 *et seq.*

25. . . . secret machinery for [his] purpose.": Thomas Jefferson, *Letter to Bishop James Madison,* January 31, 1800.

25. . . . implications on the other side of the Atlantic.: Stauffer, 210, citing Robison at 201.

26. . . . husbands," according to one Morse biographer.: Richard J. Moss, *The Life of Jedidiah Morse: A Station of Peculiar Exposure* (Knoxville: University of Tennessee Press, 1995), 70.

26. . . . sweeping into his town, Morse once lamented.: Ibid., 71, citing Morse's "Untitled Sermon" of January 6, 1799.

26. . . . political and social "defects" emerged.: James K. Morse, *Jedidiah Morse, A Champion of New England Orthodoxy,* 1939 (in *American Historical Review,* Vol. 45 (1940), 903–4), cited in Ralph Brown, *The American Geographies of Jedidiah Morse,* Annals of the Association of American Geographers, Vol. 31, no. 3 (September 1941), 214, Fn. 97.

26. . . . lost "their habits of obedience.": Moss, 62, quoting Morse's *1789 American Geography,* 113–14, 117.

27. . . . even begun to take shape.: Moss, 46.

27. . . . the present century had produced.": Stauffer, 233, citing Morse in *Independent Chronicle,* June 14, 1798.

28. . . . ordinary course of judicial proceedings.": George Washington's Annual Message to Congress, November 19, 1794.

28. . . . "ought to be read by every American.": Morse, Fast Day Sermon, 24.

29. . . . extremely unpleasant, if not unsafe.": Stauffer, 240.

29. . . . set on the destruction of the world.: Ibid., 244.

29. . . . converts to these wretched doctrines.": Timothy Dwight, *Duty of Americans, At the Present Crisis* (1798), 13.

29. . . . "been members of this society.": Ibid., 13.

29. . . . Others would soon follow suit.: See Stauffer, 253–54.

30. . . . the book was not entirely unreasonable.: Ibid., 255 *et seq.* for an analysis of Morse's articles. The articles appeared in the *Massachusetts Mercury* beginning on August 10, and continuing on the 14th, 17th, 21st, 28th, and 31st of that month.

30. . . . existence of the Illuminati was growing.: Ibid., 259, Fn. 3.

32. . . . claimed to have unearthed.: Even on the so-called facts the two authors diverged. But as Barruel wrote in the third volume of his *Memoirs,* which he penned after coming across Robison's work, "It will be perceived that we are not to be put in competition with each other; Mr. Robison taking a general view while I have attempted to descend into the particulars: as to the substance we agree." Ibid., 228.

33. . . . they are still significantly numerous.": Ibid., quoting Barruel at 226–27.

33. . . . earn the moniker "Geography Morse.": Moss, ix. Indeed, Morse is described as "the Father of American Geography" to this day. Note, also, that at the time "geography" encompassed what academics today might also call "sociology" or "culture studies."

34. . . . and spies of France in this country?": Jedidiah Morse, Thanksgiving Day Sermon, May 9, 1798, Appendix.

35. . . . under the guardianship of France?": Ibid., Appendix Note (F.).

35. . . . vigor reserved for the United States.: Ibid.

35. . . . printed in a matter of months.: William Sprague, *The Life of Jedidiah Morse, D.D.* (New York: Anson D.F. Randolph, 1874), 233.

35. . . . seventy-five-page text in six successive editions.: Ibid., 233.

36. . . . "an eighteenth-century version of a media event.": Moss, 76.

36. . . . other side of the Atlantic still be alarmed?: *Columbian Centinel and Massachusetts Federalist*, January 5, 1799. Cited in Stauffer at 279. Contents of the article were soon published in other papers.

36. . . . criminality or even of error.": *Columbian Centinel and Massachusetts Federalist*, January 19, 1799. Cited in Stauffer at 279.

36. . . . Boston to New York to Philadelphia.: Curiously, little is recorded in the South, though as we will see, plenty of people in the South, especially some of its most prominent citizens, subscribed to Morse's view of the Illuminati.

36. . . . copies to send to their constituents.": Sprague, 232.

36. . . . own printers republish it.: Ibid., 232–33.

36. . . . and Morse's longtime pen pal.: Ibid., 237.

36. . . . useful, if spread through the community.": Ibid., 232.

37. . . . mischief and misery in other countries.": John Adams, March 6, 1799, *Proclamation Recommending A National Day of Humiliation, Fasting, and Prayer.*

38. . . . compelled to sound the alarm.": Jedidiah Morse, Fast Day Sermon, April 25, 1799.

38. . . . by the Grand Orient of France.": Ibid.

39. . . . we must expect soon to fall.": Ibid.

40. . . . What do these things portend?": Moss, 68.

41. . . . the Jeffersonian challenge seemed to be a rebellion.": Ibid., 61.

41. . . . "I have disturbed a hornet's nest.": Stauffer, 303.

41. . . . Morse's most detailed accusations yet.: Ibid., 302, Fn. 1.

41. . . . "enemy to bigotry" and "a real clergyman.": For a general overview of these debates in the press, see Ibid., 304 *et seq.*

41. . . . America was now directly in its snares.: Ibid., 308–9.

42. . . . described as the "bête noire" of Morse.: William Bentley, "Jedidiah Morse and the Yale Library," *Yale University Library Gazette*, Vol. 13, no. 3 (January 1939), 80.

42. . . . most useful and important to me.": See Brown, 155–56.

42. . . . and a lifelong enemy of Morse.: Bentley, 80.

42. . . . no fistfights or punches to the jaw.: There are reasons to believe that Bentley thought Morse was responsible for the fact that Bentley's father's debt collectors had come after him, but the details surrounding this suspicion are unclear. See Stauffer 318, citing Bentley, *Diary*, Vol. iv, 241 *et seq.*

42. . . . destined to bring controversy to the clergy.: Moss, 57.

43. . . . order still exists since several years.": Bentley, 79.

44. . . . most esteemed advisor told him so.: *American Mercury*, September 26, 1799, passages of which are quoted in full in Bentley, 78–79.

44. . . . wrote Ebeling to Morse, Robison was he.: *The Bee*, November 20, 1799, cited in Stauffer at 316.

45. . . . But they were not identical.: The text of the real letter between Ebeling and Morse reads as follows: "As to illuminism, we heartily laugh at it. So our princes, except always

some few catholic governments. Wieshaupt is living peaceably under the protection
of the Duke of Gotha. Certainly not a revolutionary or irreligious prince. He lately
summoned all his adversaries, to prove before any court of justice especially in *Bavaria
& Gotha*, that the illuminati ever aimed at the overthrow of religion & state; at any
violent revolution. He will submit to the severest punishment that any law may inflict
upon him. This he published in April. He has not been brought to trial nor even
contradicted by any body till this day,—I cannot believe, and no body does, that the
order still exists since several years. . . . You will excuse that my love to America as well
as to my country and to every lawful government & to true christianity made me write
this." Reprinted in Bentley, 79–80.

46. . . . and printed at my request.: The letter is reprinted in full in Bentley, 80. See also
Sprague, 239–40.

46. . . . again capture the national spotlight.: Among Morse's many projects was the
creation of *The Panoplist*, one of the first special interest periodicals in American history.
According to one Morse biographer, "The magazine assumed a conspiracy existed
against true religion and decency, and apparently so did many readers; the monthly
became one of the most widely read publications in New England." Moss, 89.

CHAPTER 3

49. . . . "murder" while he was being dragged away.: Note that accounts of this story vary
widely. I have drawn primarily on the accounts told by Ronald P. Formisano and
Kathleen Smith Kutolowski in "Antimasonry and Masonry: The Genesis of Protest,
1826-1827," *American Quarterly*, Vol. 29, no. 2 (Summer 1977), 139–65. I have also
drawn on the admittedly biased account (in favor of the Masons) in Robert Morris's
William Morgan or Political Anti-Masonry, Its Rise, Growth and Decadence (New York:
Robert Macoy Masonic Publisher, 1883).

50. . . . before being hanged in Havana in 1838.: See Morris, 71–72.

51. . . . and extreme misery my body.": Kathleen Smith Kutolowski, "Antimasonry
Reexamined: Social Bases of the Grass-Roots Party," *Journal of American History*,
Vol. 71, no. 2 (September 1984), 271, citing, William Morgan to unknown,
November 28, 1824, individual accession no. 11289, Manuscripts and Special
Collections (New York State Library, Albany).

52. . . . especially in New York State.: In 1800, for example, Masonry had 11 Grand
Lodges, 347 subordinate lodges, and 16,000 members in the US. By 1820, New York
itself counted almost 300 lodges and 15,000 members. In the following five years,
New York would add an additional 150 lodges and 5,000 members. Formisano and
Kutolowski, 143.

52. . . . in New York were occupied by Masons.: Ibid., 144.

52. . . . in harm's way in the weeks to come.: See Morris, 74–75.

52. . . . forward in a kind of frenzy.": Formisano and Kutolowski, 147.

53. . . . were clearly to blame.": Note that others have drawn the opposite conclusion. One
historian, for example, noted that "considerable preparations had been made" to put out
the fire, including the presence of water barrels, in a sign "that Miller and his friends

were at the bottom of the matter . . . to awaken interest and compassion for them in the community." Morris, 113–14.

56. . . . government were in on the kidnapping too.: William L. Stone, *Letters on Masonry and Anti-Masonry, Addressed to the Honorable John Quincy Adams* (New York: O. Halstead, 1832), 172.

58. . . . and liberties are destined to endure.: Ibid., 201.

59. . . . upstate New York was really all about.: Paul Goodman, *Towards A Christian Republic: Antimasonry and the Great Transition in New England, 1826–1836* (New York: Oxford University Press, 1988), 36.

59. . . . the highest rates of economic development.: Between 1827 and 1833, for example, the party's candidates won every county office, averaging 69 percent of the vote. See Kutolowski, "Antimasonry Reexamined," 270.

59. . . . formed the movement's weakest base.: Ibid., 275.

59. . . . over 70 percent of the time between 1827 and 1833.: Ibid., 281.

60. . . . Freemasons, for any offices whatever.": Stone, 213.

61. . . . thought had clear national potential.: See Glyndon G. Van Deusen, "Thurlow Weed in Rochester" in *Rochester History*, eds. Dexter Perkins and Black McKelvey, Vol. 2, no. 2, April 1940.

61. . . . of 1827 were an astounding success.: Said one prominent Anti-Mason at the time, the election "astonished all—even the Antimasons themselves—and opened the eyes of politicians to the growing power of the new party." See Charles McCarthy, *The Antimasonic Party: A Study of Political Antimasonry in the United States, 1827–1840* (Washington: Government Printing Office, 1903), 374.

62. . . . populist furor and public controversy.: Formisano and Kutolowski, 148.

62. . . . for both Weed and his new party.: McCarthy, 381.

63. . . . enforcement of justice into a public spectacle.: Thurlow Weed, *Autobiography of Thurlow Weed* (Boston: Houghton Mifflin, 1883), 259.

64. . . . Bruce's trial and began packing his bags.: Ibid., 259.

65. . . . extent for political material and methods.": McCarthy, 426.

65. . . . operations of the Antimasonic party.": William Seward, *Autobiography of William H. Seward, from 1801 to 1834* (New York: D. Appleton and Co., 1877), 179.

65. . . . smooth by becoming an Anti-Mason.": Harriet Weed, ed., *Life of Thurlow Weed* (Boston: Houghton Mifflin and Co., 1884), I, 229–325, cited in Lorman Ratner, *Antimasonry: The Crusade and the Party* (Englewood Cliffs, NJ: Prentice-Hall, 1969), 74.

66. . . . Ohio, Maryland, and Michigan in attendance.: McCarthy, 398.

68. . . . sympathies" was an impossibly large group.: McCarthy, 402.

68. . . . Anti-Masonic Party was rotting from within.: *Albany Argus,* February 21, 1831, quoted in McCarthy at 409.

68. . . . Jefferson himself as his political heir.: Jefferson even identified in Wirt a man who would allow "this government (the idol of my soul) [to] continue in good hands." Goodman, 30–31.

68. . . . Jefferson had once assured him.: Ibid.

68. . . . I had attributed to our countrymen.": John P. Kennedy, *Memoirs of the Life of William Wirt*, Vol. II (Philadelphia: Lea and Blanchard, 1854), 323–24, cited in Goodman at 31.

68. . . . crept into and poisoned every public body.": William Wirt, *Letters of the British Spy*, tenth edition (New York: J. & J. Harper, 1832) 192–94, cited in Goodman at 32.

69. . . . so harmless an institution as Free Masonry.": McCarthy, 534.

69. . . . ceased to utter a word against Masonry.": Jabez D. Hammond, *Political History of New York*, II, 399, cited in McCarthy at 426.

70. . . . and practice from what it was then.": John Crary, *Albany Argus*, August 14, 1832, cited in McCarthy at 417.

70. . . . secret societies, had signally failed.": Harriet Weed, 229–325, cited in Ratner at 74.

70. . . . or two thirds of the craft, became extinct.": McCarthy, 539.

70. . . . beliefs, and many contradictions.: McCarthy, 420.

71. . . . national ambitions for their party.: In Massachusetts, for example, one Anti-Masonic convention even attempted to compile a list of all known Masons in that state's cities and towns, so that the party could keep watch over their sinister plans. In particular, the convention requested that the delegates furnish a "correct list of adhering Masons in their towns, their places of business and occupations . . . the several offices each have held or now hold; their general character for morals, temperance, charity, and [knowledge of] science, especially geometry; what number of indigent persons, widows, and orphans, are known to have been relieved in their town, and to what amount, what good or bad acts are known to have been done by Freemasons in their towns, and whether Freemasonry has tended to restrain or encourage the commission of crime." McCarthy, 519.

CHAPTER 4

73. . . . change the course of history.: Immigration records for Valdinoci indicate that he was seventeen years old in July 1913, when he arrived in Boston from Gambettola, Italy. Charles H. McCormick, *Hopeless Cases: The Hunt for the Red Scare Terrorist Bombers* (Maryland: University Press of America, 2005), 51.

74. . . . twenty pounds of dynamite.: For more details about Valdinoci's actions that night, see Michael Alexander, *Jazz Age Jews* (New Jersey: Princeton University Press, 2001), 70-72.

74. . . . words—they were serious threats.: For a detailed account of Roosevelt and Palmer's actions in the aftermath of the bombing, see Stanley Coben, *A. Mitchell Palmer: Politician* (New York: Columbia University Press, 1963), 205–6. This is, in my view, the most expansive treatment of Palmer's life, and one to which this chapter is greatly indebted.

76. . . . "no one knows where" the general strike would lead.: *Seattle Union Record*, February 4, 1919.

77. . . . *Under which flag do you stand?*: *Seattle Star*, February 5, 1919. Note that I've made slight modifications to the formatting to make these excerpts more readable (what is italicized was also bolded in the original).

77.... assert the strike was flat-out Marxist.: *Washington Post*, February 10, 1919. Quoted in Robert K. Murray, *Red Scare: A Study of National Hysteria, 1919-1920* (New York: McGraw Hill, 1964), 65. Note, also, that Murray's work has formed the basis for much of my analysis.

78.... people in Seattle to show their Americanism.": Murray, 63.

79.... Southern and Eastern Europe, to its shores.: John P. Roche, *The Quest for the Dream*, excerpted in Seymour J. Mandelbaum, ed. *The Social Setting of Intolerance* (Chicago: Scott, Foresman and Company, 1964), 111.

79.... in legislatures across twelve states.: Murray, 18.

80.... where immigrants might never adapt.: Indeed, the term "melting pot" was coined during this period.

81.... restraint, propriety and independence.: States William Siener: "Prohibitionists joined the anti-radical crusade because they feared an alliance among Germans, brewers, and radicals that threatened the country's stability." William H. Siener, "The Red Scare Revisited: Radicals and the Anti-Radical Movement in Buffalo, 1919-1920," *New York History*, Vol. 79, no. 1 (January 1998), 42.

82.... to barter away our inheritance.": Jay Feldman, *Manufacturing Hysteria: A History of Scapegoating, Surveillance, and Secrecy in Modern America* (New York: Pantheon, 2011), 77.

82.... GOVERNMENT," read another in the *Los Angeles Times*.: *New York Times*, March 11, 1919, and *Los Angeles Times*, March 11, 1919. Both quoted in Feldman at 78.

83.... "Further than that I do not care to talk.": Murray, 69.

83.... playing the part of cowardly assassins?": Murray, 70.

84.... construction or deadlier possibilities.": *New York Times*, May 1, 1919, cited in Feldman at 79.

84.... of this new and violent threat.: See Murray, 71–72.

85.... but one who can think war.": Palmer to Wilson, February 24, 1913, in Papers of A. Mitchell Palmer, box 47, Woodrow Wilson Collection, Library of Congress, cited in Robert K. Murray, "The Outer Word and the Inner Light: A Case Study," *Pennsylvania History*, Vol. 36, no. 3 (July 1969), 270.

85.... actually considered himself a friend of labor.: As a US congressman, for example, Palmer had pushed for progressive policies like expanded welfare legislation, lower tariffs to protect the middle class, and pro-labor policies. See Murray, 269.

85.... did not advocate the use of violence.: Coben, 204.

85.... Bolshevist movement is to be held in check.": Coben, 205.

86.... Palmer's reign of terror was about to occur.: States Murray: "The bombing of his own home in June 1919, however, acted as a catalytic agent which finally fused together Palmer's own fears and his intense ambition, and caused him to abandon both his prudence and his caution. There is evidence that beginning in June Palmer began to envision himself as the nation's savior." Murray, 275.

86.... to the countries from which they came.": *New York Times*, June 18, 1919. Quoted in Donald Johnson, "The Political Career of A. Mitchell Palmer," *Pennsylvania History*, Vol. 25, no. 4 (October 1958), 353.

86. . . . foundation of the Red movement.": National Popular Government League, *Report Upon the Illegal Practices of the United States Department of Justice* (Washington, DC, 1920), 64–66.

86. . . . over sixty thousand individuals themselves.: Murray, 193–94.

88. . . . "Lenin and Trotsky are on their way.": Both quoted in Murray at 130 and 129, respectively.

88. . . . would soon bring him national fame.: Murray, 132.

88. . . . "not only unjustifiable, it is unlawful.": Murray, 156.

89. . . . to develop the revolutionary implications.": See Murray, 120.

89. . . . to explain the cause of his inaction.: *Senate Resolution* 213, October 19, 1919.

90. . . . two hundred men and women were detained.: See Coben, 218–21; Murray at 196.

90. . . . I can not disclose at this time.": A. Mitchell Palmer. *Letter to the US Senate in Response to Sen. Res. 213*, November 14, 1919.

91. . . . arrest had been a mistake all along.: Murray, 214–15.

92. . . . burning up the foundations of society.": A. Mitchell Palmer, "The Case Against the 'Reds,'" *Forum* (1920), 174.

92. . . . hairsplitting over infringement of liberty.": *Washington Post*, January 4, 1929, quoted in Murray at 217.

92. . . . throughout the month of January.: Johnson, 360.

92. . . . "his method of carrying them out.": Murray, 218.

93. . . . and releasing hundreds more suspected Bolsheviks.: Coben, 231–33.

94. . . . under guard for the day "just in case.": Murray, 253.

95. . . . Despite his 71 years he seemed 25.": *Spokesman-Review*, May 8, 1920, cited in Louis F. Post, *The Deportations Delirium of Nineteen-Twenty* (Chicago; Charles H. Kerr & Co., 1928), 245.

95. . . . Constitution of the country above all fears.": Post, 250.

95. . . . anarchists of the country," Palmer asserted.: Murray, 256.

96. . . . principles of our Constitutional liberty.": Post, 300–301.

96. . . . in a word, undiluted Americanism.: See Murray, *Outer World and Inner Light*, 287.

96–97. . . . much less converted to the merits of anarchism.": Murray, *Red Scare*, 259.

97. . . . "I glory in it.": Murray, *Outer World and Inner Light*, 256.

97. . . . not long afterward, he was too.: Ibid., 288.

CHAPTER 5

100. . . . employees throughout the course of her testimony.: Hearings Regarding Communist Espionage in the United States, House Committee on Un-American Activities, July 31, 1948; see generally Lauren Kessler, *Clever Girl: Elizabeth Bentley, the Spy Who Ushered In the McCarthy Era* (New York: Harper Collins, 2003) (exact number of employees mentioned on 181–82).

101. . . . leaders of the American Communist Party.: Strictly speaking, the Justice Department moved against the Communist Party USA after Bentley revealed her misdeeds to a federal grand jury the month before. The DOJ waited until July 20, eleven days before Bentley's HUAC testimony, to indict the party's leaders as a way of

seeking cover and avoiding future embarrassment. See Larry Ceplair, *Anti-Communism in Twentieth-Century America: A Critical History* (Santa Barbara: Praeger, 2011), 88.

101. . . . loyalty test or background investigation.: Griffin Fariello, *Red Scare: Memories of the American Inquisition* (New York: W.W. Norton & Co., 1995), 40. See also James L. Gibson, "Political Intolerance and Political Repression During the McCarthy Red Scare," *American Political Science Review*, Vol. 82, no. 2 (June 1988), 514.

102. . . . from his Appleton, Wisconsin, courthouse.: One area in which McCarthy aroused ire was in his supposed tendency to grant "quickie" divorces to friendly Republican politicians. See David M. Oshinsky, *A Conspiracy So Immense: The World of Joe McCarthy* (New York: The Free Press, 1983), 24. Stated one account of his time on the bench: "He tried five cases for every one his colleagues tried; divorce trials were sometimes knocked off in five minutes; manslaughter trials took a little longer. Justice took off her robes and put on a track suit." Jack Anderson and Ronal May, *McCarthy: The Man, The Senator, The "ism"* (Boston: Beacon Press, 1952), 45, cited in Oshinsky at 24.

102. . . . and women than he did on legislating.: See Oshinsky, 56.

102. . . . and whose powers were beyond his control.: As stated by Robert Griffith, "Had the Senator from Wisconsin . . . never become a household word, what people have called 'McCarthyism' would have remained the primary characteristic of American politics during the early 1950s." Robert Griffith, "The Political Context Of McCarthyism," *Review of Politics*, Vol. 33, no. 1 (January 1971), 35.

103. . . . Roosevelt's cabinet members to resign.: Thomas I. Emerson and David M. Helfeld, "Loyalty Among Government Employees," *Yale Law Journal*, Vol. 58, no. 1 (December 1948), 9. In November 1938, for example, Dies demanded the resignation of Secretaries Harold Ickes (Department of the Interior) and Frances Perkins (Department of Labor), among other members of the executive branch.

103. . . . socialism within the United States.: Ibid., 9, Fn. 24.

103. . . . wanted its investigations to continue.: Steuart Henderson Britt and Selden C. Menefree, "Did the Publicity of the Dies Committee in 1938 Influence Public Opinion?" *Public Opinion Quarterly*, Vol. 3, no. 3 (July 1939), 449, citing *Washington Post*, December 11, 1938, Sec. III, 1.

103. . . . apprising the American people of this fact.": Emerson and Helfeld, 10, Fn. 29, citing *New York Times*, October 29, 1939, 27 col. 1.

103. . . . nation's newspapers and on Capitol Hill.: Jay Feldman, *Manufacturing Hysteria: A History of Scapegoating, Surveillance, and Secrecy in Modern America* (New York: Pantheon, 2011), 190.

104. . . . might be operating domestically.: The committee, it turns out, was created on account of the lobbying of Representative Samuel Dickstein of New York, who was principally worried about the anti-Semitic activities of the German American Bundists. Ironically, Dickstein was not deemed "American" enough by other congressmen to actually sit on the committee, as he was foreign-born. See, for example, Vern Countryman's account of the creation of the committee in Vern Countryman, "Clear And Present Danger," *New York Review of Books*, December 5, 1968.

104. . . . than he did fascism or Nazism.: Britt and Menefree, 450.

104. . . . men who had little in common with Dies.: There is a fascinating asymmetry between the perpetrators of the anti-Bolshevik hysteria, explored in the previous chapter, and the anti-communists that preceded, and were soon caught up in, McCarthyism. In the earlier episode, there is a case to be made that the movement was largely formed by white Anglo-Saxon Protestants defending their elite vision of America against Catholics and other ethnic immigrants from Western Europe. In the latter episode, however, it would be men like McCarthy—Irish, Catholic, a perfect foil to the American "WASP"—who were reasserting their vision of America by demonizing a group of elites that, presumably, would have included A. Mitchell Palmer himself.

105. . . . Communist Candidate for US Senator.": Norman Markowitz, "A View from the Left: From the Popular Front to Cold War Liberalism," in Robert Griffith and Athan Theoharis, eds., *The Specter: Original Essays on the Cold War and the Origins of McCarthyism* (New York: New Viewpoints, 1974), 98.

105. . . . bait, hook, line, and sinker.": George Brown Tindall, *The Emergence of the New South, 1913-1945* (Baton Rouge: Louisiana State University Press, 1967), 625.

105. . . . has been with us from the beginning").: *Americans All, Immigrants All*, Promotional Pamphlet, Columbia Broadcasting System, undated (held in Yale University Library).

106. . . . all but five had been founded since 1933.: Arnold M. Rose, "The Causes of Prejudice," in Francis E. Merrill et al., *Social Problems* (New York: Alfred A. Knopf, 1950), 416, cited in Philip Gleason, "Americans All: World War II and the Shaping of American Identity," *Review of Politics*, Vol. 43, no. 4 (October 1981), 499, Fn. 39.

106. . . . promote greater tolerance of diversity.": Gleason, 499–501.

107. . . . and Communism are to their adherents.": See David Holbrook Culbert, *Radio and Foreign Affairs in Thirties America* (Westport: Greenwood Press, 1976), 111; Gleason, 502.

107. . . . as equal partners in American society.": *Common Ground*, Fall 1940, cited in Gleason at 503.

107. . . . Americans had a unique "national identity.": Writes Gleason: during World War II, "the expression 'American identity' came to be used synonymously with 'American character.'" See Gleason, 505.

108. . . . subcommittee for the very same purposes.: Ceplair, 65–66.

108. . . . operating within the United States during the 1940s.: See John Earl Haynes, Harvey Klehr, and Alexander Vassiliev, *Spies: The Rise and Fall of the KGB In America* (New Haven: Yale University Press, 2009), 541.

110. . . . OSS team had come across a torpedo hole.: See Harvey Klehr and Ronald Rodosh, *The Amerasia Spy Case: Prelude to McCarthyism* (Chapel Hill: University of North Carolina Press, 1976), 4 *et seq*.

110. . . . *Amerasia's* employees had done nothing wrong.: Evidence would later indicate that the magazine staff had been approached by Soviet agents, however, and that some were "eager to participate." Harvey Klehr and Ronald Radosh, "Letter to the Editor Concerning American Anti-Communism," *Orbis*, Vol. 41, Issue 2 (Spring 1997), 283.

110. . . . Department of Justice soon dropped the case.: See Klehr and Rodosh, *The Amerasia Spy Case*, 7.

112. . . . coal, auto, electrical, steel, and railroads.: Ceplair, 76.

113. . . . rank and file, but in spite of them.": William R. Tanner and Robert Griffith, "Legislative Politics and 'McCarthyism': The Internal Security Act of 1950," in Griffith and Theoharis, 178.

113. . . . like the American Civil Liberties Union.: See, for example, Mary S. McAuliffe, "The Politics of Civil Liberties: The American Civil Liberties Union During the McCarthy Years," in Griffith and Theoharis, 154.

113. . . . number twenty-one in the national Billboard charts.: David Caute, *The Great Fear: The Anti-Communist Purge Under Truman and Eisenhower* (New York: Simon & Schuster, 1978), 27–28.

113. . . . dictatorship controlled from abroad.": Tanner and Griffith, "Legislative Politics and 'McCarthyism': The Internal Security Act of 1950," in Griffith and Theoharis, 177.

113. . . . thrive on the taxpayers' dollar.": Ibid., 175.

117. . . . Mr. Hiss: I have right here on the Potomac.: Hearings Regarding Communist Espionage in the United States Government, Monday August 16, 1948, United State House of Representatives, Special Subcommittee of the Committee on Un-American Activities, Washington, DC.

118. . . . "upon a solitary twit of a bird.": Allen Weinstein, "The Alger Hiss Case Revisited," *American Scholar*, Vol. 41, no. 1 (Winter 1971–72), 124.

118. . . . record of service to his government.": Robert L. Beisner, *Dean Acheson: A Life in the Cold War* (New York: Oxford University Press, 2006), 288.

119. . . . both him and Hiss kept on rolling.: See generally Richard M. Fried, *Nightmare in Red: The McCarthy Era in Perspective* (New York: Oxford University Press, 1990), 19 *et seq.*

119. . . . *solely* to look for the missing machine.: Ibid., 20–21; Weinstein, 127.

120. . . . espionage rings in the history of the United States.": Bruce Craig, "Politics in the Pumpkin Patch," *Public Historian*, Vol. 12, no. 1 (Winter 1990), 11.

120. . . . before the Committee in its ten-year history.": Lewis Hartshorn, *Alger Hiss, Whittaker Chambers and the Case That Ignited McCarthyism* (Jefferson: McFarland, 2013), 173.

121. . . . to turn my back upon Alger Hiss.": Beisner, 294.

122. . . . courses, according to one friend.: Oshinsky, 12.

123. . . . "It upset him to no end.": Ibid., 14–20.

123. . . . at coconut trees during danger-free joyrides.: Ibid., 32–33. Another example was that when McCarthy claimed his division had suffered heavy casualties, in truth his unit—VMSB-235—had suffered no fatalities and only one injury (a broken arm) in its eight thousand hours in the air. Ibid., 62.

123. . . . was "communistically inclined.": Ibid., 50.

123. . . . he won the election by 5,000 votes.: Writes David Oshinsky: "Poor health and the humiliation [Bob LaFollette] felt in defeat combined to destroy his fragile self-confidence. One morning in 1953 he called his wife Rachel and told her to return

home at once. Before she arrived, Bob took a loaded pistol, put it into his mouth and pulled the trigger. He died instantly. He was fifty-eight." Ibid., 49.

123. . . . his "hustling, whirlwind" style.: Ibid., 55.

124. . . . he simply opined on current events.: Robert Griffith, *The Politics of Fear: Joseph R. McCarthy and the Senate* (Lexington: University Press of Kentucky, 1970), 2.

124. . . . and screwed her on the hostess' bed.": Oshinsky, 56.

124. . . . politician seeking to rise from obscurity.: While McCarthy was certainly looking for an issue to revive his career, there is some evidence that he stumbled into the communist issue that night unintentionally. Advance press releases touting his speaking tour, for example, painted McCarthy as an expert on pensions, but left the issue of communism untouched. Indeed, he arrived at Wheeling with two speeches—one covering housing issues and another covering communism. His host apparently advised him to go with the latter, and thus history was made. See Fried, 121.

125. . . . shaping policy in the State Department.": Griffith, *Politics of Fear*, 49, citing the *Wheeling Intelligencer*, February 10, 1950. Note that the official transcript of the Wheeling speech does not exist, and the only recording of the speech was accidentally taped over by a local radio operator—as such, there is some debate about the exact details of McCarthy's outrageous claims. The evidence, however, appears to indicate that McCarthy used the number 205, though McCarthy would later claim that he had accused only fifty-seven agents of working in the government. See Griffith, at 51; Fried, 123 ("Joe's exact words in Wheeling are lost"). For McCarthy's own account of the speech, see Joe McCarthy, *McCarthyism: The Fight for America* (New York: The Devin Adiar Co., 1952), 9.

125. . . . "Solon Left Commie List in Other Bag.": *Denver Post*, February 10 and 11, 1950, cited in Griffith, *Politics of Fear*, 50, and in Oshinsky, 110.

125. . . . shapers of American foreign policy.": Oshinsky, 110.

127. . . . "seriously jeopardized, if not destroyed.": Ibid., 121–22.

127. . . . "loudmouthed" and "irresponsible.": Ibid., 122.

127. . . . the "boss" of Alger Hiss himself.: Ibid., 136.

128. . . . Red Fifth Column in the United States.": David H. Bennett, *The Party Of Fear: From Nativist Movements to the New Right in American History* (Chapel Hill: University of North Carolina Press, 1988), 298.

128. . . . more than every other senator combined.: Oshinsky, 174.

129. . . . was something rotten in the State Department.": Ibid., 167.

130. . . . communists, the failing Korean War.: Ibid., 197.

130. . . . George Marshall a traitor and a Soviet spy.: Speech delivered by Senator Joseph McCarthy before the Senate on June 14, 1951, *The Congressional Record: Proceedings and Debates of the 82nd Congress, First Session*, Volume 97, Part 5 (May 28, 1951–June 27, 1951), p. 6556 *et seq.*

131. . . . may get some rock-salt in their hides.": Wayne McKinley, "A Study of the American Right: Senator Joe McCarthy and the American Legion," unpublished master's thesis, University of Wisconsin, 1962, 219, cited in Oshinsky, 206.

131. . . . one" innocent man he had accused.: Oshinsky, 230.

131. . . . and we're against Communism.": John B. Oakes, "Report on McCarthy and McCarthyism," *New York Times Magazine*, November 2, 1952.

132. . . . but with just as much to lose.: States one historian: "Poll data indicate that 'lower classes and rural populations' gave him his most fervent following, although there was some correlation between higher socioeconomic status within these lower educational or occupational groups and McCarthyism." Bennett, 313.

132. . . . those opportunities would continue.": Arthur Herman, *Joseph McCarthy: Reexamining the Life and Legacy of America's Most Hated Senator* (New York: The Free Press, 2000), 160.

133. . . . that you have no communists.": Ceplair, 7.

134. . . . harm," boasted Senate majority leader Robert Taft.: Fried, 134.

134. . . . godfather for Robert Kennedy's first child).: Arthur Herman, excerpt of "Joseph McCarthy: Reexaming the Life and Legacy of America's Most Hated Senator," *New York Times*, www.nytimes.com/books/first/h/herman-mccarthy.html.

136. . . . and misdated the Russian Revolution.: See Oshinsky, 255.

136. . . . around the office wasn't going to kill him.": Ibid., 257.

136. . . . reached the stage of public hearings.: Griffith, *Politics of Fear*, 212–13.

136. . . . information to keep his investigations going.: Fried, 134.

136. . . . rising to 50 percent by the end of the year.: See "Chapter 3: Murrow vs. McCarthy" in W. Joseph Campbell, *Getting It Wrong: Ten of the Greatest Misreported Stories in American Journalism* (Berkeley: University of California Press, 2010).

136. . . . "lurking with intent to spy.": Fariello, 40.

136. . . . Nottingham, however, protested the move.: Fried, 34.

137. . . . throughout Hollywood in the process.: See Elizabeth Pontikes, Giacomo Negro, and Hayagreeva Rao, "Stained Red: A Study of Stigma by Association to Blacklisted Artists during the 'Red Scare' in Hollywood, 1945 to 1960," *American Sociological Review*, Vol. 75, no. 3 (June 2010), 456–78. For a quick, though admittedly legal, introduction to the blacklists, see " 'Political' Blacklisting in the Motion Picture Industry: A Sherman Act Violation," *Yale Law Journal*, Vol. 74, no. 3 (January 1965), 567–80.

137. . . . wanted to throw them in jail.: Fariello, 40.

137. . . . in the groin at a press club dinner,: Oshinsky, 180.

137. . . . plagued with "a disease of fear.": Geoffrey R. Stone, "Free Speech in the Age of McCarthy: A Cautionary Tale," *California Law Review*, Vol. 93, no. 5 (October 2005), 1400.

137. . . . people in forty-six languages and dialects.: Oshinsky, 266.

138. . . . since the beginning of time is suspect.": Ibid., 271.

138. . . . American embassy pick up the tab.: Griffith, *Politics of Fear*, 214.

138. . . . by the State Department and fired.: "The Self Inflated Target," *Time*, March 22, 1954, Vol. 63, Issue 12.

138. . . . clowns were hustling about Europe.": Oshinsky, 279.

138. . . . "Cohn and Schine, the Two London Lovers.": Andrea Friedman, "The Smearing of Joe McCarthy: The Lavender Scare, Gossip, and Cold War Politics," *American Quarterly*, Vol. 57, no. 4 (December 2005), 1114.

139. . . . riches, in the United States and beyond.: "The Self Inflated Target."

139. . . . super-secret list of spy suspects.: Griffith, *Politics of Fear*, 216.

139. . . . against McCarthy's own party, too.: Ibid., 220.

140. . . . don't think I could make it without him.": Oshinsky, 438–39.

140. . . . decided that enough was enough.: Ibid., 439.

140. . . . "No," Cohn replied, "that is a promise.": Ibid.

141. . . . every member of McCarthy's subcommittee.: Ibid., 403.

141. . . . you are not fit to wear that uniform.": Bennett, 306.

142. . . . that party whose label he wears.": Griffith, *Politics of Fear*, 273.

142. . . . charges, I make them," he boasted.: Richard Halworth Rovere, *Senator Joe McCarthy* (Berkeley: University of California Press, 1996), 39.

142. . . . his young aide, "as I am.": "The Self Inflated Target."

143. . . . dozen pages of testimony every day.: Oshinsky, 417.

144. . . . have considered him a liability.: Fisher originally accompanied Welch to Washington to help him prepare for the hearings. When Welch learned of his connection to the "subversive" organization, the National Lawyers Guild, he sent him back to Boston.

145. . . . "What did I do?": John P. Diggins, *The Proud Decades: America in War and in Peace, 1941-1960* (New York: W.W. Norton & Co., 1989), 151.

145. . . . in history to be censured by the Senate.: Note that three of these nine senators were censured after McCarthy.

146. . . . McCarthy drank himself to death.: See Fried, 140–42; Oshinsky, 505.

146. . . . expose, and combat this conspiracy.": See *Congressional Record*, 84th Congress, 1st session, 101:1, January 14, 1955, 361, cited Ceplair, 105.

146. . . . threat of domestic communist subversion.: See Fried, 194 ("[B]oth candidates agreed that the danger flowed from Moscow, not some federal agency. . . . Indeed, both candidates did their best to edge away from the McCarthy legacy in 1960.").

147. . . . who once described herself as his beard.: David Wiegand, "This Time, It's Barbara Walters' Turn to Speak," *San Francisco Chronicle*, May 6, 2008.

CHAPTER 6

149. . . . such a person serving in his administration.: For polling data, see "2012 Republican Presidential Nomination," Real Clear Politics, available at http://realclearpolitics.com/epolls/2012/president/us/republican_presidential_nomination-1452.html.

149. . . . American laws in American courts, period.": See Republican Presidential Primary Debate, June 13, 2011, CNN Transcript, available at http://transcripts.cnn.com/TRANSCRIPTS/1106/13/se.02.html.

150. . . . and in the world as we know it.": Scott Shane, "In Islamic Law, Gingrich Sees a Mortal Threat to US," *New York Times*, December 21, 2011, available at www.nytimes.com/2011/12/22/us/politics/in-shariah-gingrich-sees-mortal-threat-to-us.html?pagewanted=all&_r=0.

150. . . . "rejection of Sharia Islam.": William Petroski, "Update: Bachmann Is First to Sign Family Leader's Pro-Marriage Pledge," *Des Moines Register*, July 7, 2011,

http://caucuses.desmoinesregister.com/2011/07/07/update-bachmann-is-first-to-sign-family-leaders-pro-marriage-pledge/.

150. . . . American jurisprudence and our Constitution.": Byron Tau, "2012 Candidates Stake Out Positions on Sharia," *Politico*, April 11, 2011, www.politico.com/blogs/bensmith/0411/2012_candidates_stake_out_positions_on_sharia.html.

150. . . . from women's rights to free speech.: Though I believe such issues to be fascinating and worth discussion, I will not address the broader questions relating to Islam's place in the western world in this chapter—to do so would be to take on a topic much larger than the story of the Anti-Sharia movement alone. For those interested in further reading, however, I recommend a range of authors who have written about the subject at length, including: Andrew March, *Islam and Liberal Citizenship: The Search for an Overlapping Consensus* (New York: Oxford University Press, 2009); Marshall G. S. Hodgson, *The Venture of Islam* (Volumes I–III) (Chicago: University of Chicago Press, 1977); Seyyed Hossein Nasr, *Islam in the Modern World: Challenged by the West, Threatened by Fundamentalism, Keeping Faith with Tradition* (New York: HarperOne, 2011).

151. . . . more than 70 percent of the public's support.: The following states have enacted Sharia bans into law: North Carolina, Arizona, Kansas, Louisiana, Oklahoma, South Dakota, Tennessee, Florida, and Alabama. For more legal background on the bans, see Faiza Patel, Matthew Duss, and Amos Toh, *Foreign Law Bans: Legal Uncertainties and Practical Problems*, The Center for American Progress and the Brennan Center for Justice at New York University School of Law, May 2013, www.americanprogress.org/wp-content/uploads/2013/05/ForeignLawBans-1.pdf.

151. . . . introduced into the United States Congress, with ninety-one co-sponsors.: The bill in question, House Resolution 973, was introduced by Florida Republican Representative Sandy Adams in 2011. While the bill made no reference to Sharia by name, in one article on the necessity of the bill, Rep. Adams placed her bill alongside statewide anti-Sharia efforts as addressing the same concern. See Sandy Adams, "We Need to Keep Foreign Law Out of US Courts," *The Daily Caller*, March 30, 2011, http://dailycaller.com/2011/03/30/we-need-to-keep-foreign-law-out-of-u-s-courts/. The text of the bill itself is available at www.govtrack.us/congress/bills/112/hr973.

151. . . . in the Israeli-occupied West Bank.: Andrea Elliott, "The Man Behind the Anti-Sharia Movement," *New York Times*, July 30, 2011, www.nytimes.com/2011/07/31/us/31shariah.html?pagewanted=all&_r=0.

151. . . . dangers of the world's second-largest religion.: Ibid.

151. . . . the enemy who vowed to destroy America.": Pamela Geller, *Stop The Islamization of America: A Practical Guide to the Resistance* (New York: WND Books, 2001), 180.

152. . . . this is the deception that must be unveiled.": Ibid. ("Moderate Muslims are secular. There is nothing moderate in Islam, and this is the deception that must be unveiled.").

152. . . . "That day I was reborn as an activist.": Brigitte Gabriel, "A Personal Message from Brigitte Gabriel: Save the Date for the 2014 ACT! for America National Conference & Legislative Briefing," January 16, 2014, e-mail.

152. . . . the same opportunities as Gabriel.: As Spencer explained in a January 16, 2014, e-mail to me: "I began to speak out publicly against violent jihad right after 9/11.

9/11 did not change my thinking at all; I've been studying Islam since the early 1980s. However, after 9/11, I first began to do this work publicly."

152. . . . denigrations of the entire religion of Islam.: *Islam Unveiled: Disturbing Questions About the World's Fastest-Growing Faith* (San Francisco: Encounter Books, 2003). Other titles include *Stealth Jihad: How Radical Islam Is Subverting America Without Guns or Bombs* (Washington, DC: Regnery Publishing, 2008).

153. . . . largely untarnished in the post-9/11 world.: See, for example, Joseph Margulies, *What Changed When Everything Changed: 9/11 and the Making of National Identity* (New Haven: Yale University Press, 2013), 125 *et seq.*

153. . . . soon sprouting chapters across the country.: "Backgrounder: ACT! for America," Anti-Defamation League, March 25, 2011, http://archive.adl.org/main_interfaith/act_for_america_gabriel.html#.Us7PgvZQ2Q0.

153. . . . slept with "a crack whore" and was a secret Muslim).: Pamela Geller, "CNN Tells, Sells More Lies About Palin—It's Time to Expose the Truth About Obama," *Atlas Shrugs*, August 1, 2009, http://pamelageller.com/2009/08/cnn-tells-sells-more-lies-about-palin-its-time-to-expose-the-truth-about-obama.html/#sthash.tQO0DLBU.dpuf. See also Pamela Geller, "Report: Obama Said 'I Am a Muslim,'" AmericanThinker.com, June 16, 2010, www.americanthinker.com/articles/2010/06/report_obama_said_i_am_a_musli.html.

153. . . . sentences of twenty years in jail for practicing Islam.: See "SANE Immigration Proposal," February 14, 2007, www.saneworks.us/indexnew.php.

154. . . . dropped below 30 percent for the first time.: See Gallup's presidential tracking numbers, specifically in July 2007, www.gallup.com/poll/116500/presidential-approval-ratings-george-bush.aspx.

154. . . . national identity were beginning to arise.: See "Satisfaction With the United States," Gallup historical tracking index, available online at www.gallup.com/poll/1669/general-mood-country.aspx. Note that the polling data show that beginning in around 2006, general satisfaction levels begin to dip dramatically, at least by historical comparison, ultimately hitting their nadir in October 2008 with only 7 percent expressing a positive outlook about the future of the country.

154. . . . like Spanish, Russian, or Chinese.: Andrea Elliott, "Critics Cost Muslim Educator Her Dream School," *New York Times*, April 28, 2008, www.nytimes.com/2008/04/28/nyregion/28school.html?pagewanted=all&_r=0.

154. . . . convert Christian and Jewish students.: Daniel Pipes, "A Madrassa Grows in Brooklyn," *New York Sun*, April 24, 2007, www.nysun.com/foreign/madrassa-grows-in-brooklyn/53060/.

155. . . . and perhaps groom future radicals.": Alicia Colon, "Madrassa Plan Is Monstrosity," *New York Sun*, May 1, 2007, www.nysun.com/new-york/madrassa-plan-is-monstrosity/53557/.

155. . . . "soft jihad" carried out by Islamists.: Elliott, "Critics Cost Muslim Educator Her Dream School."

155. . . . make the project seem as alien as possible.: Ibid. See also Edith Honan, "Arabic School Opens in New York Amid Controversy," Reuters, September 4, 2007, www.reuters.com/article/domesticNews/idUSN0442469020070904.

155. . . . "PR makeover" to disguise her Islamist agenda.: "Khalil Gibran Principal Almontaser Undergoes PR Makover Switches Clothes and Headcovering in Attempt to disquise Islamist agenda [sic]," *Militant Islam Monitor*, April 16, 2007, www. militantislammonitor.org/article/id/2823.

155. . . . to sue the city and even threatening legal action against Almontaser herself.: Erin Einhorn, "Activists Sue to Open Arab Classroom Books," *New York Daily News*, October 19, 2007; Azi Paybarah, " 'Stop the Madrassa' Says It Has Been Defamed," *New York Observer*, November 27, 2007.

155. . . . every move from her popular blog.: See specifically the Coalition's acknowledgment of Geller's support ("We were also supported in this fight by many well-known blogs such as KesherTalk, Jillosophy and AtlasShrugs amongst many others."). "Our Community Coalition," Stop the Madrassa Coalition website, www. stopthemadrassa.wordpress.com/about/who-is-stop-the-madrassa/.

156. . . . "This must be monitored and stopped.": Brigitte Gabriel, "The Islam Project for Our Public Schools," published on the Stop the Madrassa Coalition website on August 7, 2007, http://stopthemadrassa.wordpress.com/2007/08/07/ from-brigitte-gabriel-the-islam-project-for-our-public-schools/.

156. . . . "America's first Muslim president").: Frank Gaffney, "Stop the Madrassa," *Washington Times*, August 14, 2007, www.washingtontimes.com/news/2007/aug/14/ stop-the-madrassa/.

156. . . . to replicate like a cancer across America.": CNN Your World Today, Transcript, "Hurricane Felix Storms Ashore in Central America; Rawalpindi Blasts Kill at Least 25 People; Court Upholds Death Sentence for 'Chemical Ali,'" September 4, 2007, 12:00 p.m. EST.

156. . . . soon elicited as a result of the Coalition's work.: Almontaser had, for example, courted controversy by describing to one reporter the history of the politically charged Arabic term "intifada," commonly used to depict the wave of Palestinian terror attacks against Israel in the 1980s and early 2000s. Andrea Peyser, "Everyday Terror at 'Intifada' HS," *New York Post*, March 18, 2010, http://nypost.com/2010/03/18/ everyday-terror-at-intifada-hs/.

157. . . . *New York Times*, "that's really just begun.": Elliott, "Critics Cost Muslim Educator Her Dream School."

157. . . . high-profile crackdown on the organization.: "Text of Remarks by President Bush, Treasury Secretary Paul O'Neill and Attorney General John Ashcroft on Freezing the Assets of Groups Allegedly Linked to Hamas," December 4, 2001, www. washingtonpost.com/wp-srv/nation/specials/attacked/transcripts/bushtext_120401. html.

157. . . . to jail on sentences ranging from fifteen to sixty-five years.: *Backgrounder: The Holy Land Foundation for Relief and Development*, The Anti-Defamation League, http:// archive.adl.org/nr/exeres/83323767-981c-4e4d-9b77-70dd604d2d75,db7611a2-02cd-43af-8147-649e26813571,frameless.html.

158. . . . 'sabotaging' its miserable house by their hands.": Mohamed Akram, "An Explanatory Memorandum On the General Strategic Goal for the Group in North America," May 22, 1991, Government Exhibit 003-0085 3:04-CR-240-G in *US*

v Holy Land Foundation, et al., 7, www.txnd.uscourts.gov/judges/hlf2/09-25-08/
Elbarasse%20Search%203.

159. . . . and the real reason behind the list.: Neil MacFarquhar, "Muslim Groups Oppose
a List of 'Co-Conspirators,'" *New York Times*, August 16, 2007 ("Technically, the
prosecution can introduce statements made by any individual or organization named
as an unindicted co-conspirator without such statements being dismissed as hearsay.
Those on the list have not been charged with anything, but they are concerned that the
label of unindicted co-conspirator will forever taint them, particularly if the Holy Land
group is convicted, and that they will have no legal recourse.").

160. . . . the government to introduce hearsay evidence.": Terry Krepel, "WND's
Klein Attacks Mainstream Islamic Organization as 'radical Muslim group,'"
Media Matters, July 27, 2010, http://mediamatters.org/research/2010/07/27/
wnds-klein-attacks-mainstream-islamic-organizat/168345.

162. . . . compared to the US average of 65 percent.: "The World's Muslims: Religion,
Politics and Society," Pew Research Center, April 30, 2013, http://www.pewforum.org/
files/2013/04/worlds-muslims-religion-politics-society-full-report.pdf; Mark Trumbull,
"How US Muslims Are Different: Pew Poll Sheds Light on Global Contrasts,"
Christian Science Monitor, May 1, 2013, www.csmonitor.com/USA/Society/2013/0501/
How-US-Muslims-are-different-Pew-poll-sheds-light-on-global-contrasts.

163. . . . all particulars with Islamic sharia law.": Robert Spencer, *Stealth Jihad: How
Radical Islam Is Subverting America Without Guns or Bombs* (Washington, DC: Regnery
Publishing, 2008), 9–11.

164. . . . and the need to protect our Constitution and country from it.": Elliott, "The Man
Behind the Anti-Sharia Movement."

164. . . . violence in pursuit of institutionalizing Sharia law.: David Yerushalmi and
Mordechai Kedar, "Shari'a and Violence in American Mosques," *Middle East Quarterly*,
Vol. XVIII, no. 3, Summer 2011, 66 ("The survey's findings . . . were that 51 percent of
mosques had texts that either advocated the use of violence in the pursuit of a Shari'a-
based political order or advocated violent jihad as a duty that should be of paramount
importance to a Muslim; 30 percent had only texts that were moderately supportive of
violence like the *Tafsir Ibn Kathir* and *Fiqh as-Sunna*; 19 percent had no violent texts at
all."). *The Middle East Quarterly* is a publication of the Middle East Forum, founded by
Daniel Pipes in Philadelphia in the early 1990s.

164. . . . incubate the Islamic holy war called jihad.": Frank Gaffney, "United Sharia of
America: Survey Shows Most US Mosques Promote Jihad," *Washington Times*, June 7,
2011, www.washingtontimes.com/news/2011/jun/7/united-shariah-of-america/.

164. . . . such rejection was beside the point.: See, for example, Robert Steinback,
" 'Study' of Mosques Reflects Anti-Muslim Bias of Co-Author," Southern
Poverty Law Center, June 13, 2011, http://www.splcenter.org/blog/2011/06/13/
study-of-radicalization-in-mosques-reflects-anti-muslim-bias-of-co-author/.

164. . . . Treasury Department, Deputy Secretary Robert M. Kimmitt.: "Gaffney catapulted
Yerushalmi onto a new platform of influence," explains Andrea Elliott, a Pulitzer-
winning investigative reporter for the *New York Times*. "Their aim seems to have been
to get people in circles of influence to understand Shariah in this totally new frame,

as a totalitarian threat akin to what the United States faced during the Cold War." See "Who's Behind The Movement To Ban Shariah Law? Interview with Andrea Elliott," *National Public Radio*, August 9, 2011, www.npr.org/2011/08/09/139168699/ whos-behind-the-movement-to-ban-shariah-law.

165. . . . "You go to the states.": Elliott, "The Man Behind the Anti-Shariah Movement."

165. . . . state Constitutions"—specifically targeting Sharia law.: Text of the American Laws for American Courts draft bill is available online at http://publicpolicyalliance. org/legislation/american-laws-for-american-courts/. Note that the actual draft law contains "state" in brackets, to allow for individuals to insert their own state's name when adopting the proposal. I have, however, removed the brackets for the purposes of readability.

165. . . . unnecessary in the view of its actual legal aims.: See Patel, Duss, and Toh, 9 *et seq* ("Foreign law is honored in both federal and state courts as long as it does not conflict with public policy. . . . Our courts do not sit in judgment of the laws and values of other countries because we do not want foreign nations to pass judgment on our own. That does not mean, however, that US courts will enforce *all* foreign laws. They will not enforce foreign laws that conflict with public policy of which the US Constitution— and in the case of state courts, the constitution of the relevant state—is surely a part.").

166. . . . the country, as Yerushalmi had once advocated.: See "SANE Immigration Proposal," February 14, 2007, www.saneworks.us/indexnew.php. The draft bill declares that any non-US citizen "who adheres to Shari'a or acts in support of the adherence to Shari'a or who makes any written or oral declaration in support of the adherence to Shari'a" shall be declared as "Alien Enemies under Chapter 3 of Title 50 of the US Code and shall be subject to immediate deportation," in addition to stating that "It shall be a felony punishable by 20 years in prison to knowingly act in furtherance of, or to support the, adherence to Shari'a."

166. . . . measures in nearly two dozen states over the last decade.: See Aaron Fellmeth, "US State Legislation to Limit Use of International and Foreign Law," *American Journal of International Law*, Vol. 106, no. 1 (January 2012).

166. . . . five co-sponsors in the Senate and thirty-four in the House.: Ibid., 107.

167. . . . politically wise to ignore our concerns.": Brigitte Gabriel, "Join ACT for America and Support the Organization," promotional video, uploaded October 8, 2007, www. youtube.com/watch?v=evh8ruYdncU. See also Ben Smith and Byron Tau, "Anti-Islamic Groups Go Mainstream," *Politico*, March 7, 2011, http://www.politico.com/ news/stories/0311/50837.html.

167. . . . organized into 573 chapters across the nation.: See The Southern Poverty Law Center's report on the organization. Ryan Lenz, "Acting Out," *Intelligence Report*, Fall 2011, Issue Number: 143, www.splcenter.org/get-informed/intelligence-report/ browse-all-issues/2011/fall/acting-out.

167. . . . and eventually even some members of Congress.: Wajahat Ali, Eli Clifton, Matthew Duss, Lee Fang, Scott Keyes, and Faiz Shakir, *Fear, Inc.: The Roots of the Islamophobia Network in America*, The Center for American Progress, August 11, 67 ("ACT! pursues a multipronged strategy for building its activist base. The

organization hosts a series of meetings to bring interested activists together and train them with best practices.").

167. . . . could not have leveraged on their own.: Elliott, "The Man Behind the Anti-Shariah Movement."

168. . . . women and children in the name of ideology.: Ron Jenkins, "Okla. lawmakers return Qurans," *USA Today*, October 24, 2007, http://usatoday30.usatoday.com/news/nation/2007-10-24-1123758280_x.htm.

168. . . . generating national headlines in the process.: Jennifer Mock, "17 State Lawmakers Refuse Quran Gifts," *Oklahoman*, October 24, 2007.

168. . . . shortly after refusing the Koran.: Ibid.

168. . . . ban Sharia law in his home state.: See Yaser Ali, "Shariah and Citizenship—How Islamophobia Is Creating a Second-Class Citizenry in America," *California Law Review*, Vol. 100, no. 4 (August 2012), 1062.

168. . . . state voters in the form of a referendum.: H.R.J. Res. 1056, 52d Leg., 2d Sess. (Okla. 2010), www.sos.ok.gov/documents/legislation/52nd/2010/2R/HJ/1056.pdf. The actual text of the measure is as follows: "The Courts provided for in subsection A of this section, when exercising their judicial authority, shall uphold and adhere to the law as provided in the United States Constitution, the Oklahoma Constitution, the United States Code, federal regulations promulgated pursuant thereto, established common law, the Oklahoma Statutes and rules promulgated pursuant thereto, and if necessary the law of another state of the United States provided the law of the other state does not include Sharia Law, in making judicial decisions. The courts shall not look to the legal precepts of other nations or cultures. Specifically, the courts shall not consider international law or Sharia Law. The provisions of this subsection shall apply to all cases before the respective courts including, but not limited to, cases of first impression."

168. . . . and a 41–2 vote in the state's Senate.: "Sharia Law Banned: Oklahoma to Become the First US State to Veto Use of Islamic Code," *Daily Mail*, November 2, 2010, www.dailymail.co.uk/news/article-1325986/Sharia-law-banned-Oklahoma-US-state-veto-Islamic-code.html.

169. . . . "beginning to be cited in a few US courts.": Matt Smith, "Judge Blocks Oklahoma's Ban on Islamic Law," CNN.com, November 8, 2010, www.cnn.com/2010/POLITICS/11/08/oklahoma.islamic.law/.

169. . . . more than 70 percent of the electorate voted to ban Sharia law.: "Sharia Law Banned: Oklahoma to Become the First US State to Veto Use of Islamic Code."

169. . . . violating constitutional protections on religious freedom.: James C. McKinley Jr., "Judge Blocks Oklahoma's Ban on Using Shariah Law in Court," *New York Times*, November 29, 2010, www.nytimes.com/2010/11/30/us/30oklahoma.html?_r=0.

169. . . . more support for their growing war on Islam.: According to the *Columbia Journalism Review*, for example, Yerushalmi would soon draft "a new template for anti-Sharia legislation that would be less vulnerable to court challenges." Deron Lee, "Creeping Sharia Legislation," *Columbia Journalism Review*, June 7, 2013, www.cjr.org/united_states_project/creeping_sharia_legislation_kansas_missouri_islamic_law_bans.php?page=all. In particular, Yerushalmi created a "continuing legal education" page on

his website, containing instructions on how to modify his draft law. David Yerushalmi, "CLE Course on Draft Uniform Act: American Laws for American Courts," Personal website, www.davidyerushalmilaw.com/CLE-Course-on-Draft-Uniform-Act-American-Laws-for-American-Courts-b25-p0.html.

170. . . . West," as Geller described the event on her blog.: Pamela Geller, "Brussels: Counter Jihad Resistance," *Atlas Shrugs*, http://pamelageller.com/2007/10/one-for-the-age-2.html/#ixzz2r3JKcvHc.

171. . . . girl brutally murdered by her father and brother.: "Aqsa Parvez's Father, Brother Get Life Sentences," *CBC News*, June 16, 2010, www.cbc.ca/news/canada/aqsa-parvez-s-father-brother-get-life-sentences-1.920103.

171. . . . not have died in vain," wrote Geller on her blog.: Pamela Geller, "Canada: No Headstone Marking Honor Killing Victim Help Atlas Buy Aqsa Parvez A Headstone," *Atlas Shrugs*, http://pamelageller.com/2008/12/canada-no-heads.html/#.

171. . . . disgusting publicity stunts I think I've ever heard of.": Charles Johnson, "How Not to Memorialize Aqsa Parvez," *Little Green Footballs*, February 20, 2009, http://littlegreenfootballs.com/article/32843_How_Not_to_Memorialize_Aqsa_Parvez/comments/.

171. . . . to resonate with most Americans.: Anne Barnard and Alan Feuer, "Outraged, and Outrageous," *New York Times*, October 8, 2010, www.nytimes.com/2010/10/10/nyregion/10geller.html?pagewanted=all&_r=0.

171. . . . conservative activists, on the dangers of Islam.: The talk at CPAC the following year was unofficial as well, with the official conference organizers including the event on the official conference schedule but highlighting the fact that it was sponsored by outside groups. See Kelley Beaucar Vlahos, " 'Unofficial' CPAC Event Takes On Islam," *FoxNews.com Liveshots Blog*, February 19, 2010, http://liveshots.blogs.foxnews.com/2010/02/19/unoffical-cpac-event-takes-on-islam/.

171. . . . Islamophobia is the height of common sense.": Robert Marquand, "Why 'Islamophobia' Is Less Thinly Veiled in Europe: How Anti-Muslim Sentiment Is Different in European Countries than in America," *Christian Science Monitor*, September 5, 2010, www.csmonitor.com/World/Europe/2010/0905/Why-Islamophobia-is-less-thinly-veiled-in-Europe/%28page%29/2.

172. . . . none other than David Yerushalmi.: Robert Spencer, "Major Victory For Free Speech and Religious Freedom: SOIA Bus Ads Are Going Back Up," JihadWatch.org, April 21, 2010, www.jihadwatch.org/2010/04/major-victory-for-free-speech-sioa-religious-liberty-bus-ads-are-going-back-up/#.

172. . . . It's not Islamophobia, it's Islamorealism.": Robert Mackey, "Anti-Islam Ads Remixed in San Francisco and New York," *New York Times Lede Blog*, August 21, 2012, http://thelede.blogs.nytimes.com/2012/08/21/anti-islam-ads-remixed-in-san-francisco-and-new-york/.

172. . . . that is not felt about other issues.": Barnard and Feuer, "Outraged, and Outrageous."

173. . . . as a way of giving back to the people.": Diana L. Eck, "Civility in the Face of Organized Hostility," in *Civility and American Democracy: Nine Scholars Explore the History, Challenges and Role of Civility in Public Discourse*, University of Massachusetts

Center for Civil Discourse, 2012, 6, www.centerforcivildiscourse.org/wp-content/
uploads/2012/08/Civility-and-American-Democracy-Nine-Scholars.pdf.

173. . . . describing Islam as a "religion of hate.": Joe Jackson and Bill Hutchinson,
"Plan for Mosque Near World Trade Center Site Moves Ahead," *New
York Daily News*, May 11, 2010, www.nydailynews.com/new-york/
plan-mosque-world-trade-center-site-moves-article-1.444850.

173. . . . on 9/11 and look at a mosque.": Ibid.

174. . . . buildings brought down by Islamic attack?": Pamela Geller, "Monster Mosque
Pushes Ahead in Shadow of World Trade Center Islamic Death and Destruction,"
Atlas Shrugs, http://pamelageller.com/2010/05/monster-mosque-pushes-ahead-in-
shadow-of-world-trade-center-islamic-death-and-destruction.html/#.

174. . . . this was too good an opportunity to miss.: Press Release, "SIOA Rally June
6 Against Islamic Supremacist Mosque at Ground Zero," June 1, 2010, www.
prnewswire.com/news-releases/sioa-rally-june-6-against-islamic-supremacist-mosque-
at-ground-zero-95376819.html.

174. . . . stop the jihadis from marking their territory.": Pamela Geller, "No 9/11 Mosque!,"
Human Events, May 14, 2010, www.humanevents.com/2010/05/14/no-911-mosque/.

174. . . . and murder three thousand Americans.": Pamela Geller, "Excelsior! Upwards
of Eight Thousand Protest 911 Mega Mosque on D Day!," *Atlas Shrugs*, http://
pamelageller.com/2010/06/excelsior-five-thousand-protest-911-mega-mosque.html/#;
Robert Spencer, "SIOA Rally with Robert Spencer at Ground Zero," video, uploaded
June 6, 2010, www.youtube.com/watch?v=GK5EEjozbs0.

174. . . . "a symbol of conquest of [the] West.": Pamela Geller, "Another Historic D-Day
Anniversary," *Atlas Shrugs*, http://pamelageller.com/2013/06/another-historic-d-day-
anniversary-ground-zero-mosque-offense.html/#.

174. . . . controversy could not have been more perfect.: See, for example, the press
release promoting the first rally, set for June 6, noting the pair's upcoming book. Press
Release, "SIOA Rally June 6 Against Islamic Supremacist Mosque at Ground Zero,"
June 1, 2010, www.prnewswire.com/news-releases/sioa-rally-june-6-against-islamic-
supremacist-mosque-at-ground-zero-95376819.html.

174. . . . their larger project of demonizing Islam.: Pamela Geller, "Another Historic
D-Day Anniversary" (including a quotation from Robert Spencer as saying that
"Pamela Geller did interviews with Al-Jazeera, AP, Chilean television, Italian television
and many others; I was interviewed by Italian television and TV Asia.").

175. . . . a platform on national television.": Jocelyn Fong and Brooke Obie, "Memo
to Media: Pamela Geller Does Not Belong on National Television," *Media
Matters for America*, July 14, 2010, www.mediamatters.org/research/2010/07/14/
memo-to-media-pamela-geller-does-not-belong-on/167700.

175. . . . categorize as irrational or bigoted," he explained.: Michael Barbaro, "Debate Heats
Up About Mosque Near Ground Zero," *New York Times*, July 30, 2010, www.nytimes.
com/2010/07/31/nyregion/31mosque.html?pagewanted=all.

175. . . . This is a basic issue of respect.": Rep. John Boehner, "Boehner Statement on
Construction of Mosque Near Ground Zero," Speaker.gov website, www.speaker.gov/

press-release/boehner-statement-construction-mosque-near-ground-zero #sthash.8ijMdgUP.

175. . . . where the real insensitivity is.": "9/11 Families and the Mosque Controversy," *Frontline*, September 27, 2011, www.pbs.org/wgbh/pages/frontline/religion/man-behind-mosque/911-families-and-the-mosque-controversy/.

175. . . . speaking for the opposition to the community center as a whole.: Abby Phillip, "Obama Defends Ground Zero Mosque," *Politico*, August 15, 2010, www.politico.com/news/stories/0810/41060.html#ixzz2rWXUmE2o.

176. . . . year (ironically, without much fanfare).: Mark Jacobson, " 'Ground Zero Mosque Furor a Faint Memory at Park51 Opening," *New York Magazine*, September 22, 2011, http://nymag.com/daily/intelligencer/2011/09/ground_zero_mosque_furor_a_fai.html.

176. . . . Americans faced during the Cold War.: Frank Gaffney et al., *Shariah: The Threat to America: An Exercise in Competitive Analysis*, Center for Security Policy Press, 2010, www.centerforsecuritypolicy.org/upload/wysiwyg/article%20pdfs/Shariah%20-%20The%20Threat%20to%20America%20%28Team%20B%20Report%29%2009142010.pdf.

176. . . . by any court in the United States.": Evan McMorris-Santoro, "Gingrich Calls for Federal Ban on Shariah Law in US," *Talking Points Memo*, September 18, 2010, http://talkingpointsmemo.com/dc/gingrich-calls-for-federal-ban-on-shariah-law-in-us.

176. . . . would "be the downfall of America.": Terry Krepel, "At Newsmax, Palin Joins Fellow Conservatives with False, Inflammatory Attacks on Obama," *Media Matters*, October 12, 2010, http://mediamatters.org/research/2010/10/12/at-newsmax-palin-joins-fellow-conservatives-wit/171847.

176. . . . spread throughout the United States.": Anna M. Tinsely, "Texas Lawmakers Considering Sharia Law Ban," *McClatchy DC*, April 11, 2011, www.mcclatchydc.com/2011/04/11/111934/texas-lawmakers-considering-sharia.html#storylink=cpy.

176. . . . has caused a problem in a state court.": Marc Caputo, "Two Florida Lawmakers Target 'Sharia' Law," *Tampa Bay Times*, March 9, 2011, www.tampabay.com/news/politics/stateroundup/two-florida-lawmakers-target-sharia-law/1156309.

176. . . . imposed Sharia law in lieu of local laws.": Eric Lach, "South Carolina Lawmakers Hop On the Sharia Ban Bandwagon," Talking Points Memo, January 31, 2011, http://talkingpointsmemo.com/muckraker/south-carolina-lawmakers-hop-on-the-sharia-ban-bandwagon.

177. . . . thirty-six measures were introduced in fifteen states.: Omar Sacirbey, "Anti-Shariah Movement Changes Tactics and Gains Success," Religion News Service, May 16, 2013, www.religionnews.com/2013/05/16/anti-shariah-movement-changes-tactics-and-gains-success/. See also Kimberley Railey, "More States Move to Ban Foreign Law in Courts," *USA Today*, August 4, 2013, www.usatoday.com/story/news/nation/2013/08/04/states-ban-foreign-law/2602511/.

177. . . . vote to ban Sharia in their state as well.: Greg Garrison, "Amendment Banning 'Foreign Law' in Alabama Courts Passes; Will Be Added to Alabama Constitution," AL.com, November 4, 2014, www.al.com/news/index.ssf/2014/11/amendment_banning_foreign_law.html.

177. . . . almost one in five states in the union.: Note that these statistics do not include Missouri, where Democratic governor Jay Nixon vetoed a ban on foreign law that had successfully made its way through the state legislature in 2013 (though they do include Oklahoma, where the law was passed but then blocked by the courts). See Omar Sacirbey, "Sharia Law in the USA 101: A Guide to What It Is and Why States Want to Ban It," Religion News Service, July 29, 2013, www.huffingtonpost. com/2013/07/29/sharia-law-usa-states-ban_n_3660813.html.

178. . . . divided, and less religious than ever before.: Support for the Anti-Sharia movement, for example, "increases with age and religiosity, and the most enthusiastic supporters are the elderly, white, conservative Protestants." Margulies, 181.

178. . . . wrote Geller and Spencer in their 2010 book.: Pamela Geller and Robert Spencer, *The Post-American Presidency: The Obama Administration's War on America* (New York: Simon & Schuster, 2010), 328.

178. . . . Islamists' goals for societal domination.: Andrew C. McCarthy, *The Grand Jihad: How Islam and the Left Sabotage America* (New York: Encounter Books, 2010), 17.

178. . . . "transforming the country right before our own eyes.": Ginni Thomas, "Brigitte Gabriel Calls on President Obama to Step Down," *Daily Caller*, July 7, 2013, http:// dailycaller.com/2013/07/07/brigitte-gabriel-calls-on-president-obama-to-step-down/ #ixzz2ru27Ge4I.

179. . . . in "destroying Western civilization from within.": Reps. Michele Bachmann (R-MN), Trent Franks (R-AZ), Louie Gohmert (R-TX), Tom Rooney (R-FL), Lynn Westmoreland (R-GA), "Letter to Ambassador Harold W. Geisel, Deputy Inspector General, Department of State," June 13, 2012. See also Michele Bachmann, "Letter to The Honorable Keith Ellison," July 13, 2012.

179. . . . as the representatives must have predicted.: The editorial boards of papers ranging from *USA Today* to the *New York Times* dismissed the charges as "McCarthyism redux." See editorial, "Bachmann's Islamist Scare Relaunches McCarthyism," *USA Today*, July 25, 2012, http://usatoday30.usatoday.com/news/opinion/editorials/story/2012-07-25/ Bachmann-Huma-Abedin-letters/56492480/1; editorial, "McCarthyism Redux," *New York Times*, July 18, 2012, www.nytimes.com/2012/07/19/opinion/mccarthyism-redux. html?_r=1&ref=todayspaper; editorial, "Michele Bachmann's Baseless Attack On Huma Abedin," *Washington Post*, July 19, 2012, www.washingtonpost.com/opinions/ michele-bachmanns-baseless-attack-on-huma-abedin/2012/07/19/gJQAFhkiwW_ story.html.

179. . . . dedicated American, and a loyal public servant.": Ed Rollins, "Bachmann's Former Campaign Chief—Shame on You, Michele," FoxNews.com, July 18, 2012, www.foxnews.com/opinion/2012/07/18/bachmann-former-campaign-chief-shame- on-michele/#ixzz214gTcXTm.

179. . . . in a crude bid for its members' support.: So too did Newt Gingrich reveal that the movement's base remained viable. In a lengthy article for *Politico*, Gingrich publicly defended the representatives, calling them "the National Security Five." In standing up to the elites, Gingrich wrote, who are too scared to view radical Islam for the threat that it truly poses, "the National Security Five were doing their duty in asking difficult questions designed to make America safer." Newt Gingrich, "In Defense of Michele

Bachmann, Muslim Brotherhood Probes," *Politico*, July 12, 2012, www.politico.com/news/stories/0712/79104_Page6.html#ixzz2riJ9F39k.

179. . . . and higher levels of condemnation in the process.: Following the Boston Marathon bombing, for example, their organization released a platform calling for Islam to "be regarded as an authoritarian and supremacist political system," in addition to the "surveillance of mosques and regular inspections of mosques in the U.S.," among other points. Press Release, "American Freedom Defense Initiative Announces Platform for Defending Freedom In Wake of Boston Jihad," April 24, 2013, http://news.yahoo.com/american-freedom-defense-initiative-announces-platform-defending-freedom-064500056.html.

179. . . . condemning the duo's activities as extremist.: See: Hatewatch Staff, "Islamophobes Geller and Spencer Banned from Britain," Southern Poverty Law Center, June 27, 2013, http://www.splcenter.org/blog/2013/06/27/islamophobes-geller-and-spencer-banned-from-britain/.

179. . . . 270,000 members and supporters nationwide.: E-mail from Brigitte Gabriel, "Important Legislative Action Alert: Protect America from the Iranian Threat," January 13, 2014 ("That is exactly where you, ACT! for America's 270,000-strong members and supporters come in.").

180. . . . a prime agent of the Muslim Brotherhood in America.: See Melanie Hunter, "Former Sen. Alan Simpson: Grover Norquist Is 'Most Powerful Man in America,' " *CNS News*, May 21, 2012, http://cnsnews.com/news/article/former-sen-alan-simpson-grover-norquist-most-powerful-man-america. See also Neil Swidey, "Grover Norquist: Emperor of No: How Anti-Tax Crusader Norquist Rose from Weston to Washington," *Boston Globe Magazine*, March 16, 2012, www.bostonglobe.com/magazine/2012/03/16/read-grover-norquist-lips/HYhyPVdyay7oMNf3ETRyYI/story.html?camp=pm.

180. . . . operating out of his office suite?'": Erica Ritz, "Glenn Beck Presents 'Just the Beginning' of Why You Need to Pay Attention to Grover Norquist," *Center for Security Policy*, October 21, 2013, www.centerforsecuritypolicy.org/2013/10/21/glenn-beck-presents-just-the-beginning-of-why-you-need-to-pay-attention-to-grover-norquist/. In 2011, conservative columnist David Frum covered the Gaffney-Norquist feud on his website. See David Frum, "The Secret History of the Gaffney-Norquist Feud," FrumForum.com, February 17, 2011, www.frumforum.com/the-secret-history-of-the-gaffney-norquist-feud/.

180. . . . news outlets like CNN and Fox News.: Joe Strupp, "Columnist's Departure for Breitbart Is News to *Washington Times*," MediaMatters.org, February 27, 2014, http://mediamatters.org/blog/2014/02/27/columnists-departure-for-breitbart-is-news-to-w/198262.

180. . . . former attorney general Michael Mukasey.: *Agent of Influence: Grover Norquist and the Assault on the Right*, Center for Security Policy Press, February 2014, www.centerforsecuritypolicy.org/grovermustgo/.

181. . . . 62 percent of Republicans and 29 percent for Democrats.: "After Boston, Little Change in Views of Islam and Violence," Pew Center for the People and the Press, May 7, 2013, www.people-press.org/2013/05/07/

after-boston-little-change-in-views-of-islam-and-violence/. Note, however, that younger Americans have managed to avoid these negative perceptions as a whole.

CHAPTER 7

184. . . . they cause during the times of crisis.": William J. Brennan Jr., *The Quest to Develop a Jurisprudence of Civil Liberties in Times of Security Crises*, 9, www.brennancenter.org/ sites/default/files/analysis/A%20Quest%20to%20Develop%20a%20Jurisprudence%20 of%20Civil%20Liberties.pdf, and quoted in Nancy Murray and Sarah Wunsch, "Civil Liberties in Times of Crisis: Lessons from History," 87 Massachusetts Law Review 72, 82 (2002). The full quote is as follows: "The rumors of French intrigue during the late 1790s, the claims that civilian courts were unable to adjudicate the allegedly treasonous actions of Northerners during the Civil War, the hysterical belief that criticism of conscription and the war effort might lead droves of soldiers to desert the Army or resist the draft during World War I, the wild assertions of sabotage and espionage by Japanese Americans during World War II, and the paranoid fear that the American Communist Party stood ready to over-throw the government, were all so baseless that they would be comical were it not for the serious hardship that they cause during the times of crisis."

185. . . . points to two important conclusions.: Dan M. Kahan, "Making Climate-Science Communication Evidence-Based—All the Way Down," in Deserai A. Crow and Maxwell T. Boykoff, eds., *Culture, Politics and Climate Change* (New York: Routledge Press, 2014). Note that while Kahan specifically refrains from recommending specific strategies—"What are those strategies? I *refuse* to answer"—I take his conclusions about communal motivated reasoning and local self-interest to be in line with the two lessons I abstract from his work. Crow and Boykoff, eds., 11.

189. . . . majority-minority nation in less than three decades.: Sabrina Tavernise, "Whites Account for Under Half of Births in US," *New York Times*, May 17, 2012, www.nytimes.com/2012/05/17/us/whites-account-for-under-half-of-births-in-us. html?pagewanted=all&_r=0; "US Census Bureau Projections Show a Slower Growing, Older, More Diverse Nation a Half Century from Now," Census Bureau, Press Release, December 12, 2012, www.census.gov/newsroom/releases/archives/population/cb12-243.html.

189. . . . with the way things are going: Gallup Poll, "Satisfaction With the United States," available at www.gallup.com/poll/1669/general-mood-country.aspx. See also Rasmussen's weekly "Right Direction or Wrong Track" poll of likely US voters, stretching back to 2009, an overview of which is available at www.rasmussenreports. com/public_content/politics/mood_of_america/right_direction_or_wrong_track.

189. . . . and corporations than they did ten or fifteen years ago.: Mark Murray, "Faith in the American Dream—But Not Much Else," *NBC News*, March 30, 2011, http:// firstread.nbcnews.com/_news/2011/03/30/6375569-faith-in-the-american-dream-but-not-much-else, citing a March 2011 survey by Xavier University's Center for the Study of the American Dream.

189. . . . loss of faith as "chronic disillusionment.": Maureen Dowd, "Who Do We Think We Are?" *New York Times*, July 4, 2014, www.nytimes.com/2014/07/06/opinion/ sunday/maureen-dowd-who-do-we-think-we-are.html?_r=0.

189. . . . twelfth graders actually declined from its 2006 low.: Sandra Day O'Connor, "The Democratic Purposes of Education: From the Founders to Horace Mann to Today," in David Feith ed., *Teaching America: The Case for Civic Education* (Lanham: Rowman and Littlefield, 2011), 7.

190. . . . "American students lost 450 school days of civics instruction.": Bob Graham with Chris Hand, "A Failure of Leadership: The Duty of Politicians and Universities to Salvage Citizenship," in David Feith, ed., *Teaching America*, 64.

191. . . . about how best to confront hysteria.: Note that, in line with Kahan's two lessons highlighted earlier in the chapter, Post was exactly the sort of figure that the supporters of the hysteria could trust—at least by appearance. Post was a pure blue-blooded Protestant American, of the type to trace his ancestry back to Stephen Post, a native of Kent, England, who settled in Massachusetts as early as 1630, as the *New York Times* obituary of Post would note. "L.F. Post, Friend of Single Tax, Dies," *New York Times*, January 11, 1928, http://query.nytimes.com/mem/archive-free/pdf?res=9905EED9133 DE73ABC4952DFB7668383639EDE.

192. . . . because you call him a high-brow anarchist.: *Investigation of Administration of Louis F. Post Assistant Secretary of Labor, in the Matter of Deportation of Aliens,* Hearing before the Committee on Rules of the House of Representatives, Sixty-Sixth Congress, Second Session, 232.

193. . . . wives and children upon the community.": Ibid., 78.

193. . . . when there is doubt as to the guilt.": Ibid., 79.

194. . . . American citizens, in this country.": Ibid., 195.

195. . . . "I am willing to be impeached.": Ibid., 222–24.

196. . . . where reason is left free to combat it.": Thomas Jefferson, First Inaugural Address (March 4, 1801).

INDEX

A

Abedin, Huma, 179, 181
Abt, John, 115
Acheson, Dean, 121
Adams, Elisha, 63–64
Adams, John, 21, 27, 29, 50
  Fast Day
    Proclamation, 37
Adams, John G., 140, 141
Adams, John Quincy, 61,
  62, 65
Adler, Solomon, 100
AIG (American
  International Group), 1
Akram, Mohamed, 158–59,
  160–61, 163, 178
  memorandum of,
    162, 163
al-Banna, Hassan, 158
Albany Evening Journal,
  67, 70
Almontaser, Debbie,
  155, 156
Alter, Irene, 155
Amerasia (magazine),
  109–10, 111, 114
America
  and *Amerasia* case,
    108–11, 114
  anti-Bolshevism in, 73,
    80–85, 86–94, 95–97
  anti-communism in,
    112–14
  Anti-Illuminati
    movement in, 32–33,
    35–37, 37, 40, 41–42
  anti-intellectualism in, 8
  Anti-Masonic Party in,
    46, 60–62, 65–71
  anti-Semitism in, 106

Anti-Sharia movement in,
  2, 149–54, 156–57, 160,
  162–67, 168–72, 173–81
  bailout of AIG, 1–2
  confronting political
    hysteria in, 183–91,
    195–96
  early political parties in,
    27–28
  idea of multiculturalism
    in, 105–7
  immigrants in, 79–80
  independence of, 26–27
  industrialization in, 58–60
  and Korean War, 129
  labor movement and
    strikes in, 75–76,
    87–88, 112
  mail bombings in, 83–84
  Masons in, 51–52
  McCarthyism in, 101–2,
    131–33, 136–37
  national identity of, 7,
    9, 11–16, 26–27, 183,
    187–88, 189
  New Deal policies in,
    104–5
  polls of Muslims in,
    161–62
  relationship with France,
    21, 28
  style of politics in, 8–10
  and Wall Street bombing,
    96–97
American Civil Liberties
  Union, 113
American Communist
  Party, 88–89, 101
American Congress for
  Truth, 153

  See also Gabriel, Brigitte
American Creed, 14
  See also America
American Freedom Defense
  Initiative, 172
"Americans All, Immigrants
  All" (radio show), 105
American Socialist Party, 79
Anti-Masonic Party, 60–62,
  65–71
  conventions of, 67, 68–69
Atlas Shrugs (blog), 153

B

Bachmann, Michele, 150,
  178, 179
Barruel, Abbé Augustin,
  32–33
Beck, Glenn, 2
Bentley, Elizabeth, 99–101,
  102, 108, 114, 115
Bentley, William, 42
Berlin, Irving, 113
Berman, Leo, 176
Black Panthers, 18
Blair, Fred Bassett, 105
Boehner, John, 175
Bolshevik Revolution, 76
Bolshevism, 80–81
  perceived threat of, 81–97
Bolton, John, 2, 174
Brennan, William, 184
Bruce, Eli, 62–63, 64
Bush, George W., 151,
  152, 189
  on Hamas support
    group, 157

C

Cain, Herman, 149

Campbell, Philip, 192, 193
Caplan, Charles, 83–84
Chambers, David
  Whittaker,
  114–15, 146
  and Hiss, 116–20
Chesebro, Nicholas, 56, 57
Chiang Kai-shek, 121
Chicago (IL), bomb plot in,
  83, 84
China, communism in, 121
civics, importance of,
  189–90
Clark, Tom, 113
Clinton, DeWitt, 50, 52
Cohn, Roy Marcus,
  134–35, 136,
  138–41, 142
  death of, 146–47
  hearings on McCarthy,
  143–44
Collins, Henry, 115
Colon, Alicia, 155
Committee on
  Un-American
  Activities, 102, 103,
  105, 108
  See also Dies, Martin
Common Council for
  American Unity, 103
communism
  and Dies, 103–4
  spread of, 121–22
  See also McCarthyism
Communist Party of the
  United States, 146
Coolidge, Calvin, 88
Cordoba House, 173–75
Council for Democracy, 107
Crary, John, 69–70
Cronin, Father John, 116
Crosby, Bing, 113
Crowd, The: A Study of
  the Popular Mind
  (Le Bon), 6
crowds, psychology of, 6–7,
  8, 10
Currie, Lauchlin, 100

D
Davis, John W., 120
deism, 51
Democratic Party
  and communism, 121
  on immigrants, 80
  and McCarthy, 131
  and Tydings
  Committee, 128
Democratic-Republican
  Societies, 27–28
Dewinter, Filip, 170
Dies, Martin, 102–4, 105,
  107, 108, 111, 188
Donohue, Bill, 156
Duncan, Rex, 2,
  167–68, 169
Dwight, Theodore, 29
Dwight, Timothy, 29

E
Ebeling, Christoph, 42,
  43–45
Eisenhower, Dwight D., 8,
  133, 145
El-Gamal, Sharif, 172–73
Enlightenment
  and deism, 51
  ideals of, 23, 25, 26
  extremism, 17–18
  See also political hysteria

F
Fair, Mike, 176
Federalists, 27, 32, 40
Federman, Minnie, 91
Fillmore, Millard, 71
Fisher, Fred, 144
Flanders, Ralph, 141–42
Foster, Dwight, 36
Foxman, Abraham, 175
France, 21, 27, 34–35
  French Revolution, 7, 26
  and XYZ Affair, 28
Frankfurter, Felix, 96,
  115, 120
Franklin, Benjamin, 51–52
Franks, Trent, 178

Freemasonry, 23, 24,
  51–52, 59
  committees investigating,
  54–55
  and kidnapping trials,
  56–58, 62–65, 69
  and Miller and Morgan,
  52–56
  See also Anti-Masonic
  Party
Freud, Sigmund, 6
Fuchs, Klaus, 122

G
Gabriel, Brigitte, 152, 153,
  177, 179
  and American Congress
  for Truth, 167,
  168, 174
  on Obama, 178
  opposition to school,
  155–56
Gaffney, Frank, 156, 174,
  177, 179, 180
  collaboration with
  Yerushalmi,
  163–67, 170
  report by, 178–79
  study on Sharia by, 176
Geller, Pamela, 151–52,
  153, 178, 179
  collaboration with
  Spencer, 170–72,
  173–75
  opposition to school, 155
Gingrich, Newt, 150, 176
Gleason, Philip, 106, 107
Goethe, Johann Wolfgang
  von, 5
Gohmert, Louie, 178
Golos, Jacob, 99–100
Goodman, Paul, 59
Graham, Bob, 190
Grand Jihad, The
  (McCarthy), 3, 178
Great Depression,
  104, 106
Gusfield, Joseph, 15

H

Haiti, slave revolt in, 25
Hamas, 157
Hamilton, Alexander, 27
Hanson, Ole, 78, 83, 90
Harding, Warren G., 97
Hardwick, Thomas W., 83
Harper, Robert
  Goodloe, 36
Hiss, Alger, 115–16
  and Chambers, 116–20
  conviction of, 120–22
Hoch, Homer, 93
Hoffman, Clare E., 113
Hofstadter, Richard, 8–10
Holmes, Oliver Wendell,
  Jr., 115
Holy Land Foundation
  for Relief and
  Development, 157–60,
  161, 162
Hoover, J. Edgar, 86
  on communist influence,
  112–13
Hopkins, Samuel
  Miles, 68
House Civil Service
  Committee, 112
House Un-American
  Activities Committee
  (HUAC), 188
  Chambers testimony,
  114–15
hysteria, definition of, 4–5
  See also political hysteria

I

Illuminati
  banning of, 24–25
  Barruel's theories on,
  32–33
  perceived threat of, 36, 37,
  38, 39–40, 46–47
  theories about, 23–24, 27,
  28–32
  See also Morse, Jedidiah
Islam, 150
  Islamism ideology, 158

Khalil Gibran
  International Academy,
  154–55, 156, 157
  proposed NYC mosque,
  173–75, 176
  and Sharia law, 1, 2
  See also Sharia law

J

Jackson, Andrew, 65–66, 68
  reelection of, 69, 70
Jaffe, Philip, 110
Jay, John, 36
Jefferson, Thomas, 25, 27,
  42, 47, 196
  death of, 50
  and Illuminati, 22, 40
  and Wirt, 68
Jihad Watch (website), 153
Jung, Carl Gustav, 6

K

Kaghan, Theodore, 138
Kahan, Dan, 184–85
Kane, Francis, 92
Kaplan, Raymond, 138
Kennedy, John F., 134
Kennedy, Robert F., 134
Kenyon, Dorothy, 127
Khalil Gibran International
  Academy, 154–55,
  156, 157
Kimmitt, Robert M., 164
Koh, Harold, 2
Kohut, Andrew, 189
Korean War, 129

L

Labor Council, 78
  See also labor movement
labor movement, 75
  May Day rallies, 84–85
  Seattle strike, 75–78
  1919 strikes, 87–88, 89
  1945-46 strikes, 112
Lattimore, Owen, 127
Lawson, Loton, 56, 57
Le Bon, Gustave, 5–8

Levey, Stuart A., 165
Lincoln, Abraham, 12, 71
Luce, Henry, 107

M

MacArthur, Douglas, 129
Magon, Enrique Flores,
  193–94
Mao Tse-tung, 121
Marshall, George
  Catlett, 130
Mason, Noah, 103
Masonry. *See* Freemasonry
Masons, 23, 24
  See also Freemasonry;
  Illuminati
McCain, John, 179
McCarthy, Andrew C.,
  3, 178
McCarthy, Eugene, 17, 18
McCarthy, Joseph, 101–2,
  122–46, 188
  attack on Marshall,
  129–31
  and 1952 campaign and
  election, 131, 133
  censure of, 145
  and Cohn, 134–35,
  138–41, 142
  death of, 146
  hearings on, 143–45
  prominence of, 128–29
  and Schine, 135–36,
  138–41
  1950 speech and tour by,
  124–26
  and Subcommittee on
  Investigations, 134,
  137–38, 142
  and Tydings Committee,
  126–28
  See also McCarthyism
McCarthyism, 8, 101,
  132–33, 136–37, 146
  beginnings of, 101–8
  confronting, 187–88,
  190–91
  See also McCarthy, Joseph

McDowell, John, 117
McKinley, William, 74
McPhail, Clark, 10
*Memoirs Illustrating the
History of Jacobinism*
(Barruel), 32
Miles-LaGrange,
Vicki, 169
Miller, David C., 50–51, 56
and Masonry, 52–55
Mitchell, Kate, 110
Morgan, Lucinda, 54, 71
Morgan, William, 51
disappearance of, 49–50,
55–56, 57, 64
and Masonry, 52, 54, 55
Morse, Jedidiah, 21–22, 33
and Bentley, 42, 45–46
church of, 26
conspiracy theories of,
21–22, 23–24, 25, 26
and Ebeling, 42, 43–45
first sermon on Illuminati,
28–29
and Jefferson, 40–41
legacy of, 46–47
and Robison's book, 27,
30–32
Thanksgiving sermon,
33–35, 35–37
third sermon on
Illuminati, 38–39, 41
and Wolcott, 39–40
Morse, Samuel F. B., 3, 47
Mukasey, Michael, 180
Mundt, Karl, 120
Murray, Kevin J, 1–2
Murrow, Edward R., 142
Muslim Brotherhood,
158–59, 161, 178,
179, 181
Myrdal, Gunner, 14

N
New York City (NY)
Arabic school in, 154–57
proposed mosque in,
173–75, 176

Nixon, Richard M., 114
and Chambers and Hiss,
116–17, 119
Norquist, Grover, 180, 181

O
Oakes, John B., 131
Obama, Barack, 3, 153,
154, 178
on NYC mosque, 175
Office of Strategic Services
(OSS), 108–10
Oklahoma, Sharia law
legislation in, 2, 168–69
Overman, Lee, 81–82

P
Paine, Thomas, 22
Palin, Sarah, 176
Palmer, A. Mitchell, 75, 89,
94, 97, 191, 195
anti-Bolshevism of, 85–87
death threat to, 84
denouncement of, 95–96
explosion at home of, 74
orders raids, 89–92
and Post, 93, 95
Parvez, Aqsa, 170–71
Pearson, Drew, 137
Perlo, Victor, 115
Pipes, Daniel, 154–55,
157, 164
political hysteria, 5, 9–11,
15–17, 18–19, 183–87
confronting, 183–91
and extremism, 17–18
See also specific examples
of
Populist Party, 3
Post, Louis F., 92–94,
190–95
testimony of, 94–95
*Post-American Presidency:
The Obama
Administration's War
on America* (Spencer &
Geller), 174
Pound, Roscoe, 96

*Proofs of a Conspiracy
Against All the Religions
and Governments of
Europe* (Robison), 23,
25, 30

R
Rankin, John E., 100
Rauf, Feisal Abdul, 172–73
Reagan, Ronald, 146
"Red Scare," 73
See also Bolshevism
Reed, Stanley, 120
Republican Party, 40, 71
Democratic-Republican
Societies, 27
and domestic
communism, 113
and Illuminati theory, 32
and McCarthy, 131–32,
133–34
and Morse's claims, 41
rift in, 177
and Sharia law, 149–50
and Tydings
Committee, 128
view of Islam, 181
Republic of Indian
Stream, 50
Riches, Jim, 173
Robison, John, 23, 33
Ebeling's opinion on,
44, 45
influence on Morse, 28,
30, 31
Rodgers, Guy, 167
Rombin, Hillevi, 147
Rooney, Brian, 156
Rooney, Tom, 178
Roosevelt, Eleanor,
107, 118
Roosevelt, Franklin Delano,
74, 103, 104
Roosevelt, Theodore, 80
Rove, Karl, 2
Russia
congress on Bolshevism,
82–83

revolution in, 76
See also Soviet Union

S
Santorum, Rich, 150
Sawyer, Edward, 56, 57
Schine, G. David, 135–36,
   138–41, 142
   death of, 147
Scott, Rick, 177
Seattle (WA)
   attempted bombing in, 83
   strike in, 75–78
Seirafi-Pour, Marjan, 168
Service, John Stewart, 110
Seward, William, 71
Sharia law, 1, 2
   movement against,
   149–54, 156, 160–67,
   168–72, 173–81
Sheldon, John, 56, 57
Silvermaster, Nathan
   Gregory, 100
Smith, Joseph, 71
Smith Act, 102
Social Security Act, 104
Society of Americans for
   National Existence, 153
Sorrows of Young Werther,
   The (Goethe), 5
Soviet Union
   atomic bomb test, 121
   spread of communism,
   100–101, 111
Spencer, Robert, 152, 153,
   174, 178, 179
   collaboration with Geller,
   170–72, 173–75
   treatise of, 163
Stealth Jihad: How Radical
   Islam Is Subverting
   America Without
   Guns or Bombs
   (Spencer), 163
Stevens, Thaddeus, 71

Stevenson, Adlai, 8,
   120, 133
Stop the Madrassa
   Coalition, 155–57
strikes. See labor movement
Studebaker, John W., 113

T
Taft, Robert, 134
Tallon, Rosaleen, 175
Tallon, Sean, 175
Tea Party, 177
Thomas More Law
   Center, 1
Thompson, Richard, 1
threats, symbolic, 16–17
Throop, Enos T., 57–58
Truman, Harry, 19,
   102, 112
   on Hiss, 118
trust, importance of, 185
Twain, Mark, 3
Tydings, Millard E., 126
   committee of, 126–28

U
unconscious, theory of, 5–8
Union of Russian Workers,
   89–90
United States. See America

V
Valdinoci, Carlo, 73–74, 86
values, importance of, 185
Van Beuren, Archibald, 109
Velde, Harold, 134
Voice of America, 137–38

W
Walters, Barbara, 146–47
Washington, George, 26, 51
   on Morse's sermon,
   36–37, 47
   and Whiskey
   Rebellion, 28

Weather Underground, 18
Webster, Daniel, 50
Weed, Thurlow, 60–61,
   62, 65
   and Adams, 63–64
   and Anti-Mason party,
   67–68, 70
   prominence of, 71
   and Wirt, 68, 69
   See also Anti-Masonic
   Party
Weishaupt, Adam, 24,
   25, 43
Welch, Joseph Nye,
   143–45
Wells, Kenneth, 108–9
   See also Office of Strategic
   Services
Westmoreland, Lynn, 178
Whig Party, 70
Whiskey Rebellion, 28
Wiesenfeld, Jeffrey, 155
Wilders, Geert, 171
Wilson, Woodrow, 13, 80
   on strikes, 88
Wirt, William, 68–69
Wolcott, Oliver, Jr., 29, 36,
   39–40
Woolsey, James, 168–69
Works Progress
   Administration, 104

X
XYZ Affair, 28

Y
Yerushalmi, David, 151,
   153, 172, 177, 179–80
   collaboration with
   Gaffney, 163–67, 170
   opposition to school, 155
   study on Sharia by, 176

Z
Zwicker, Ralph, 141

About the Author

A former reporter for *US News & World Report*, Andrew Burt is a Visiting Fellow at Yale Law School's Information Society Project. His articles have appeared in *Slate*, *Politico*, and *The Atlantic*, among other publications. *American Hysteria* is his first book.